Tongue-Tied

Tongue-Tied

*The Lives of Multilingual Children
in Public Education*

Edited by
Otto Santa Ana

ROWMAN & LITTLEFIELD PUBLISHERS, INC.
Lanham • Boulder • New York • Toronto • Oxford

ROWMAN & LITTLEFIELD PUBLISHERS, INC.

Published in the United States of America
by Rowman & Littlefield Publishers, Inc.
A wholly owned subsidiary of The Rowman & Littlefield Publishing Group, Inc.
4501 Forbes Boulevard, Suite 200, Lanham, MD 20706
www.rowmanlittlefield.com

P.O. Box 317, Oxford OX2 9RU, UK

British Library Cataloguing in Publication Information Available

Library of Congress Cataloging-in-Publication Data
    Tongue-tied : the lives of multilingual children in public education /
edited by Otto Santa Ana.
        p.   cm.
    Includes bibliographical references and index.
    ISBN 0-7425-2382-9 (cloth : alk. paper)—ISBN 0-7425-2383-7 (pbk. :
alk. paper)
        1. Children of minorities—Education—United States. 2. Linguistic
minorities—United States. 3. Bilingualism in children—United States.
    I. Santa Ana, Otto, 1954–
    LC3731.T65 2004
    370.117—dc22   2003022739

Printed in the United States of America

∞ ™ The paper used in this publication meets the minimum requirements of American
National Standard for Information Sciences—Permanence of Paper for Printed Library
Materials, ANSI/NISO Z39.48-1992.

To Thelma

I hear nothing in my ear
But your voice
I see nothing in my mind
But our dreams

Contents

Foreword

Ofelia Zepeda

At a recent conference on endangered American Indian languages, one speaker lamented his frustrations regarding the "brainwashing" of our people. He referred to instances where learners of a second language viewed their heritage language as "backward." For example, some Native American people saw their language as being "backwards" because it maintained a word order that did not match that of the English language. It was a feature that they, as heritage language learners, did not expect. It was a feature that they did not appreciate, hence, making this linguistic difference a major stumbling block to fully accepting and learning their heritage language. On another occasion I have heard language teachers of an Athabascan language fret at having to teach the rich complex morphology that is characteristic of these American Indian languages. They wish out loud, "Why can't our language be more like English?" a language that appears to them to have an "easier" morphological system. Such attitudes are a reminder that language colonization is complete and that it compounds the struggle to recover or maintain the American Indian languages that are now endangered. This colonialized attitude is prevalent among many speakers of minority languages and dialects.

Other people have chosen to verbalize their struggle to win acceptance of their home languages and its full richness. They are ones who share experiences with many of the unsilenced voices found in this collection. The voices in *Tongue-Tied* sing for the many still quiet voices that have yet to say something about their language and language experience, whether good or bad.

The wide range of writing that appears in *Tongue-Tied* in part describes the frustration, anxiety, shame, and embarrassment that people who have minority languages experience when they are unable to fully participate in the dominant language community—in this case, English—or when they are discouraged from holding their own language up high. As one whose second language is English, I empathize completely with many of the stories and experiences presented here. The stories and poems pull me back to my childhood, my school experience of sitting in the classroom and hearing the sounds of a strange language that my parents and their parents and all the people before them did not speak or hear on a regular basis. As a child I knew only one language, Tohono 'O'odham (known formerly as Papago), spoken in southern Arizona and northern Mexico. This language was the core of my parents; it was the rhythm my grandmother, my uncles, and my aunts moved to throughout their lives. It was comfort and love; it was a language of safety, of laughter, of spirituality, of sadness, of imagination. It was a rich, rich language. I had it in myself as a child and held it quietly, close to my chest, as the English language bounced and rattled all around me.

I learned the English language and began to move in it with some fluidity. But at the same time, I continued to hold my first language close. I needed 'O'odham. I needed it because of my parents, my aunts and uncles, my brothers and sisters. And later, as an adult, I realized that I needed it because of the people that had gone before all of us. 'O'odham connected me back to them and the things they knew and left with us to carry on. In this sense I have been very fortunate to be able to hold on to my first language, considering the pressures of the English language and U.S. culture. Holding on to 'O'odham compelled me to struggles—many of them expressed by the eloquent voices in this collection.

Otto Santa Ana brings together many voices. Whether young, well known, or less well known, over thirty authors who once were language minority students present their essays, novels, and poems. Santa Ana sets off these literary pieces with a tight collection of excerpts and synopses that describe relevant research on bilingualism, language, law, and schooling in the United States. *Tongue-Tied* also restates the history of U.S. language colonialization—our history and memory of pain for defending our languages and, in some instances, for giving up our languages.

Walking with Language

Some have carried it, held it close, protected.
Others have pulled it along like a reluctant child.
Still others have waved it like a flag, a signal to others.
And still, some have filled the language with rage and
Dare others to come close.
And there are those who find their language a burdensome
Shackle.
They continually pick at the lock.

In this wide-ranging collection one thing is held in common, and that is the hopefulness—the hopefulness that rings true in all these voices.

Ofelia Zepeda
Member, Tohono 'O'odham Nation
Professor of Linguistics and American Indian Studies
University of Arizona, Tucson

Student Preface

Erika Villegas

The raucous 1998 campaign in California to pass Proposition 227, a public referendum to rid public schools of bilingual education, generated an atmosphere of turmoil, uncertainty, and despair for the state's language minority communities.

Supporters of Proposition 227 spoke primarily about the failures of California's bilingual educational system—how, according to them, children were not acquiring English quickly enough or well enough to succeed in school. As evidence, they noted that these children did not become monolingual English speakers fast enough to justify the program expenditures.

For their part, opponents of Proposition 227 emphatically voiced their concern for the future of these children. Without bilingual education, California's 1.3 million non-English-speaking public school students would be left with fewer options in an already weak instructional environment. Proposition 227 would add salt to the wounds already inflicted on these children. With significant, abiding problems—like large classroom sizes, inadequate facilities, and poorly trained teachers—bilingual education (even in its feeble formulation) was a good choice for many non-English-speaking children. Moreover, in its optimal formulations, bilingual education is without doubt a better method on pedagogic and linguistic grounds for non-English-speaking students.

In November 1998, California's overwhelmingly monolingual English-speaking electorate passed Proposition 227. This vote prompted a group of students from the University of California, Los Angeles, to respond to a professor's call to take action in the face of the discouraging events. The professor and students agreed to set aside the manifestos, slogans, and half-truths that had been noisily recited for front-page headlines and television sound bites. By working together, we had hoped to support the children and the teachers most affected by this ill-conceived referendum.

Tongue-Tied is the result. Together—students and professor—we formulated a course of action: compile an attractive anthology that speaks personally and authoritatively about the experiences of language minority students. We acted because most public school educators, and the general public, know next to nothing about these children—even if they see their red, yellow, brown, and black faces in classrooms each day. We believe that such an anthology would provide an introduction to a crucial aspect of the lives of these children. We offer this volume to begin to expose the lives of language minority students to an audience who, for the most part, comprises monolingual English speakers.

Our endeavor is not founded on abstract altruism. Many of us personally know the pain and defiance expressed in this anthology—from our own school years. It is our own lived experiences as language minority students that impel us to act on behalf of other language minority students.

We began this project feeling the urgency to respond to reactionary politics. However, the scope of *Tongue-Tied* eclipses misguided legislation, such as California's Proposition 227. By providing an introduction to the historical, cultural, and linguistic character of minority education in the United States, our goal is to inform the electorate about limited-English-proficient and non-Standard-English-speaking students—immigrant, Latino, American Indian, Asian American, or African American. Narrating these children's educational experiences will also empower their teachers with knowledge about cultural and linguistic issues that are key to the success of the educational process.

As only a single step on the long path to educational equity, *Tongue-Tied* speaks to the needs of communities who have historically been silenced within the educational system. We hope to bring educators to a point where they not only understand but also embrace our most marginalized children. Only then will we be able to help develop all the potential these children possess.

Erika Villegas, on behalf of the student editors

Acknowledgments

In 1998 the student editors of the first version of *Tongue-Tied* helped me develop the idea of this anthology; gathered some of the first essays, poems, and excerpts; and shaped the first versions of the synopses. I deeply appreciate the verve and ideas of these dedicated people: Dewi Faulkner, Gerardo Felix, Marilena Franco, Edna Guevara, Antonio Guzmán, Roseanna Guzmán, Nikolai Ingistov-García, Jo Anna Ley, Mirna Loughlin-Morales, Yvonne Marrón, Micaela Millán, Moisés Merino, Érica Ramírez, May Relaño Pastor, Martha Rivas, Claudia Rodríguez, Christina Torres, Marco Tello, Erika Villegas, and Mimi Thanh Vo. In the ensuing years, Erika Villegas and Roseanna Guzmán served successively as my research assistants. These strong, silent women cultivated our slender sapling of a book. They tended it patiently, pruned it vigorously, loosened its knotted roots, and staked it so that it would grow straight. It would not have flourished without Erika and Roseanna. These people are accountable for the dream we christened *Tongue-Tied*, but they are not to blame for any of the anthology's shortcomings; I am.

Four colleagues, three from University of California, Los Angeles, one from University of California, Santa Barbara, also worked to bring *Tongue-Tied* to your hands. I am grateful for the support of Claudia Mitchell-Kernan (Vice Chancellor of UCLA Graduate Studies and Dean of the Graduate Division), Scott Waugh (Dean of Social Sciences for the UCLA College of Letters and Sciences), and Guillermo Hernández (past Director of the UCLA Chicano Studies Research Center). They provided the means to bring these many authors into one book. Thanks are due to Carl Gutiérrez-Jones (Chair, Department of English, UCSB) and the Rockefeller Foundation for the support I received to prepare this volume when I was a Rockefeller fellow in Gutiérrez-Jones's Dynamics of Chicana/o Literacy Program.

I remain responsible for the final version of synopses and editing decisions. Moreover, the plethora of views and differing opinions expressed herein are those of the authors, or my own. As such, these views do not—cannot—represent those of the Rockefeller Foundation, any individual UCLA or UCSB faculty member, or the Regents of the University of California. I am responsible for all misstatements.

I wish to thank the poets, novelists, essayists, and scholars for working with me—too often an exasperating editor—to bring their creative beauty and exacting craft to this project. I am indebted to two artists in particular for bringing special beauty to *Tongue-Tied*. Elizabeth Gómez Freer captures the hopeful expectation of the Silent waiting their turn to speak in her painting "Siblings," which is reproduced on the book cover. I am deeply honored that the renown poet and activist scholar Ofelia Zepeda offers us her sage words. Ofelia, my esteemed friend, has written a compassionate foreword that she graces with a poem, "Walking with Language," which appears for the first time.

I dedicate this anthology to Dr. Thelma Esther Meléndez. She inspires me to persevere against the silencing with her words, dreams, and actions. She takes up the good fight each day, as do many truly committed education professionals throughout the country, so that all our children can sing out.

Introduction: The Unspoken Issue That Silences Americans

Otto Santa Ana

> My native English, now I must forego;
> And now my tongue's use is to me no more
> Than an unstringèd viol or a harp. . . .
> And dull unfeeling barren ignorance
> Is made my jailor to attend on me. . . .
> What is thy sentence then but speechless death,
> Which robs my tongue from breathing native breath?
>
> —Richard II[1]

Each day, many millions of Americans are denied their right to speak in their own words. Remarkably, civil rights advocates still do not roundly condemn this silencing. The formal rules and prevalent norms of U.S. society are rarely questioned, much less disputed. Social institutions and empowered individuals coolly go about their day proscribing a large portion of our society from speaking their mind. It may be surprising in this day and age that the American public continues to believe that certain kinds of people should be silenced for their own good. Muteness, it seems, will make them better citizens. Their lives, it is believed, will be better for the experience.

This anthology is a forum for them to speak.

When I went to kindergarten and had to speak English for the first time, I became silent. A dumbness—a shame—still cracks my voice in two, even when I want to say "hello" casually, or ask an easy question in front of the check-out counter, or ask

1

directions of a bus driver. I stand frozen, or I hold up the line with the complete, grammatical sentence that comes squeaking out at impossible length. "What did you say?" said the cab driver, or "Speak up," so I have to perform again, only weaker the second time. A telephone call makes my throat bleed and takes up that day's courage. It spoils my day with self-disgust when I hear my broken voice come skittering out into the open.*

The largest silenced group is millions of American school children who do not speak English, or Standard English. They do not constitute a tiny portion of today's students. These students, including children who are English monolinguals, make up the 40 percent of all our public schools, 68 percent of the largest school districts of the country.[2]

At first blush, the reader might think that it is not a problem that the school's standard operating procedure tries to silence them, believing once these children learn the correct way of speaking, that they will recover their voice. In utter contrast, most educational theorists and all linguists reject this falsehood. Such practices stifle educational advancement and are neither necessary nor efficient. The youngest children mistakenly internalize the school practices as signs of their own personal inadequacy. Older students rightly take them as insults. To this contempt for their humanity, the children reply with resignation, and with resistance. By all means, they continue to speak their home languages and dialects. Institutional silencing practices impose significant personal costs. Children's entire education and life chances often hinge on their response to the repression. For the nation, moreover, the costs of these pointless methods of linguistic oppression are enormous.

The public's views about language are based on repudiated learning theories. These theories falsely demand that language minority children give up their home language to learn English quicker. The basis of these obsolete views was presented in 1913 in Edward Lee Thorndike's *The Principles of Teaching Based on Psychology*. This antiquated research, which extended Thorndike's theory of animal intelligence to human learning, dates from a time when the U.S. Cavalry still used horses and suffragettes were marching on Washington to seek the right to vote. In conspicuous contrast to Thorndike, all the most important educational theorists of the past century, such as Dewey, Piaget, Bruner, Freire, and Vygotsky, have all stressed that to silence students is to place a great hurtle on their educational path. It denies them an equal opportunity to learn. Yet, it is still common—even mandated—to silence non-English-speaking students. Such silencing practices also hurt non-Standard-English-speaking children, when they are not allowed to speak with their own voices.

---

*From Maxine Hong Kingston's *The Woman Warrior,* in part I.

Because they are children, their anguish at the daily repudiation of their home languages for educational purposes is customarily disregarded, if it is heard at all. These students' tongues are tied. Moreover, they are not the only ones who are silenced.

> He retired into silence. . . . His children grew so accustomed to his silence that, years later, they would speak routinely of his shyness. . . . But my father was not shy, I realized, when I'd watch him speaking Spanish with relatives. Using Spanish, he was quickly effusive. Especially when talking with other men, his voice would spark, flicker, flare alive with sounds. In Spanish, he expressed ideas and feelings he rarely revealed in English. With firm Spanish sounds, he conveyed confidence and authority English would never allow him.*

Another tongue-tied segment of the U.S. population is the parents of these children. An antidemocratic linguistic ideology discredits their home language or home dialect, as it falsely exalts Standard English. Most often, the warranted outrage of these adults is often dismissed as so much garbled ingratitude.

Another group of throttled Americans include the schoolteachers who are constrained by the prevailing linguistic ideology. The teachers speak English, of course, but their heartfelt desire to provide the best education for each student is undercut—often unintentionally—by their unquestioned acceptance of the monolingual ideology. English-only instruction restricts the range of pedagogical methods available to teachers. This ideology also insists that dialects, such as Chicano English,† African American English, Neoriquen English, American Indian English, Native Hawaiian English, working-class white English dialects, among others—all legitimate dialects of home communities— must be cut out of the children's mouths to advance their education.

The linguistic ideology that oppresses our children is five hundred years old, as old as the contact between Europe and the Americas. It was an essential part of the process that falsely raised the so-called superior European colonist over the so-called inferior native, the civilized over the savage, the sophisticated over the primitive. In short, it was part of the racist project of colonialism. Speech, because its rich variation both unites and differentiates people, was appropriated to mark specious social hierarchies. While racism based on skin

---

*From Richard Rodriguez's "Aria," in part I.
†Chicano English is the ethnic dialect that Chicanos and Spanish-speaking immigrant children acquire—as native English speakers—in their home communities. Chicano English is not the mispronounced English of Spanish speakers who are presently learning English as a second language.³ As for terms of reference, *Chicano* and *Chicana* are alternative terms for Mexican American, used by Chicanos/as who reject total assimilation to Anglo-American mores while reaffirming the cultural and social values of their home community.

color has been publicly discredited, the linguistic reflex of colonialism remains largely unexamined by U.S. society. The most damaging effect of linguistic ideology is that it reinforces the all-too-familiar and utterly false refrain: "It's no wonder *those* kids do badly in school; they speak English so poorly!"

> Those who steal the words of others develop a deep doubt in the abilities of the others and consider them incompetent. Each time they say their word without hearing the word of those whom they have forbidden to speak, they grow more accustomed to power and acquire a taste for guiding, ordering, and commanding. They can no longer live without having someone to give orders to. Under these circumstances, dialogue is impossible.—Paulo Freire[4]

The ideology of monolingualism provides a false excuse to blame these children for their educational circumstances. It absolves the economic and other structural inadequacies of the U.S. public school system that are the real sources of the plight of the marginalized student. Moreover, these structural inequities and social prejudices often relegate the least-experienced teachers to the very classrooms filled with language minority students. These teachers, who are very often unfamiliar with the language and culture of their students, easily succumb to an unspoken misconception: the smartest child is the one who speaks the language and the dialect of the teacher. As has been thoroughly documented, teachers accept this false premise, which lowers their expectations for non-English-speaking or non-Standard-English-speaking children. This preconception creates a self-fulfilling prophecy that is extremely difficult for the elementary school student to overcome. Thus the linguistic ideology compounds the socioeconomic predicament of the student with an entirely unnecessary educational disadvantage.

Tongue-Tied is designed to address these abuses by creating an opportunity for language minority children to speak up in their own defense. It brings together two kinds of writing. First, it includes select literary works by authors of every color who recount their own experiences as language minority students. Second, it includes my abridgments of key commentaries and scientific readings about such students. By interweaving gripping compositions about the lives of language minority students with critical readings about their education, *Tongue-Tied* may sensitize those readers who lived their lives speaking only English, and often only Standard English. Such readers are often unaware of the costs that hurtful English-only and Standard English values impose on other Americans.

Tongue-Tied attempts to open up people's hearts by way of literature. First-person accounts of Latino, Asian American, African American, American

Indian, working-class white, and others form its core. These literary selections are contextualized with readings that are designed to contribute scientific and pedagogic perspectives. The technical complexities of research-based essays have been eliminated to better inform the reader about the capacities of these marginalized students and the oppression of the current linguistic ideology. By making readers aware of the chauvinism of monolingualism, it may become much less acceptable to silence these children.

This anthology balances its negative exposé with positive recommendations for schools. Its six sections depict both the pain and the promise of American multilingual communities.

The child is at the center of *Tongue-Tied*. Part I, "The Child's Struggle against Silencing" comprises first-person literary accounts of language minority children's distress and their response to chauvinistically monolingual U.S. public schools. Part I is rounded out by part II, "The History of Silencing Children," which consists of a 300-year chronology of key events, court decisions, and legislation that have affected language minority children in American public education. Americans generally do not know the basic history of U.S. public education and its adverse impact on language minority students.

Part III, "The Potential and Vulnerability of Multilingual Children," offers somber scientific descriptions of the defenselessness of these children, as well as hopeful expositions on their special capabilities.

The next parts deal with the adults in the world of the child. Part IV, "Mother Tongue," is a set of recollections of the child's home language, the true medium of emotional and cultural sustenance of all children. These poignant contemplations gently underline the dreadful loss for the child and family when this spiritual link is unnecessarily severed by a school system's practicing linguistic exclusion. Part V, "Excellence and Neglect in the Schooling of Multilingual Children," brings together a number of wise statements on the educational practice that teachers should use with these children. Included are descriptions of highly successful schools for language minority children. This part serves as guidance on the best practices for teachers and schools to follow—and for parents to call for—to provide the greatest opportunities for these students.

The last set of literary pieces and social commentaries, in part VI, "Rage, Regret, and Resistance," are writers' critical reflections on their own experiences as language minority children who were subjected to the English-only and Standard English ideology of U.S. public schooling. They all come to the same conclusion—at times stated subtly, at other times more forcefully. At their most subdued, they counsel for greater recognition of the child's vulnerability, and they plead for more-humane treatment. At their most strident, they demand these children's linguistic rights, to ensure their equal treatment in school and in society at large.

～

The numbers of language minority children in American public schools has never been greater. Since 1996, Latino students made up at least 44 percent, a plurality, of California public school students. Again in the nation's bellwether state, nearly half of Latino, Asian, and Pacific Islander children are limited English-proficient students. Statewide, 24 percent of *all* California public school students were limited English-proficient students.[5] Language minority children now constitute the largest portion of urban school districts, for example, making up over 70 percent of the Los Angeles Unified School District kindergartners. And just as their numbers soar, national concern for American public education is increasing. While the real origins of the educational crisis are structural and economic, the social marginalization of these children, which resonates with American xenophobia and racism, makes them the prime scapegoat for the institutional failure of public schools. The direction of the public's backlash is quite predictable. One example was the national outrage vented at the 1997 Oakland California School Board decision to acknowledge the home language of the children, Ebonics, in its schools. Another, in 1998, was the passage of a statewide referendum in California, Proposition 227, which eliminated bilingual education for 1,380,000 non-English-speaking children. These controversies—like all matters of linguistic discrimination—are spectacles of latent racism, in which speech plays proxy for race. Linguistic chauvinism, assessing people's intellect by how they speak, rather than by what they say, penalizes millions of non-English-speaking and non-Standard-English-speaking schoolchildren.

> In human intercourse the tragedy begins, not when there is misunderstanding about words, but when silence is not understood. Then there can never be an explanation.—Henry David Thoreau[6]

In the first half of the twenty-first century, the English-only issue will not disappear. It will draw greater attention to itself as multilingualism becomes more apparent throughout the country. For the bilingual American, this future is natural and welcome. However, for many monolingual English-speaking citizens, this same future portends the end of a parochial way of life. We have already suffered the first political volleys to retain and reassert the archaic ideology of monolingual and Standard English superiority. Meanwhile, these children's multilingual richness is deemed a liability to scorn and eliminate, rather than a personal gift to nurture and a national resource to build upon. *Tongue-Tied* provides some relief from their plight, by creating a setting where these silenced millions may finally be heard. It is not difficult to hear their voices calling for respect for diversity, if one is willing to listen:

> The people were created
> sacred.
> There was a gift within them.
> A sound to make.
> A song.
> A praising to the creator of All
> Things.
> A voice in Thanksgiving.
> The centers within them were
> very strong.
> When they spoke
> they addressed the Creator.
> When they spoke
> they spoke to All things.
> The vibration of voice was
> Powerful.
>
> This is language.
>
> —Dorene Day, age seventeen[7]

Tongue-Tied offers a much-needed dialogue that, for once, will include these silenced children and their parents. With an inclusive conversation, the linguistic ideology in this country, which most easily perpetuates itself in silence, can finally be cross-examined.

Notes

1. William Shakespeare, *The Tragedy of Richard II,* act 1, scene 3, in *The New Folger Library,* ed. Barbara A. Mowat and Paul Werstine (Boston: Washington Square Press, division of Simon and Schuster, 1996), 37.

2. National Center for Educational Statistics, "Characteristics of the 100 Largest Public Elementary and Secondary School Districts in the United States: 1999–2000" (U.S. Department of Education, October 2001).

3. See Otto Santa Ana and Robert Bayley, "Chicano English Phonology," in *Handbook of World Varieties of English,* ed. Edgar Schneider (Berlin: Mouton de Gruyter, forthcoming).

4. Paulo Freire, *Pedagogy of the Oppressed* (New York: Seabury Press, 1970), 129.

5. Reynaldo Macías, Raymond E. Castro, and Yolanda Rodríguez-Ingle, "Looking for Needles in a Haystack: Hispanics in the Teaching Profession," in *Readings on Equal Educa-*

tion, vol. 16 of *Education of Hispanics in the United States*, ed. Abbas Tashakkori and Salvador Hector Ochoa (New York: AMS Press, 1999), 50–51.

6. Henry David Thoreau, "A Week on the Concord and Merrimack Rivers," in *The Writings of Henry David Thoreau*, vol. 1 (New York: Houghton Mifflin, 1906), 295.

7. Dorene Day, "The People's Gift," in *Angwamas Minosewag Anishinabeg: Time of the Indian,* St. Paul Community Programs in the Arts and Sciences (St. Paul, MN: Indian Country Communications, 1977).

PART ONE

THE CHILD'S STRUGGLE AGAINST SILENCING

What has happened to me in this new world? I don't know. I don't see what I've seen, don't comprehend what's in front of me. I'm not filled with language anymore, and I have only a memory of fullness to anguish me with the knowledge that, in this dark and empty state, I don't really exist.

—Eva Hoffman

Silence is as full of potential wisdom and wit as the unhewn marble of great sculpture.

—Aldous Huxley[1]

If images, as some philosophers theorize, congeal out of the matrix of language, then perhaps I've had to wait to have enough linguistic concentrate for hope to arise. Or perhaps I've had to gather enough knowledge of my new world to trust it, and enough affection for it to breathe life into it, to image it forth.

—Eva Hoffman

Cut into Me

Carole Yazzie-Shaw

The autumn air is cold   crisp
   and I have never been so all alone

        Blood flows through my veins like ice
           hurting my hands as I hang on tightly to the cold chains
         but I cannot let go

Alone on the swing I sit   thinking
    wanting to go away   to disappear like fog
       slow movement   back and forth
         Afraid
          Fear holds me in place for you

I am Diné like shimá   shizhé'é*
   They want me to learn to survive in your world
      But I don't know how to tell them   about you
       stealing away my language

Why do you do this?
   I am only five   a girl   a child
     and I am afraid
       I swing back and forth   holding secrets inside

   You beat me with your words
     You beat me with my own hands
       because I cannot speak your language   though I try   I can't

Fear holds me in place for you

   Your voice has anger   words with hard edges that cut
     They cut into my heart   into my spirit
       I feel my insides ripping and shredding

---

*Diné 'the People', *shimá* 'my mother', *shizhé'é* 'my father'.

You kill my spirit　　　　　slowly　　　　tearing away my people
　　　making me feel dirty
　　　　　making me feel shame

Tears of pain flow from my eyes
　　　turning into ice crystals as I am left alone
　　　　　and I don't know who I am

back or fight back if need be. All we had to do was study hard and apply ourselves. So every day after school I would load my bag full of textbooks and walk up two hills to where we lived the first few years after we landed here. I remember opening each book and reading out loud a paragraph or two, skipping over words I didn't know until I gave up in frustration.

My parents thought that by mastering the English language, I would be able to attain the Chinese American dream: a college education, a good-paying job, a house in the suburbs, a Chinese husband and children. They felt intimidated and powerless in American society and so clung tightly to me to fulfill their hopes and dreams. When I objected to these expectations using my limited Chinese, I received endless lectures. I felt smothered by their traditional values of how a Chinese girl should behave and this was reason enough not to learn more Chinese. Gradually language came to represent our two or more opposing sets of values. If I asserted my individuality, wanted to go out with my friends, had opinions of my own, or disagreed with their plans for me, I was accused of becoming too smart for my own good now that I had grown wings. "*Cheun neuih*, stupid girl. Don't think you're better than your parents just because you know more English. You don't know anything! We've eaten more salt than you've eaten rice." Everything I heard in Chinese was a dictate. It was always one more thing I wasn't supposed to do or be, one more way I wasn't supposed to think. At school I felt stupid for not knowing the language. At home I was under attack for my rebellious views. The situation became intolerable after I came out to my parents as a lesbian.

When I ran away from home at sixteen, I sought refuge in the women's community working part-time at a feminist bookstore. I felt like I had no family, no home, no identity or culture I could claim. In between hiding from my parents and crashing at various women's houses, I hung out in the Mission playing pool with other young dykes, got high, or took to the streets when I felt like I was going to explode. Sometimes at night I found myself sitting at the counter of some greasy spoon Chinese restaurant longing for a home-cooked meal. I was lonely for someone to talk to who could understand how I felt, but I didn't even have the words to communicate what I felt.

At the bookstore, I was discovering a whole other world: women, dykes, feminists, authors, political activists, artists—people who read and talked about what they were reading. As exciting as it all was, I didn't understand what people were talking about. What was political theory? What was literary criticism? Words flew over my head like planes over a runway. In order to communicate with other feminists, most of whom were white or middle class or both, educated, and at least ten years older than me, I had to learn feminist rhetoric.

Given my uprooted and transplanted state, I have a difficult time explaining to other people how I feel about language. Usually they don't understand or will even dispute what I'm saying. A lot of times I'll think it's because I don't have the right words, I haven't read enough books, or I don't know the language. That's how I felt all the time while working at a feminist bookstore. It wasn't only white, educated people who didn't understand how I felt. Women of color or Third World women who had class privilege and came from literary backgrounds thought the problem was more my age and my lack of political development. I often felt beaten down by these kinds of attitudes while still thinking that my not being understood was the result of my inability to communicate rather than an unreceptive environment.

Even though feminist rhetoric does give me words to describe how I'm being oppressed, it still reflects the same racist, classist standards of the dominant society and of colleges and universities. I get frustrated because I constantly feel I'm being put down for what I'm saying or how I talk. For example, in a collective meeting with other women, I spoke about how I felt as a working class person and why I felt different from them. I told them they felt 'middle class' to me because of the way they behaved and because of the values they had, that their 'political vision' didn't include people with my experience and concerns. I tried to say all of this using feminist rhetoric, but when I used the term "working class," someone would argue, "You can't use that term. . . ." Because they were educated they thought they owned the language and so could say, "You can't use 'middle class,' you can't use 'working class,' because nowadays everybody is working class and it's just a matter of whether you're poor or comfortable." They did not listen to the point I was trying to make. They didn't care that I was sitting there in the circle stumbling along, struggling to explain how I felt oppressed by them and the structure and policies of the organization. Instead of listening to why I felt that way, they invalidated me for the way I used language and excluded me by defending themselves and their positions and claiming that my issues and feelings were 'personal' and that I should just get over them.

Another example of my feeling excluded is when people in a room make all sorts of literary allusions. They make me feel like I should have read all those books. They throw around metaphors that leave me feeling lost and confused. I don't get to throw in my metaphors. Instead of acknowledging our different backgrounds and trying to include me in the discussion, they choose to ignore my feelings of isolation. I find that among feminists, white and colored, especially those who pride themselves on being progressive political activists with credentials, there's an assumption that if a person just read more, studied more, she would find the right words, the right way to use them, and even the right thoughts. A lot of times my language and the language of other working class, non-academic people become the target of scrutiny and criticism when others don't want to hear what we have to say. They convince themselves we're using the wrong words: "What definition are you using?" "What do you mean by that?" And then we get into debate about what was meant, we get lost in semantics and then we really don't know what we're saying.

Why should I try to use all of these different words when I'm being manipulated and suppressed by those whose rhetoric is more developed, whether it's feminist, academic, or leftist?

Those of us who feel invisible or misunderstood when we try to name what is oppressing us within supposedly feminist or progressive groups need to realize that our language is legitimate and valid. It comes from our families, our cultures, our class backgrounds, our experiences of different and conflicting realities. And we don't need to read another book to justify it. If I want to say *I'm working class*, I should be able to *say* I'm working class without having to read or quote Marx. But just saying that I'm working class never gives me enough of the understanding that I want. Because our experiences and feelings are far too complex to be capsulized in abstractions like "oppression," "sexism," "racism," etc., there is no right combination of these terms which can express why we feel oppressed.

I knew that I needed to go some place where some of my experiences with language would be mirrored. Through the Refugee Women's Program in the Tenderloin district of San Francisco, I started to tutor two Cambodian refugee girls. The Buth family had been in the U.S. for one and a half years. They lived, twelve people to a room, in an apartment building on Eddy Street half a block from the porno theaters. I went to their home one evening a week and on Sundays took the girls to the children's library. The doorbells in the building were out of order, so visitors had to wait to be let in by someone on their way out. Often I stood on their doorsteps watching the street life. The fragrant smell of jasmine rice wafting from the windows of the apartment building mixed with the smell of booze and piss on the street. Newspapers, candy wrappers and all kinds of garbage swept up by the wind colored the sidewalks. Cars honked and sped past while Asian, Black and white kids played up and down the street. Mothers carrying their babies weaved through loose gatherings of drunk men and prostitutes near the corner store. Around me I heard a medley of languages: Vietnamese, Chinese, Cambodian, English, Black English, Laotian.

Sometimes, I arrived to find Yan and Eng sitting on the steps behind the security gate waiting to let me in. Some days they wore their school clothes, while on other days they were barefooted and wore their traditional sarongs. As we climbed the stairs up to their apartment, we inhaled fish sauce and curry and rice. Six-year-old Eng would chatter and giggle but Yan was quieter and more reserved. Although she was only eight years old, I couldn't help but feel like I was in the company of a serious adult. I immediately identified with her. I noticed how, whenever I gave them something to do, they didn't want to do it on their own. For example, they often got excited when I brought them books, but they wouldn't want to read by themselves. They became quiet and withdrawn when I asked them questions. Their answer was always a timid "I don't know," and they never asked a question or made a request. So I read with them. We did everything together. I didn't want them to feel like they were supposed to automatically know what to do, because I remembered how badly that used to make me feel.

Play time was the best part of our time together. All the little kids joined in and sometimes even their older brothers. Everybody was so excited that they forgot they were learning English. As we played jigsaw sentences and word concentration and chickens and whales, I became a little kid again, except this time I wasn't alone and unhappy. When they made Mother's Day cards, I made a Mother's Day card. When they drew pictures of our field trip to the beach, I sketched pictures of us at the beach. When we made origami frogs and jumped them all over the floor, I went home and made dinosaurs, kangaroos, spiders, crabs and lobsters. Week after week, I added to my repertoire until I could feel that little kid who used to sit like the piece of unmolded clay in front of her in art class turn into a wide-eyed origami enthusiast.

As we studied and played in the middle of the room surrounded by the rest of the family who were sleeping, nursing, doing homework, playing cards, talking, laughing or crying, Yan would frequently interrupt our lesson to answer her mother. Sometimes it was a long conversation, but I didn't mind because English was their second language. They spoke only Cambodian with their family. If they laughed at something on television, it was usually at the picture and not at the dialogue. English was used for schoolwork and to talk to me. They did not try to express their thoughts and feelings in English. When they spoke to each other, they were not alone or isolated. Whether they were living in a refugee camp in the Philippines or in Thailand or in a one-room apartment on Eddy Street, they were connected to each other through their language and their culture. They had survived war, losing family members, their country and their home, but in speaking their language, they were able to love and comfort each other. Sitting there on the bamboo mat next to the little girls, Eng and her younger sister Oeun, listening to their sweet little voices talking and singing, I understood for the first time what it was like to be a child with a voice and it made me remember my first love, the Chinese language.

While searching for an address, I came across a postcard of the San Francisco–Oakland Bay Bridge. I immediately recognized it as the postcard I had sent to my schoolmate in Hong Kong when I first got here. On the back was my eight-and-a-half-year-old handwriting.

In English it says:

Dear Kam Yee, I received your letter. You asked if I've been to school yet. Yes, I've already found a school. My family has decided to stay in America. My living surroundings are very nice. Please don't worry about me. I'm sorry it has taken so long for me to return your letter. Okay let's talk some more next time. Please give my regards to your parents and your family. I wish you happiness. Signed: Your classmate, Yuen Kit, August 30th.

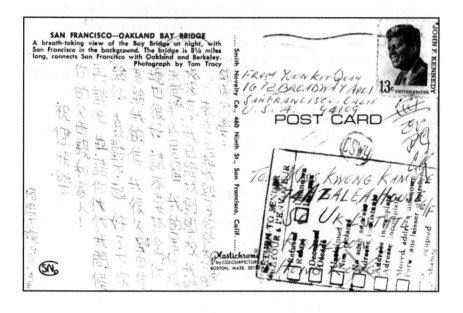

The card, stamped "Return To Sender," is postmarked 1970. Although I have sketchy memories of my early school days in Hong Kong, I still remember the day when Kam Yee and I found each other. The bell rang signaling the end of class. Sitting up straight in our chairs, we had recited "Goodbye, teacher" in a chorus. While the others were rushing out the door to their next class, I rose from my desk and slowly put away my books. Over my left shoulder I saw Kam Yee watching me. We smiled at each other as I walked over to her desk. I had finally made a friend. Soon after that my family left Hong Kong and I wrote my last Chinese letter.

All the time that I was feeling stupid and overwhelmed by language, could

I have been having the Chinese blues? By the time I was seven, I was reading the Chinese newspaper. I remember because there were a lot of reports of raped and mutilated women's bodies found in plastic bags on the side of quiet roads. It was a thrill when my father would send me to the newsstand on the corner to get his newspaper. Passing street vendors peddling sweets and fruit, I would run as quickly as I could. From a block away I could smell the stinky odor of *dauh fuh fa*, my favorite snack of slippery, warm, soft tofu in sweet syrup.

Up until a year ago, I could only recognize some of the Chinese characters on store signs, restaurant menus and Chinese newspapers on Stockton and Powell Streets, but I always felt a tingle of excitement whenever I recognized a word or knew its sound, like oil sizzling in a wok just waiting for something to fry.

On Saturdays I sit with my Chinese language teacher on one of the stone benches lining the overpass where the financial district meets Chinatown and links Portsmouth Square to the Holiday Inn Hotel. We have been meeting once a week for me to practice speaking, reading and writing Chinese using whatever material we can find. Sometimes I read a bilingual Chinese American weekly newspaper called the East West Journal, other times Chinese folk tales for young readers from the Chinatown Children's Library, or bilingual bro- chures describing free services offered by non-profit Chinatown community agencies, and sometimes even Chinese translations of Pacific Bell Telephone inserts. I look forward to these sessions where I reach inward to recover all those lost sounds that once were the roots of my childhood imagination. This exercise in trying to use my eight-year-old vocabulary to verbalize my thoughts as an adult is as scary as it is exhilarating. At one time Chinese was poetry to me. Words, their sounds and their rhythms, conjured up images that pulled me in and gave me a physical sense of their meanings. The Chinese characters that I wrote and practiced were pictographs of water, grass, birds, fire, heart and mouth. With my calligraphy brush made of pig's hair, I made the rain fall and the wind blow.

Now, speaking Chinese with my father is the closest I have felt to coming home. In a thin but sage-like voice, he reflects on a lifetime of hard work and broken dreams and we slowly reconnect as father and daughter. As we sit across the kitchen table from one another, his old and tattered Chinese dictionary by his side, he tells me of the loving relationship he had with his mother, who encouraged him in his interest in writing and the movies. Although our immi- grant experiences are generations apart and have been impacted differently by American culture, in his words I see the core of who I am. I cannot express my feelings fully in either Chinese or English or make him understand my choices. Though I am still grappling with accepting the enormous love behind the sacrifices he has made to give me a better life, I realize that with my ability to move in two different worlds I am the fruit of his labor.

For 85 cents, I can have unlimited refills of tea and a *gai mei baau* at The Sweet Fragrance Cafe on Broadway across from the World Theatre. After the first bite, the coconut sugar and butter ooze down my palm. Behind the pastry counter, my favorite clerk is consolidating trays of walnut cupcakes. Pointing to some round fried bread covered with sesame seeds, she urges the customer with "Four for a dollar, very fresh!"

Whole families from grandparents to babies sleeping soundly on mothers' backs come here for porridge, pastries and coffee. Mothers stroll in to get sweets for little ones waiting at home. Old women carrying their own mugs from home come in to chat with their buddies. Workers wearing aprons smeared with pig's blood or fresh fish scales drop in for a bite during their break. Chinese husbands sit for hours complaining and gossiping not unlike the old women in the park.

A waitress brings bowls of beef stew noodles and pork liver porridge. Smokers snub out their cigarettes as they pick up their chopsticks. The man across from me is counting sons and daughters on the fingers of his left hand: one son, another son, my wife, one daughter. He must have family in China waiting to immigrate.

The regulars congregate at the back tables, shouting opinions from one end of the long table to the other. The Chinese are notorious for their loud conversations at close range that can easily be mistaken for arguments and fights until someone breaks into laughter or gives his companion a friendly punch. Here the drama of life is always unfolding in all different dialects. I may not understand a lot of it, but the chuckling, the hand gestures, the raising of voices in protest and in accusation, and the laughter all flow like music, like a Cantonese opera.

Twenty years seems like a long time, but it has taken all twenty years for me to understand my language blocks and find ways to help myself learn. I have had to create my own literacy program. I had to recognize that the school system failed to meet my needs as an immigrant and that this society and its institutions doesn't reflect or validate my experiences. I have to let myself grieve over the loss of my native language and all the years wasted in classrooms staring into space or dozing off when I was feeling depressed and hopeless. My various activities now help to remind me that my relationship with language is more complex than just speaking enough English to get by. In creative activity and in anything that requires words, I'm still eight years old. Sometimes I open a book and I still feel I can't read. It may take days or weeks for me to work up the nerve to open that book again. But I do open it and it gets a little easier each time that I work through the fear. As long as there are bakeries in Chinatown and as long as I have 85 cents, I know I have a way back to myself.

Prospectus

Joe Nieto

I was raised on the Reservation
In an adobe house, with neither
A running water.
My bed was cradleboard
A sheepskin and the earth.
My food was my Mother's breast,
Goat's milk and cornmeal.
My play partners were puppies,
The lamb and the lizards.
I ate with my fingers,
I went barefoot at most time,
I washed my hair with yucca roots,
I carried water from the ditch.
My Mom ground corn for food.
Sometimes I went without eating.
I only spoke my language.
I prayed to the Great Spirit.
Someday I'll learn to speak English.

Tenth grader of Chilocco Indian School, Oklahoma, originally from Santo Domingo Pueblo, New Mexico.

Learning Silence

Maria Mazziotti Gillan

By the time I am in the first grade, I know enough
to be frightened, to keep my hands folded
on my desk and try to be quiet 'as a mouse.'
I am nervous most of the time,
feel sick to my stomach.
I am afraid to raise my hand, afraid
to ask for the bathroom pass, afraid
of the bigger children, but most of all,
afraid of Miss Barton who does not like me.

We read the *Dick and Jane* books. The world of these books,
painted in bright primary colors, seems so free and perfect.
When I open the pages, I feel I can walk through them,
like Alice stepping through the looking glass,
into that clean world,
those children with their wide open faces,
their blonde curls, their cute, skipping legs,
their black-and-white dog with its perky tail,
their big, white house with its huge lawn of manicured grass.
In those books, I can forget Miss Barton and her icy
eyes and the grimy, shopworn classrooms of P.S. 18,
with their scarred wooden desks,
their dark green blackout shades,
reminders of the war that has just ended.
In that house, where even the doghouse is perfect,
there would be no reason to be afraid.

I try to be good. I try to be quiet.
I hope Miss Barton will not curl her lip
when she looks at me.
I would gladly turn into Jane
if some magic could transform me,
make me blonde and cute, instead of sad

and serious and scared, with my sausage curls
my huge, terrified eyes,
my long nose, my dark, olive-toned skin,
the harsh cheap cotton of my clothes.

~

From *Always Running*

Luis Rodríguez

The first day of school said a lot about my scholastic life to come. I was taken to a teacher who didn't know what to do with me. She complained about not having any room, about kids who didn't even speak the language. And how was she supposed to teach anything under these conditions! Although I didn't speak English, I understood a large part of what she was saying. I knew I wasn't wanted. She put me in an old creaky chair near the door. As soon as I could, I sneaked out to find my mother.

I found Rano's class with the mentally disabled children instead and decided to stay there for a while. Actually, it was fun; they treated me like I was everyone's little brother. But the teacher finally told a student to take me to the main hall.

After some more paperwork, I was taken to another class. This time the teacher appeared nicer, but distracted. She got the word about my language problem.

"Okay, why don't you sit here in the back of the class," she said. "Play with some blocks until we figure out how to get you more involved."

It took her most of that year to figure this out. I just stayed in the back of the class, building blocks. It got so every morning I would put my lunch and coat away, and walk to my corner where I stayed the whole day long. It forced me to be more withdrawn. It got so bad, I didn't even tell anybody when I had to go to the bathroom. I did it in my pants. Soon I stunk back there in the corner and the rest of the kids screamed out a chorus of "P.U.!" resulting in my being sent to the office or back home.

In those days there was no way to integrate the non-English speaking children. So they just made it a crime to speak anything but English. If a Spanish word sneaked out in the playground, kids were often sent to the office to get swatted or to get detention. Teachers complained that maybe the children were saying bad things about them. An assumption of guilt was enough to get one punished.

A day came when I finally built up the courage to tell the teacher I had to go to the bathroom. I didn't quite say all the words, but she got the message and promptly excused me so I didn't do it while I was trying to explain. I ran to the bathroom and peed and felt good about not having that wetness trickle down my pants leg. But suddenly several bells went on and off. I hesitantly stepped out of the bathroom and saw throngs of children leave their classes. I had no idea what was happening. I went to my classroom and it stood empty. I looked into other classrooms and found nothing. Nobody. I didn't know what to do. I really thought everyone had gone home. I didn't bother to look at the playground where the whole school had been assembled for the fire drill. I just went home. It got to be a regular thing there for a while, me coming home early until I learned the ins and outs of school life.

Not speaking well makes for such embarrassing moments. I hardly asked questions. I just didn't want to be misunderstood. Many Spanish-speaking kids mangled things up; they would say things like "where the beer and cantaloupe roam" instead of "where the deer and antelope roam."

That's the way it was with me. I mixed up all the words. Screwed up all the songs.

From *Lost in Translation*

Eva Hoffman

On about the third night at the Rosenbergs' house, I have a nightmare in which I'm drowning in the ocean while my mother and father swim farther and farther away from me. I know, in this dream, what it is to be cast adrift in incomprehensible space; I know what it is to lose one's mooring. I wake up in the middle of a prolonged scream. The fear is stronger than anything I've ever known. My parents wake up and hush me up quickly; they don't want the Rosenbergs to hear this disturbing sound. I try to calm myself and go back to sleep, but I feel as though I've stepped through a door into a dark place. Psychoanalysts talk about "mutative insights," through which the patient gains an entirely new perspective and discards some part of a cherished neurosis. The primal scream of my birth into the New World is a mutative insight of a negative kind—and I know that I can never lose the knowledge it brings me. The black, bituminous terror of the dream solders itself to the chemical base of my being—and from then on, fragments of the fear lodge themselves in my consciousness, thorns and pinpricks of anxiety, loose electricity floating in a psyche that has been forcibly pried from its structures. Eventually, I become accustomed to it; I know that it comes, and that it also goes; but when it hits with full force, in its pure form, I call it the Big Fear.

After about a week of lodging us in his house, Mr. Rosenberg decides that he has done enough for us, and, using some acquired American wisdom, explains that it isn't good for us to be dependent on his charity: there is of course no question of kindness. There is no question, either, of Mrs. Rosenberg intervening on our behalf, as she might like to do. We have no place to go, no way to pay for a meal. And so we begin.

"Shut up, shuddup," the children around us are shouting, and it's the first word in English that I understand from its dramatic context. My sister and I stand in the schoolyard clutching each other, while kids all around us are running about, pummeling each other, and screaming like whirling dervishes. Both the boys and the girls look sharp and aggressive to me—the girls all have bright lipstick on, their hair sticks up and out like witches' fury, and their skirts are held up and out by stiff, wiry crinolines. I can't imagine wanting to talk their harsh-sounding language.

We've been brought to this school by Mr. Rosenberg, who, two days after our arrival, tells us he'll take us to classes that are provided by the government to teach English to newcomers. This morning, in the rinky-dink wooden barracks where the classes are held, we've acquired new names. All it takes is a brief conference between Mr. Rosenberg and the teacher, a kindly looking woman who tries to give us reassuring glances, but who has seen too many people come and go to get sentimental about a name. Mine—Ewa—is easy to change into its near equivalent in English, *Eva*. My sister's name—Alina— poses more of a problem, but after a moment's thought, Mr. Rosenberg and the teacher decide that *Elaine* is close enough. My sister and I hang our heads wordlessly under this careless baptism. The teacher then introduces us to the class, mispronouncing our last name—Wydra—in a way we've never heard before. We make our way to a bench at the back of the room; nothing much has happened, except a small, seismic mental shift. The twist in our names takes them a tiny distance from us—but it's a gap into which the infinite hobgoblin of abstraction enters. Our Polish names didn't refer to us; they were as surely us as our eyes or hands. These new appellations, which we ourselves can't yet pronounce, are not us. They are identification tags, disembodied signs pointing to objects that happen to be my sister and myself. We walk to our seats, into a roomful of unknown faces, with names that make us strangers to ourselves.

When the school day is over, the teacher hands us a file card on which she has written, "I'm a newcomer. I'm lost. I live at 1785 Granville Street. Will you kindly show me how to get there? Thank you." We wander the streets for several hours, zigzagging back and forth through seemingly identical suburban avenues, showing this deaf-mute sign to the few people we see, until we eventually recognize the Rosenbergs' house. We're greeted by our quietly hysterical mother and Mrs. Rosenberg, who, in a ritual she has probably learned from television, puts out two glasses of milk on her red Formica counter. The milk, homogenized, and too cold from the fridge, bears little resemblance to the liquid we used to drink called by the same name.

Every day I learn new words, new expressions. I pick them up from school exercises, from conversations, from the books I take out of Vancouver's well-lit, cheerful public library. There are some turns of phrase to which I develop strange allergies. "You're welcome," for example, strikes me as a gaucherie, and I can hardly bring myself to say it—I suppose because it implies that there's something to be thanked for, which in Polish would be impolite. The very places where language is at its most conventional, where it should be most taken for granted, are the places where I feel the prick of artifice.

Then there are words to which I take an equally irrational liking, for their sound, or just because I'm pleased to have deduced their meaning. Mainly they're words I learn from books, like *enigmatic* or *insolent*—words that have only a literary value, that exist only as signs on the page.

But mostly, the problem is that the signifier has become severed from the signified. The words I learn now don't stand for things in the same unquestioned way they did in my native tongue. *River* in Polish was a vital sound, energized with the essence of riverhood, of my rivers, of my being immersed in rivers. *River* in English is cold—a word without an aura. It has no accumulated associations for me, and it does not give off the radiating haze of connotation. It does not evoke.

The process, alas, works in reverse as well. When I see a river now, it is not shaped, assimilated by the word that accommodates it to the psyche—a word that makes a body of water a river, rather than an uncontained element. The river before me remains a thing absolutely other, absolutely unbending to the grasp of my mind.

When my friend Penny tells me that she's envious, or happy, or disappointed, I try laboriously to translate not from English to Polish but from the word back to its source, to the feeling from which it springs. Already, in that moment of strain, spontaneity of response is lost. And anyway, the translation doesn't work. I don't know how Penny feels when she talks about envy. The word hangs in a Platonic stratosphere, a vague prototype of all envy, so large, so all-encompassing that it might crush me—as might disappointment or happiness.

I am becoming a living avatar of structuralist wisdom; I cannot help knowing that words are just themselves. But it's a terrible knowledge, without any of the consolations that wisdom usually brings. It does not mean that I'm free to play with words at my wont; anyway, words in their naked state are surely among the least satisfactory play objects. No, this radical disjoining between word and thing is a desiccating alchemy, draining the world not only of significance but of its colors, striations, nuances—its very existence. It is the loss of a living connection.

The worst losses come at night. As I lie down in a strange bed in a strange house—my mother is a sort of housekeeper here, to the aging Jewish man who has taken us in in return for her services—I wait for that spontaneous flow of inner language which used to be my nighttime talk with myself, my way of informing the ego where the id had been. Nothing comes. Polish, in a short time, has atrophied, shriveled from sheer uselessness. Its words don't apply to my new experiences; they're not coeval with any of the objects, or faces, or the very air I breathe in the daytime. In English, words have not penetrated to those layers of my psyche from which a private conversation could proceed.

This interval before sleep used to be the time when my mind became both receptive and alert, when images and words rose up to consciousness, reiterating what had happened during the day, adding the day's experiences to those already stored there, spinning out the thread of my personal story.

Now, this picture-and-word show is gone; the thread has been snapped. I have no interior language, and without it, interior images—those images through which we assimilate the external world, through which we take it in, love it, make it our own—become blurred too. My mother and I met a Canadian family who live down the block today. They were working in their garden and engaged us in a conversation of the "Nice weather we're having, isn't it?" variety, which culminated in their inviting us into their house. They sat stiffly on their couch, smiled in the long pauses between the conversation, and seemed at a loss for what to ask. Now my mind gropes for some description of them, but nothing fits. They're a different species from anyone I've met in Poland, and Polish words slip off of them without sticking. English words don't hook on to anything. I try, deliberately, to come up with a few. Are these people pleasant or dull? Kindly or silly? The words float in an uncertain space. They come up from a part of my brain in which labels may be manufactured but which has no connection to my instincts, quick reactions, knowledge. Even the simplest adjectives sow confusion in my mind; English kindliness has a whole system of morality behind it, a system that makes "kindness" an entirely positive virtue. Polish kindness has the tiniest element of irony. Besides, I'm beginning to feel the tug of prohibition, in English, against uncharitable words. In Polish, you can call someone an idiot without particularly harsh feelings and with the zest of a strong judgment. Yes, in Polish these people might tend toward *silly* and *dull*—but I force myself toward *kindly* and *pleasant*. The cultural unconscious is beginning to exercise its subliminal influence.

The verbal blur covers these people's faces, their gestures with a sort of fog. I can't translate them into my mind's eye. The small event, instead of being added to the mosaic of consciousness and memory, falls through some black hole, and I fall with it. What has happened to me in this new world? I don't know. I don't see what I've seen, don't comprehend what's in front of me. I'm not filled with language anymore, and I have only a memory of fullness to anguish me with the knowledge that, in this dark and empty state, I don't really exist.

Name Giveaway

Phil George

That teacher gave me a new name . . . again.
   She never even had feasts or a giveaway!

Still I do not know what "George" means;
   and now she calls me: "Phillip."

      TWO SWANS ASCENDING FROM STILL WATERS
must be a name too hard to remember.

Masks and Acculturation

Abridged from an article by Margaret Montoya

I put on my masks, my
costumes and posed for each
occasion. I conducted myself
well, I think, but
an emptiness
grew
that no thing
could fill. I think

I hungered for myself.[2]

One of the earliest memories from my school years is of my mother braiding my hair, making my *trenzas*. In 1955, I was seven years old and in second grade at the Immaculate Conception School in Las Vegas, New Mexico. Our family home with its outdoor toilet was on an unpaved street, one house from the railroad track. I remember falling asleep to the subterranean rumble of the trains.

Nineteen-fifty-five was an extremely important year in my development, in my understanding of myself in relation to Anglo society. I remember 1955 as the year I began to think about myself in relation to my classmates and their families. I began to feel different and to adjust my behavior accordingly.

My sister, brother, and I dressed in front of the space heater in the bedroom we shared with my older brother. Catholic school girls wore uniforms. We wore blue jumpers and white blouses. I remember my mother braiding my hair and my sister's. I can still feel the part she would draw with the point of the comb. She would begin at the top of my head, pressing down as she drew the comb down to the nape of my neck. "Don't move," she'd say as she held the two hanks of hair, checking to make sure that the part was straight. Only then would she begin, braiding as tightly as our squirming would allow, so the braids could withstand our running, jumping, and hanging from the monkey bars at recess. "I don't want you to look *greñudas*," my mother would say.*

Hearing my mother use both English and Spanish gave emphasis to what she was saying. She used Spanish to talk about what was really important: her

---

*"I don't want you to look uncombed."

feelings, her doubts, her worries. She also talked to us in Spanish about gringos, Mexicanos, and the relations between them. Her stories were sometimes about being treated outrageously by gringos, her anger controlled and her bitterness implicit. She also told stories about Anglos she admired—those who were egalitarian, smart, well-spoken, and well-mannered.

Sometimes Spanish was spoken so as to not be understood by Them. Usually, though, Spanish and English were woven together. *Greñuda* was one of many words encoded with familial and cultural meaning. My mother used the word to admonish us, but she wasn't warning us about name-calling: *Greñuda* was not an epithet that our schoolmates were likely to use. Instead, I heard my mother saying something that went beyond well-groomed hair and being judged by our appearance—she could offer strategies for passing *that* scrutiny. She used the Spanish word, partly because there is no precise English equivalent, but also because she was interpreting the world for us.

The real message of *greñudas* was conveyed through the use of the Spanish word—it was unspoken and subtextual. She was teaching us that our world was divided, that They-Who-Don't-Speak-Spanish would see us as different, would judge us, would find us lacking. Her lessons about combing, washing and doing homework frequently relayed a deeper message: be prepared, because you will be judged by your skin color, your names, your accents. They will see you as ugly, lazy, dumb, and dirty.

As I put on my uniform and my mother braided my hair, I changed; I became my public self. My *trenzas* announced that I was clean and well-cared-for at home. My *trenzas* and school uniform blurred the differences between my family's economic and cultural circumstances and those of the more economically comfortable Anglo students. I welcomed the braids and uniform as a disguise which concealed my minimal wardrobe and the relative poverty in which my family lived.

Aria

Richard Rodriguez

Supporters of bilingual education today imply that students like me miss a great deal by not being taught in their family's language. What they seem not to recognize is that, as a socially disadvantaged child, I considered Spanish to be a private language. What I needed to learn in school was that I had the right— and the obligation—to speak the public language of *los gringos*. The odd truth is that my first-grade classmates could have become bilingual, in the conventional sense of that word, more easily than I. Had they been taught (as upper-middle-class children are often taught early) a second language like Spanish or French, they could have regarded it simply as that: another public language. In my case such bilingualism could not have been so quickly achieved. What I did not believe was that I could speak a single public language.

Without question, it would have pleased me to hear my teachers address me in Spanish when I entered the classroom. I would have felt much less afraid. I would have trusted them and responded with ease. But I would have delayed—for how long postponed?—having to learn the language of public society. I would have evaded—and for how long could I have afforded to delay?—learning the great lesson of school, that I had a public identity.

Fortunately, my teachers were unsentimental about their responsibility. What they understood was that I needed to speak a public language. So their voices would search me out, asking me questions. Each time I'd hear them, I'd look up in surprise to see a nun's face frowning at me. I'd mumble, not really meaning to answer. The nun would persist, 'Richard, stand up. Don't look at the floor. Speak up. Speak to the entire class, not just to me!' But I couldn't believe that the English language was mine to use. (In part, I did not want to believe it.) I continued to mumble, I resisted the teacher's demands. (Did I somehow suspect that once I learned public language my pleasing family life would be changed?) Silent, waiting for the bell to sound, I remained dazed, diffident, afraid.

Because I wrongly imagined that English was intrinsically a public language and Spanish an intrinsically private one, I easily noted the difference between classroom language and the language of home. At school, words were directed to a general audience of listeners. ('Boys and girls.') Words were meaningfully ordered. And the point was not self-expression alone but to make oneself understood by many others. The teacher quizzed: 'Boys and girls, why do we use that word in this sentence? Could we think of a better word to use there?

Would the sentence change its meaning if the words were differently arranged? And wasn't there a better way of saying much the same thing?' (I couldn't say. I wouldn't try to say.)

Three months. Five. Half a year passed. Unsmiling, ever watchful, my teachers noted my silence. They began to connect my behavior with the difficult progress my older sister and brother were making. Until one Saturday morning three nuns arrived at the house to talk to our parents. Stiffly, they sat on the blue living room sofa. From the doorway of another room, spying the visitors, I noted the incongruity—the clash of two worlds, the faces and voices of school intruding upon the familiar setting of home. I overheard one voice gently wondering, 'Do your children speak only Spanish at home, Mrs. Rodriguez?' While another voice added, 'That Richard especially seems so timid and shy.'

That Rich-heard!

With great tact the visitors continued, 'Is it possible for you and your husband to encourage your children to practice their English when they are home?' Of course, my parents complied. What would they not do for their children's well-being? And how could they have questioned the Church's authority which those women represented? In an instant, they agreed to give up the language (the sounds) that had revealed and accentuated our family's closeness. The moment after the visitors left, the change was observed. '*Ahora*, speak to us *en inglés*,' my father and mother united to tell us.

At first, it seemed a kind of game. After dinner each night, the family gathered to practice 'our' English. (It was still then *inglés*, a language foreign to us, so we felt drawn as strangers to it.) Laughing, we would try to define words we could not pronounce. We played with strange English sounds, often over-anglicizing our pronunciations. And we filled the smiling gaps of our sentences with familiar Spanish sounds. But that was cheating, somebody shouted. Everyone laughed. In school, meanwhile, like my brother and sister, I was required to attend a daily tutoring session. I needed a full year of special attention. I also needed my teachers to keep my attention from straying in class by calling out, *Rich-heard*—their English voices slowly prying loose my ties to my other name, its three notes, *Ri-car-do*. Most of all I needed to hear my mother and father speak to me in a moment of seriousness in broken—suddenly heartbreaking—English. The scene was inevitable: One Saturday morning I entered the kitchen where my parents were talking in Spanish. I did not realize that they were talking in Spanish however until, at the moment they saw me, I heard their voices change to speak English. Those *gringo* sounds they uttered startled me. Pushed me away. In that moment of trivial misunderstanding and profound insight, I felt my throat twisted by unsounded grief. I turned quickly and left the room. But I had no place to escape to with Spanish. (The spell was broken.) My brother and sisters were speaking English in another part of the house.

Again and again in the days following, increasingly angry, I was obliged to hear my mother and father: 'Speak to us *en inglés.*' (*Speak.*) Only then did I determine to learn classroom English. Weeks after, it happened: One day in school I raised my hand to volunteer an answer. I spoke out in a loud voice. And I did not think it remarkable when the entire class understood. That day, I moved very far from the disadvantaged child I had been only days earlier. The belief, the calming assurance that I belonged in public, had at last taken hold.

Shortly after, I stopped hearing the high and loud sounds of *los gringos.* A more and more confident speaker of English, I didn't trouble to listen to *how* strangers sounded, speaking to me. And there simply were too many English-speaking people in my day for me to hear American accents anymore. Conversations quickened. Listening to persons who sounded eccentrically pitched voices, I usually noted their sounds for an initial few seconds before I concentrated on *what* they were saying. Conversations become content-full. Transparent. Hearing someone's *tone* of voice—angry or questioning or sarcastic or happy or sad—I didn't distinguish it from the words it expressed. Sound and word were thus tightly wedded. At the end of a day, I was often bemused, always relieved, to realize how 'silent,' though crowded with words, my day in public had been. (This public silence measured and quickened the change in my life.)

At last, seven years old, I came to believe what had been technically true since my birth: I was an American citizen.

But the special feeling of closeness at home was diminished by then. Gone was the desperate, urgent, intense feeling of being at home; rare was the experience of feeling myself individualized by family intimates. We remained a loving family, but one greatly changed. No longer so close; no longer bound tight by the pleasing and troubling knowledge of our public separateness. Neither my older brother nor sister rushed home after school anymore. Nor did I. When I arrived home there would often be neighborhood kids in the house. Or the house would be empty of sounds.

Following the dramatic Americanization of their children, even my parents grew more publicly confident. Especially my mother. She learned the names of all the people on our block. And she decided we needed to have a telephone installed in the house. My father continued to use the word *gringo.* But it was no longer charged with the old bitterness or distrust. (Stripped of any emotional content, the word simply became a name for those Americans not of Hispanic descent.) Hearing him, sometimes, I wasn't sure if he was pronouncing the Spanish word *gringo* or saying gringo in English.

Matching the silence I started hearing in public was a new quiet at home. The family's quiet was partly due to the fact that, as we children learned more and more English, we shared fewer and fewer words with our parents. Sentences needed to be spoken slowly when a child addressed his mother or father. (Often the parent wouldn't understand.) The child would need to repeat himself. (Still the parent misunderstood.) The young voice, frustrated, would end up saying, 'Never mind'—the subject was closed. Dinners would be noisy with the clinking of knives and forks against dishes. My mother would smile softly between her remarks; my father at the other end of the table would chew and chew at his food, while he stared over the heads of his children.

My *mother!* My *father!* After English became my primary language, I no longer knew what words to use in addressing my parents. The old Spanish words (those tender accents of sound) I had used earlier—*mamá* and *papá*—I couldn't use anymore. They would have been too painful reminders of how much had changed in my life. On the other hand, the words I heard neighborhood kids call *their* parents seemed equally unsatisfactory. *Mother* and *Father*, *Ma, Papa, Pa, Dad, Pop* (how I hated the all-American sound of that last word especially)—all these terms I felt were unsuitable, not really terms of address for *my* parents. As a result, I never used them at home. Whenever I'd speak to my parents, I would try to get their attention with eye contact alone. In public conversations, I'd refer to 'my parents' or 'my mother and father.'

My mother and father, for their part, responded differently, as their children spoke to them less. She grew restless, seemed troubled and anxious at the scarcity of words exchanged in the house. It was she who would question me about my day when I came home from school. She smiled at small talk. She pried at the edges of my sentences to get me to say something more. (What?) She'd join conversations she overheard, but her intrusions often stopped her children's talking. By contrast, my father seemed reconciled to the new quiet. Though his English improved somewhat, he retired into silence. At dinner he spoke very little. One night his children and even his wife helplessly giggled at his garbled English pronunciation of the Catholic Grace before Meals. Thereafter he made his wife recite the prayer at the start of each meal, even on formal occasions, when there were guests in the house. Hers became the public voice of the family. On official business, it was she, not my father, one would usually hear on the phone or in stores, talking to strangers. His children grew so accustomed to his silence that, years later, they would speak routinely of his shyness. (My mother would often try to explain: Both his parents died when he was eight. He was raised by an uncle who treated him like little more than a menial servant. He was never encouraged to speak. He grew up alone. A man of few words.) But my father was not shy, I realized, when I'd watch him speaking Spanish with relatives. Using Spanish, he was quickly effusive. Especially when talking with other men, his voice would spark, flicker, flare alive with sounds. In Spanish, he expressed ideas and feelings he rarely revealed in English. With firm Spanish sounds, he conveyed confidence and authority English would never allow him.

The silence at home, however, was finally more than a literal silence. Fewer words passed between parent and child, but more profound was the silence that resulted from my inattention to sounds. At about the time I no longer bothered to listen with care to the sounds of English in public, I grew careless about listening to the sounds family members made when they spoke. Most of the time I heard someone speaking at home and didn't distinguish his sounds from the words people uttered in public. I didn't even pay much attention to my parents' accented and ungrammatical speech. At least not at home. Only when I was with them in public would I grow alert to their accents. Though, even then, their sounds caused me less and less concern. For I was increasingly confident of my own public identity.

I would have been happier about my public success had I not sometimes recalled what it had been like earlier, when my family had conveyed its intimacy through a set of conveniently private sounds. Sometimes in public, hearing a stranger, I'd hark back to my past. A Mexican farmworker approached me downtown to ask directions to somewhere. '¿Hijito . . . ?' he said. And his voice summoned deep longing. Another time, standing beside my mother in the visiting room of a Carmelite convent, before the dense screen which rendered the nuns shadowy figures, I heard several Spanish-speaking nuns—their busy, singsong overlapping voices—assure us that yes, yes, we were remembered, all our family was remembered in their prayers. (Their voices echoed faraway family sounds.) Another day, a dark-faced old woman—her hand light on my shoulder—steadied herself against me as she boarded a bus. She murmured something I couldn't quite comprehend. Her Spanish voice came near, like the face of a never-before-seen relative in the instant before I was kissed. Her voice, like so many of the Spanish voices I'd hear in public, recalled the golden age of my youth. Hearing Spanish then, I continued to be a careful, if sad, listener to sounds. Hearing a Spanish-speaking family walking behind me, I turned to look. I smiled for an instant, before my glance found the Hispanic-looking faces of strangers in the crowd going by.

Today I hear bilingual educators say that children lose a degree of 'individuality' by becoming assimilated into public society. (Bilingual schooling was popularized in the seventies, that decade when middle-class ethnics began to resist the process of assimilation—the American melting pot.) But the bilingualists simplistically scorn the value and necessity of assimilation. They do not seem to realize that there are *two* ways a person is individualized. So they do not realize that while one suffers a diminished sense of *private* individuality by becoming assimilated into public society, such assimilation makes possible the achievement of *public* individuality.

Language and Consciousness

Simon Ortiz

When I was born in the early 1940's, the first sounds of language I heard were those of the Aacqumeh hanoh—namely, my family and community. The Acoma people, according to oral traditional mythology, since leaving Kashkah-trutih, an immemorial time and place in the epic Acoma narrative of our development, have spoken our language. Even the language known and used in that ancient time and place is no longer spoken except in memory. "Kash," my mother told me, "means white. For example, kashshehshi. White corn. Now, there is another, more recent word, for it. 'Kash' is of the old language." Upon leaving Kashkahtrutih, it was required of the people to speak their own language which would come about from their intelligence, perception and expression, creativity, their consciousness.

Most of the first songs and chants I heard were in our native dzehni of Acoma, because that was what my mother and father and my grandparents mainly spoke—although I am sure I heard a small amount also of Mericano songs and childhood ditties from my older sisters who were in school. In our home and community of Deetseyamah as well as Acoma Pueblo as a whole, the main language was Acoma although, since Spanish colonization in the sixteenth century, some people spoke Spanish, as they did English when American occupation began in the 1840's. The cultural and linguistic integrity of Aacqu was relatively secure, though shaky, in the first half of the twentieth century, although it was constantly under attack by U.S. education, values, attitudes, influences, politics, and its economy—really by everything on all sides. Aacqu, like other Pueblos and Native American people, had to be constantly on the defensive, protecting its self-government, culture, livelihood, rights, land, language, its very lifeblood and spirit, everything. Within family and community, the Acoma language was a vital link to the continuance of the hanoh, the people, as a whole. The prayers, many of which are in song and chant, were for that, and I am sure the first murmur of prayer I heard and understood was in the Acoma language.

Years later, when I learned English well and began to use it fluently, at least technically and intellectually, I found myself "objectifying" my native language, that is, in translation. And it felt awkward, almost like I was doing something I was forbidden but doing it anyway. I've posed myself the frequent question: Is it possible to translate from the Acoma language to another? Yes, I've insisted, but I'm not sure I am convinced of it or of how complete the

Native American people, many, many children were sent away to federal and Christian mission boarding schools far from their homelands. The policy was to break or sever ties to culture, family, and tribe, to change indigenous people into "Americans." It was a severe and traumatic form of brainwashing, literally to destroy the heritage and identity of native people, ostensibly to assimilate them into an American way of life. "Mericano nehyahwihtraa skquwaahdrumaah," as the Aacqumeh hanoh would say. "To make us into American white people," as the Acoma people saw it. It was fearful to be faced by this, and my mother used to say that some grandparents would hide the children whenever a Mericano was seen driving a buckboard wagon toward Acoma. "They would sweep kahnee branches behind them to wipe away their tracks as they hid on the mesas," she said.

This official U.S. educational policy in its most extreme practice was implemented into the 1950's. My mother and father were sent in the 1920's to St. Catherine's Indian School and my older sisters, when I started school at McCartys, were at Albuquerque Indian School. It was exciting, however, "to go to school," even though I hardly spoke or knew any English except what I'd been coached to say by my sisters. I could say my "ABCs" and "Good morning, Miss Oleman," and I soon learned, "May I please be excused to go to the boys' bathroom," which is not easy for an Acoma child to say simply to go to the toilet. Most of us six- and seven-year-old children looked forward in any case to meeting and knowing each other, playing games, coloring pictures, and sharing a further sense of community and bonding which sometimes took the form of resistance against school and teachers. Though it was forbidden and punishable with a hard crack by the teacher's ruler across the back or knuckles, we continued to speak in our Aacqumeh dzehni, surreptitiously in the classroom and openly on the playground unless teachers were around. I have some fond memories of being in Peekqikqih, the beginning grade, although the reality of it then was harsher than my recollections.

Reading was fun. I quickly learned how to read. I know it was because I loved language and stories. All my life up to that point I loved the sounds of language and what was being told, and I would listen avidly to just about anything and I eavesdropped a lot, about which my father teased me by calling me a "reporter." As early on I associated reading with oral stories, it was not difficult to learn to read and subsequently to write. All in English, of course, as there was no such thing as bilingual education then, though now very minimally a few schools provide it. My mother read to us, too, perhaps even to a small extent before I started school, but my real interest and love of reading had to do with stories. I'd heard stories all my life, ranging from the very traditional to the history of Acoma-Mericano relations to current gossip. Stories were told about people of the Aacqumeh community, our relatives, both living and long ago, and there were stories of mythic people and beings who were wondrous and heroic and even magical. Some stories were funny, some sad; all were interesting and vitally important to me because, though I could not explain it then, they tied me into the communal body of my people and heritage. I could never hear enough of the stories. Consequently, when I learned to read and write, I believe I felt those stories continued somehow in the new language and use of the new language and they would never be lost, forgotten, and finally gone. They would always continue.

In writing *Going for the Rain* and later *A Good Journey,* I was very aware of trying to instill that sense of continuity essential to the poetry and stories in the books, essential to Native American life in fact, and making it as strongly apparent as possible. Without worrying about translation, I tried to relate them directly to their primary source in the oral tradition as I knew it. This quality of continuity or continuance I believe must be included and respected in every aspect of Native American life and outlook. I have often heard Native American elders repeat, "We must always remember," referring to grandmothers and grandfathers, heritage, and the past with a sense of something more than memory or remembering at stake. It is knowing present place and time, being present in the here and now essentially, just as past generations knew place and time whether they were Acoma, Lakota, or Mayan people. Continuance, in this sense, is life itself.

Since I was in school from Peekqikqih to the sixth grade at Deetseyamah mostly, I was still within the hold of family and community; this was fortunate as many others had been taken away to school and still were at that time. I had a strong, continuing social-cultural connection with my people, for which I am grateful. "Education" and "learning" were stressed by parents, Acoma elders, and tribal leaders; they were deemed to be essential to our future and ability to live in the American way of life. Though it was not definitively pointed out, it was implied that education was necessary for employment and to live a bountiful, better life.

I began to feel stirrings of thoughts that focused upon our way of Acoma life compared with the American way of life. At moments, I even heard and perceived the idea that being Aacqumeh was not quite as good as being Mericano, although it was not until much later that I would find the words to describe and define racism, discrimination, and colonialism. However, the loving hold of its children by the Acoma family and community was insisted on, especially with reference to school. The social and cultural integrity and future of Aacqu would be maintained and strengthened by education and learning. Often and again, I heard elders repeat, "Go to school, stay in school, and get educated so you can help our people." Later when I learned the language to think and talk about colonialism, I knew the Aacqumeh hanoh were in resistance against the more destructive elements of American education and policy.

In 1954 when I was in the fifth grade, our family lived in Skull Valley, Arizona, for one year, and this was the first time I became surely aware of a world beyond Acoma. I knew there was one of course before then, since our teachers at McCartys were white and not Acoma people (Miss Oleman was from Missouri, wherever that was) and I read books (other than the school fare of Dick and Jane and Spot) where I learned of faraway places like South America, Africa, New York, Denver. And we had battery-powered radios that received broadcasts from El Paso and Shreveport which could have been on mysterious planets I read about. And definitely there were people howchaatya— "outside"—who were Mericano white, in great numbers and very different (we thought of them as rich and powerful), and there were Kashtuurrlah (what we called our Hispanic neighbors), and Muurrlahtoh (African Americans), and Chinese (usually anyone who was Asian American). There were also Lagunas and Navajos, Native American people nearby.

Acoma people had been outside, away from Aacqu, usually working, especially for the railroad and in the military, and they brought back knowledge and stories of California, Texas, Kansas, the Pacific Ocean, World War II, the Philippines, and Korea. My father had worked for the Santa Fe railroad since the late 1930's, and so I knew to some extent of places he had been, and it seemed to be a strange, very different, exciting, and somewhat scary world outside.

For me, this fear of the other world had to do not only with its difference from our familiar one but also with a feeling of not belonging in that world. It was a Mericano world where people were well off and in control, and we were Acoma people who were poor, who, I had been told, were taken care of by Shrahnaishtiyahshi Tsihchuu-hoochani, Our Father Big Government. As a fifth grader, a child of colonialism, I had doubts that Big Government would protect and take care of us if we left Aacqu. There were also other signs that it was not exactly safe away from Acoma. When young people, such as my older sisters (and later myself), were taken away by the busload every August for Indian boarding school, parents, grandparents, and other elders would advise and warn them of bad and dangerous influences they would face. These included alcohol use, bad people, and "wrong ways" in general. They were to remember family, home, community, and the ways of the Acoma culture. Many had been lost as a result of leaving home and of powerful influences, especially alcohol. Like many Native American communities and tribes, Acoma was afflicted by the destruction caused by liquor. Our family directly experienced the disease as my beloved father and other relatives abused alcohol, which caused family tension, arguments, distrust, fear, pain, all of the trauma of alcoholism.

Although I listened eagerly to stories about California or Arizona or other places, I also noticed there was something less than positive about them. I think it had to do with an awareness that it was socially difficult to live within the Mericano world and its way of life. I also noticed that Acoma people who went and lived howchaatya dhuuh—outside out there—were different, and when they came back home, they were different. They dressed, acted, talked differently, and even thought and felt differently, I sensed. I had perceived this in reading about American life in *Reader's Digest, True Romance,* "Our Weekly Reader," and school books with the famous Dick and Jane characters. They lived with Mother and Father in a house with a lawn and white picket fence, and I knew they were different. But I really didn't know about Acoma people outside. Did they also come to live in houses with white picket fences and have dogs named Spot? So when we moved to Skull Valley where my father worked for the railroad, I had some knowledge of Mericano society, although a lot of it was wrought in my imagination and speculation. And we did not come to live in that mythical American home but in drab, substandard housing the railroad company provided for its section crew laborers.

Beyond and Not Beyond Acoma

Beyond Acoma, howchaatya dhuuh, was not the best of all possible worlds. For the first time in my life, away from our tiny enclave of Native and Mexican American railroad laborers' families, I felt like a minority. I couldn't talk about it, however, much less describe the feeling; up to then, I don't think I'd ever heard terms like "segregation" or "discrimination" or even "minority." But the feeling of being physically outnumbered was there, especially in that small farming and ranching community in north central Arizona and at the school where my younger sister and brothers and I were the only Native Americans. It was a tiny, one-room school, much smaller than the one at home, and I believe this helped us socially to "integrate" the all-white school, although we were regarded with curiosity and topical interest which was at times very uncomfortable. I was eleven years old, growing into adolescence, experiencing new sensations, finding girls enticingly interesting, and discovering new emotions especially about my identity. And I read voraciously just about anything I could get my hands on. The schoolteacher encouraged students to check books out of the three-shelf library, and I read *Robinson Crusoe, The Adventures of Huckleberry Finn,* and books by H. G. Wells and Arthur Conan Doyle, and many others.

Feeling like a minority in an American world was definitely not a good feeling. It meant feeling that you were looked at differently or feeling excluded, which did take place from time to time. There was something else, though, which didn't have much to do with race and culture. It had to do with being poor. My father as a railroad laborer was paid very low wages, and we got all our clothes and food from the company store, the Holmes Supply, on credit billed against my father's paycheck. We dressed as best we could but cheaply, and we kept our shoes until they were really worn.

Back in Those Days

Carole Yazzie-Shaw

Grandma sat on the dirt floor of the hogan singing a morning song as she ground corn. Her strong hands were tightly wrapped around the mono as she rocked back and forth. The sound of grinding as the mono crushed corn woke her granddaughter, Desbah, from sleep. She sat up with a puzzled look, as she combed her fingers through her hair. She got up from her sheepskin bedding and folded her blanket. Yawning, Desbah rubbed sleep from her eyes and began to walk outside, when Grandma called out to her.

"Shi yazhi, on your way back in, bring some firewood with you."

"Yes Masani, I'll be back in a little while. You want me to get water too?" Desbah asked, scratching her back.

"I already got it while you were sleeping."

Desbah stood watching her grandmother's large hands as they gripped the mono. They looked like the hands of a man, and her fingernails were yellow with jagged edges. Desbah was still very sleepy. Grandma looked up to see why she hadn't left yet. The light from the kerosene lamp showed years in Grandma's once dark brown eyes. They were fading with age, causing them to have a light ring around the iris.

"What's the matter with you silly girl, are you sleepwalking?"

Desbah looked down embarrassed.

"You shouldn't stare at people. Now hurry up! You mustn't waste the morning!"

Closing the door behind her, Desbah looked out to the horizon and tied her shoestrings. It was a beautiful morning, and the birds had already begun to sing. The air was fresh and cool, and the stars were still shining. The morning shadows were dark on the bluish light from the white line of the horizon.

When Desbah started toward the East, she heard a coyote somewhere far away in the canyons howling as it made its kill. The sheep in the brush corral shuffled around because of the howling, so Desbah ran faster in fright, avoiding big sagebrush. The farther she ran, the more light dawned upon her. She felt as if she were running into the early morning.

Desbah was breathing fast when she stopped and could feel tiny beads of sweat forming around her face and dry lips. When she stood for a moment to catch her breath, the cool air burned her throat and warm streams of sweat ran down her neck. She looked past the hills covered with piñon trees and sagebrush and saw hints of yellow light as the sun began to come up. She reached into her pocket, took out a medicine pouch and made an offering to the Sun and to Mother Earth, the way Grandma taught her to do. She felt good and began to pray.

"Holy People of the early morning, it is I your granddaughter. I pray to you for a good day. Bring us health and happiness. Watch over my Masani and Mom and Dad, and all my people. May Mother Earth provide enough food for all living things—may all things be good."

Desbah felt a rush of happiness. She felt good all over while she listened to the birds and Mother Earth waking with life. She took a deep breath and headed for home. As she ran home, the sun began to rise, and the sagebrush smelled of early morning dew. When Desbah returned home, sunlight was hitting the tips of trees and bushes. She picked up some firewood before she entered the hogan. Her Masani was kneading dough from the corn.

"Shi yazhi, put some more wood in the fire."

"Masani, when will Mom and Dad come to see me?"

"I don't know. . . . Go let out the sheep. We have much to do."

Grandma did not know what to tell her granddaughter. She didn't know when the girl's mother or father would come back. Desbah's mother said she was going to find work in Gallup, but she was drunk when she said this. She said she would return to get Desbah when she found a place to stay, but that was months ago. Ester was with another man. She had tears in her eyes when she left with this man. Grandma wondered where her daughter was now. Many times she watched Desbah stand in the doorway listening and watching the road to the hogan, hoping to see her parents walking up the road. She often said, "They'll probably bring me something when they come. Maybe some candy."

Desbah walked to the brush corral she and Masani were always having to repair. The main support posts were made of juniper, but the rest was made of sticks and brush tied together with baling wire and pieces of rope. The odor from the sheep stung her nose while she removed the poles to let the sheep out. Desbah thought of her parents while the sheep ran out one at a time. She remembered their fights and the drinking. Her father would frighten her when he hit her mother. Both she and Mom would sit outside and cry while they hid from him. Mother was usually drunk, too, and she would start to say strange things. She often spoke of dying or killing father. Desbah felt tightness inside of her. Mother told her she would come back soon when she left her with Grandma. Suddenly, Desbah heard Masani yelling and waving her arms.

"Come in, it's time to eat!"

"I'll be there in a little while," Desbah said as she waited for the last sheep to run out.

Summer was ending, and Desbah liked living with Grandma. They did many things together. Sometimes Masani would surprise her with a new clay animal she had made, and they would play with them together. While the sheep were grazing, they would make little hogans and brush corrals made of twigs, but Masani always quit playing too soon. Today she and Masani were to pick piñons while they herded sheep.

When Desbah went back into the hogan, Grandma had made breakfast—mutton, fried bread made of ground corn, and coffee. Everything smelled so good. The juices in Desbah's mouth began to stir.

"Wash your hands."

"Are we going to look for piñons today?" Desbah asked while she washed her face and hands in icy cold water.

"Yes, and what you pick, you can sell at the trading post and buy anything you want," Grandma said, putting out two metal cups and the salt shaker.

"I'll pick a lot so I can buy you a new shawl, the kind with a lot of different colors and long fringes. What's your favorite color, Masani, what color do you like? Mine is red—I like red," Desbah said while she tore a piece of fried bread and wrapped it around mutton. She jerked when she sipped her coffee too fast because it was too hot. Grandma laughed, covering her mouth with her hand to hide her missing teeth.

"I guess I like blue. But I don't think you'll make enough money to buy a shawl from picking piñons. Maybe you should buy yourself a doll."

"Yes, Masani, one with a real pretty red dress and little shoes. Let's hurry and eat. We need to start picking right away!" Desbah said, trying to imagine what the doll would look like. She wanted one with long black hair and shiny shoes—like the one she saw in an old catalog that someone had thrown away.

The door was open while Grandma and Desbah sat eating as sun threw light on their faces. Desbah noticed that in the light, her Masani's hair looked almost yellow instead of white. Then a small puppy came up to the doorway, wagging his tail begging for scraps. Desbah was going to give it a piece of bread, when she saw Masani glare at her.

"Shoooo!" Grandma threw a piece of wood at the puppy.

"The puppy eats too much, even if he doesn't help us much, does he Masani?"

"Yes but he's still learning—like you. . . . You came back from running later than yesterday," Grandma said, picking her teeth with a splinter she broke off the firewood.

"Yes Masani, I ran farther today. The sun is making me strong like you said it would if I pray for strength," Desbah said in between bites.

"Yes, but you must run every day. Then you will be strong."

After breakfast, Desbah sat on a slab of rock outside by the door finishing her cup of coffee. She was watching the sheep far off in the field. It was a cool morning, but the sun felt warm on her skin.

"Masani, I'm afraid the sheep might get lost. There's nobody watching them."

"No, they won't go very far—they didn't eat all night so they won't have the energy," Grandma said, cleaning up after breakfast.

"But aren't you afraid that the coyotes will get them? I heard them crying this morning when I was running, and they kind of scared me."

"No, sheep dogs will take care of them. Besides they won't come out this far unless they are starving. You have much to learn."

"Well, what would you do if they came too close and started to kill the sheep, Masani? What would you do?"

"I'd use that to scare them!" Grandma said, pointing at an old Winchester hanging on the wall.

"Really? You would shoot a coyote?"

"Don't be silly. The gun is just for making noise. You just shoot up into the air several times—then the coyotes get scared and run off. Only certain people can kill them, not just anyone like you or me. It would be dangerous for just anyone to kill them."

"How come only certain people can kill them?"

"Because coyotes are like holy people. They give people messages—that's why they're special. One has to have a special ceremony before they have the right to harm the coyote."

"Gosh Masani, I didn't know that." But Desbah didn't ask anymore questions because she saw that Grandma was getting annoyed.

"Let's go before the sheep go too far," Masani said.

When Grandma and Desbah reached the sheep, they gathered them up and followed them toward the hills where the piñon trees were. They both carried flour sacks for the nuts, the kind with the blue bird on it.

Desbah could feel the tiny pine needles poking through her skirt while she knelt to pick the nuts, one at a time. She carefully picked each nut, for when she picked piñons the first time, she had been scolded for picking empty shells. Now she knew well enough to pick the fresh red ones and not the gray ones. A few feet away, Masani was hitting the trees with a long stick to make the cones fall to the ground. When they hit, the cones would burst and nuts would fall out. After a while, she stopped to rest.

"Shi yazhi, climb up there and shake the tree."

She lifted Desbah into the tree. Desbah started to shake the piñon tree as hard as she could. Desbah was laughing while she shook the tree, because the cones were hitting her Masani in the head.

"Ah Yah! Wait until I'm out of the way," Grandma scolded.

Desbah stopped for a moment to check on the sheep when she suddenly saw two men wearing white men's clothes walking toward them.

"Look Masani! Somebody's coming."

Grandma lifted her out of the tree and set her on the ground. Desbah was frightened so she ran behind her Masani's long skirt. When they came closer, the smaller man was a Navajo and the taller one was a white man with a mustache.

"Who are they, Masani? I wonder what they want," Desbah said in fright. She had never seen a white man this far out before.

"They must be Gáámaliis, missionaries from the Mormon Church. They usually come around here trying to make believers out of the Navajo," Grandma said.

Desbah wondered what believers were; she wondered what they believed in. As the two men approached, they both had smiles on their faces.

"Yah-ta-hey!" The white man said. He reached out to shake Grandma's hand.

"Yá'at'eeh, Hello," Grandma said and shook both men's hands. Grandma didn't know how to speak English so she looked at the Navajo questioningly.

"Old one, we have come to take the little girl. She must go to school."

Grandma was not surprised. She knew this would happen soon. She looked down and seemed to notice her worn-out shoes for the first time. Desbah was frightened. She couldn't understand why she had to go to school.

"Masani, am I a bad person? Why does the white man want to take me? What did I do?" Desbah asked almost crying.

"Shh! Don't ask so many questions," Grandma said, putting her finger to her lips.

Desbah tried to focus her sight, but the blur wouldn't go away. She had always been told that if she was a bad girl, the Bilagaana—white man would come and take her away. He is said to have hair all over his body. Desbah stared at the white man's mustache, and she could see glimpses of the hair on his chest sticking out of his shirt. He even had hair on his hands. She was shaking with fright.

"Masani, no! Please don't let the white man take me away. They might kill me!" Desbah was so frightened, she remembered her mother telling her that the Bilagaana kills bad children. "He'll carry you off in a bag and club you so you don't know where he's taking you, or what he does to you. Then he kills you," Mother used to say. She always had stories like that.

"Please Masani, I've been good. I even prayed to the sun like you told me to. I don't want to die." Tears were running down Desbah's cheeks. She was holding her grandma's hand tight. Grandma looked at her pitiful grandchild.

"What has your mother told you? You mustn't talk like that, it's wrong. No one is going to hurt you." She put her arms around Desbah and squeezed her.

"No!" she said, staring at both men.

"She has no parents. You cannot take her away. She'll be too lonely. T'ah yee' 'awee' 'at'eh, she's still a baby. She does not understand this thing called school."

"Please old one, it's the law. You know that. You could be sent to jail. Then who's going to take care of her?"

The white man began to speak.

"Tell her that the school is good. It has good food, and there are other Indian children there. We'll take good care of her."

The Navajo interpreted the message.

"She's old enough to be in school. The younger they are, the better," the white man said.

"Please, old one, we have to do this, you know that. She's old enough to start learning the white man's ways. She'll have a better chance of getting a job when she grows up. I know they will take good care of her. I've been to the school. They even give the children new clothes," the Navajo explained. He did not like doing this, but it was worse when the parents said no. Many were threatened with jail until they agreed to put their children in school. He just wanted to help these people. Many just did not understand.

"And what's wrong with being a sheep herder," the old woman said. But she knew there was no arguing with these men. She remembered hearing such stories before, and she knew that there was no way out. School ruined the children. They would come home like babies, not knowing how to care for the sheep and unable to fend for themselves. School made the children forget about their people, their language, and their religion. Many returned home only to laugh at the old ones. Grandma looked at her granddaughter with tears in her eyes. They were just getting to know one another, but there was no choice.

"My little one, I don't think we can say no. I have taught you that the sheep keep us strong and if I say no, then they will take you and me away. There will be no one to take care of the sheep. Without the sheep, we will surely lose our strength."

Desbah looked down at the ground because she didn't want to see the tears in her Masani's eyes.

"We have a new program. The little girl will come home several times a year. She will have a good place to live," the Navajo said.

"What else can I say. You know I have no choice. You've already made up your minds. There's nothing else to do. I'm sure you will take good care of her," Grandma said.

"We'll have a truck to pick her up tomorrow. There will be other Navajo children on the truck."

The White man smiled and reached out to Desbah.

"There, there little girl, everything's going to be okay. Tell the old woman to have her ready by morning."

Desbah jerked away from the white man. The Navajo interpreted the message and told them good-bye. Both Desbah and her Masani were very quiet the rest of the day. They didn't pick any more piñons. They just followed the sheep in silence.

Indian Boy Love Song (#2)

Sherman Alexie

I never spoke
the language
of the old women

visiting my mother
in winters so cold
they could freeze
the tongue whole.

I never held my head
to their thin chests
believing in the heart.

Indian women, forgive me.
I grew up distant
and always afraid.

Wašicuia ya he? Do you speak English?

Delphine Red Shirt

I did not learn how to write a composition in English until I left the government school and entered seventh grade at a small school run by nuns from the Notre Dame order. I discovered that despite their shortcomings, the nuns brought people, volunteers, to the school, who were intent on teaching. There, at the school with its simple white buildings closely nestled in a small valley, I learned to read, write, and finally how to converse in English.

I learned to read properly in a program at the school, which they called a "reading lab." The lab was actually a trailer house that was equipped with small reading booths, where there were no books, only strips of film in darkened reading booths where we were required after every reading session to answer a set of comprehension questions. While there, I watched sentences flow by at a speed which I controlled and therefore could read. I could not rewind or review before answering the questions at the end of the session. I started slowly, reading at a speed that allowed me to answer the questions correctly. I enjoyed the darkened room, the quiet trailer, and the chance to learn without someone looking over my shoulder.

I remember one girl in my class who was fond of bypassing all the work. She showed me where the answers were one day when she lingered behind to point out the answer sheets in a file hidden at the end of a cabinet. I think she did it because she wanted to be my friend. We were friends all through high school. I tried to look past her shortcomings, particularly her inclination to cheat. In those early years, I seemed to have accepted people as what they were more readily than I do now. I continued painstakingly, and many times erroneously, to learn to read properly. I forced myself to try to comprehend the language I did not speak at home, the language I felt self-conscious speaking, the language I will never fully comprehend.

I learned more at that small school run by the nuns and volunteers than I learned at the government school, where I entered in the fourth grade and stayed through sixth grade. The government school, which had all the modern conveniences that the small Catholic school didn't have, seemed, by comparison, to be massive, sterile, and empty in an inexplicable way. It had desks, chairs, blackboards, and books, but it lacked something which I was not able to pinpoint until I met the nuns and teachers at the Catholic school. It had all the trappings of a school, but it did not educate the way the Catholic school did, with heart and feeling for the children in it.

The government school was worlds away from the bright classrooms I left behind in rural Nebraska. There were no sweet-smelling teachers in rouge who hung snowflakes and valentines in the windows. There was no daily reminder to "Put on your thinking cap," and no daily practice with reading or writing. There were no libraries or music classes. Instead, at the government school we had teachers who were past retirement and who fell asleep in the classroom, teachers who were more eager to keep order in the classroom than to teach. They were more eager to put you in your place and gladly shunned you after school. I do not remember having one conversation with any of my teachers at the government school. What I did learn, I still carry with me. I learned shame there, as they pulled our hair and checked it for lice. I learned silence there, as I stood in line and watched the teacher pull a girl's hair to keep her in line. I learned fighting there, as we channeled our energy the wrong way, for we took our frustrations out on one another. There was no positive regard or positive reinforcement, only suspicion and mistrust.

Despite it all, I had a favorite teacher in that school run by the Bureau of Indian Affairs. This teacher, a black man or *ha sapa*, as the people called him, 'skin that is black', was considered a *wašicu*, a 'black "white" man'. He seemed to belong to that category of "white man," and Kah-kah said that in all his mannerisms, this person, the "black man," seemed closer to the wašicu than anyone else on the reservation. He was the first and only black person I remember seeing in my early life. My world back then was only Lakota and wašicu. It was said that at one time, the black teacher had brought a wife, a son, and a daughter to the reservation. They left, but he stayed. I know how he must have felt as the only black man in our midst; for many years I was the only "Indian" in the classroom in rural Nebraska.

I liked him because he was my first teacher on the reservation, and my first year there I celebrated the whole year. I celebrated because it was the first time in my life that I was not the only "Indian" in the classroom. All the girls and all the boys were just like me. They had hair, skin, and eyes that were the same color as mine. They spoke English as I did, some better than others. I looked at my friends, cousins, and other children at the school with happy eyes. They were kids who had families like mine, who lived in houses like mine, *miye s'e*, meaning 'just like me'. I finally belonged somewhere.

This soon gave way to the realization, even as a young child, that a prison is a prison, no matter how pleasant it may seem, and I know that I soon realized that while we lived within the confines of the reservation, we were all under the constant eye and supervision of a benevolent but neglectful government. I soon realized that the isolation we all felt made us despair silently and that it drove some adults to alcohol and others to insanity. We children, at least, had the school to distract us; for the adults there was nothing, day after day. My father didn't stay on the reservation, and in that he was like other fathers, and some mothers. They had nothing there; only the patient ones, the old ones, the children, and those who clung to the old ways could find comfort in the land, the language, and the occasional powwow or dance celebrating some event. For anyone else, the reservation and its schools were a black hole in which your energy is eventually drained. By the time I left the government school in seventh grade, I was a shadow of the happy little girl who had gone skipping out to play at recess in fourth grade. I had become silent and belligerent, but I did not despair.

I had known freedom outside the reservation, and I knew that if I just bided my time, I could someday leave and find something more. I was ready for something to restore me. I wanted to grow stronger, to replenish my spirit, which I knew was on the wane. I could go forward at that critical age, or I could succumb to what others, who were in the same place I was, did. Some tried suicide, others tried alcohol, and still others dropped out of the government schools and followed their parents somewhere, to Denver or Minneapolis, to get away from that demoralizing place called the government school. I was one of those kids who didn't play a sport in school, but I wish I had. I needed to vent my energy in some way. My way was as always in the realm of thought, and perhaps books would have offered me solace. But we had no library; music and art would have consoled me, but they didn't offer those things at that school.

The only music I remember in the government school came from the kindergarten classroom where a senile teacher often sang. Her favorite song was from the *Wizard of Oz*. She would sing, "Somewhere over the rainbow, blue birds fly." When I hear that song, I can still see the tall gray-haired woman in kindergarten who, perhaps because she was somewhat senile, was the happiest person on the teaching staff. She would sing as she wandered from her classroom to the principal's office. When she wasn't singing, she was fond of napping.

The other person who loved music was our fourth grade teacher, the large black man whose baritone voice rang out, "Nobody knows the trouble I've seen. Nobody knows but Jesus." We played tricks on him. We knew that he would not punish us in any way, that he was the only one who seemed to have a sense of humor, so we played harmless tricks on him. One of our favorite tricks was to have someone stand behind him when he sang one of his favorite songs, which was often. He would stop whatever he was doing and lean back in his desk chair, close his eyes, and break into song. We would have someone creep up behind him and have that person pretend to shine the bald spot on the back of his head with the chalkboard eraser, keeping time to the song he was singing. He would always catch on after a few stanzas of his song, when he opened his eyes and saw us all giggling. He would reach behind him to grab whoever was there. His singing seemed to break the monotony of the long days we spent at our desks. He seemed to know that if he sang, we listened and joined in, by being playful in our own way. I liked him because he allowed us to be kids in his classroom.

There were many things that my old school in Nebraska had that I missed at the government school I attended on the reservation. I missed the smell of new books that seemed a natural part of my life in my old school; the clear sound of the triangle when the music teacher played a note to get our attention for music class; the Friday afternoon art class when we could bring bubble gum to class and chew it while we worked unhurried and unsupervised on some art project. Somewhere between my old school and my new one, someone had made the judgment that books, music, and art were no longer important, but I knew they were and I missed them. I remember the year my older brother gave me a pad of drawing paper and charcoal for my birthday. I was already in junior high, but, I felt as if I was back in that sunny classroom in Nebraska, in first grade, when I took a large blank sheet of paper and a new box of crayons and sat down to create something. I don't remember that same freedom in any classroom in the government school.

In contrast, my first year at the Catholic school, I listened to Haydn, Bach, and Mozart. The volunteer the nuns hired at fifty dollars a month plus room and board brought out an ancient record player and played classical music while she had us rest our heads on our desks. I remember "Poppa Haydn" the best. I was in seventh grade at the school, an adolescent ready and able to learn, despite what the government school thought I could or could not learn, what I should or should not be exposed to, what freedom I should or should not be given, even with a simple box of crayons and a blank piece of art paper.

My teacher, a balding woman in her thirties, brought new things to us: she brought books and music—but not art. Her specialties were books, music, and composition. I wrote my first short story for her. I wrote about a ghetto where a young boy died when he broke his promise to his mother to stay away from drugs. The last words he spoke were to his mother, to whom he said, "I'm sorry I broke my promise." The story was called "Broken Promise." I remember it because I wrote it after I had pilfered my older brother's book about a boy growing up in a ghetto and had read it in secret.

It was a time when I was like an empty vessel, ready to hold whatever was poured into me. It was also a time when I realized that I had the power to pour into myself those things that I thought were interesting and new. I "borrowed" my brother's books whenever I could. I read about Hiroshima in secret, suffering nightmares about my skin melting like butter and not being able to die before it happened. It was a time during which I covered my ears when I heard the nightly news because I didn't want to hear the body counts of how many died in Vietnam that day. It was a fearful time, to be in seventh grade, in knee highs and dresses that were one inch below the knee, and feel that the world I read about in my "stolen" books was much more interesting but terrifying than my own.

It was there at that school, in that small valley with the large cottonwood, apple orchards, and statues of the Virgin Mary, that I found the freedom to enjoy all the things in which I have always felt a certain solace: especially books, but also music and art. I was now able to learn, finally to read and write well; *Owagahnige*, meaning 'I understood'. I also learned how to converse with my teachers in a playful way. The teachers I was exposed to at the Catholic school were not government employees; they were real people. They came to the school to volunteer their talents for the grace of their church, and they were real.

In my second year there, I was finally given a teacher who was an artist. He became my mentor, my substitute for my older brother, who no longer had time for me. My brother had married his high school girlfriend, and they both went away to college. I needed someone to replace him, and this teacher who had come all the way from the East Coast, from Schenectady, New York, with his young child and wife, became the perfect replacement. In secret he called me *wanahca*, meaning 'flower or blossom', and he tended to me like a careful gardener, just like my older brother had done in his own way.

My teacher-friend taught me many things, but one of the most important things I learned was from watching him, how he vented his creative energy. I remember well how he seemed to have a deep well within him from which he drew the sweetest water. He was able to go off alone and come back with something he created, something beautiful and admirable, whether it was a simple watercolor, a poem, a story, or a piece of dry wood that he had cleaned and varnished. In whatever way he chose to give expression to his creative tendencies, he always produced something tangible to give or share. He gave me many things, but the most important thing that he gave me was time, the time he spent talking to me.

I liked sitting in his living room and swapping stories with him. He listened well. No matter when I showed up at his door, he would sit down with me and we would talk. The house he and his wife and small child lived in had two bedrooms and a large kitchen and living room combination. They had one couch, an armchair, and a kitchen table and four chairs, which was all that could fit in the small space. The things he seemed to cherish the most in his living space were his books and his music—there were stacks of books and records everywhere. To me, he seemed rich in the things he had, and I have tried to imitate him in what I fill my house with today.

I know now that the most important thing he taught me, neither of us had known then. He taught me in his direct and honest way how to converse in English. He spent time with me, time that up until then no other *wašicu*, or 'English-speaking person', had. I admired that in him, his acceptance of others who were different. He insisted that we were not so different, the Lakota and the Irish-Catholic. He had been to Ireland, the Ireland that James Joyce had written about. He even made a list of the similarities between what happened to the "Indians" in America and to the Irish in Ireland. He talked about concepts like oppression, things about which I had not heard before. It was not until after he had died, many years later, that I understood what he had told me about his people and mine. I often wish that I could go back to his living room, back to that time, only with the knowledge and understanding that I have now, and have a real conversation with him.

I remember the nuns who ran the school. The women, some of whom had been orphans before coming to the convent, had turned to the church to give them families. They cooked wholesome foods, taught literature, and celebrated the mass among themselves without the Pope looking over their shoulders. I liked their clear minds, practical nature, and calm faith. I respected them, and deep inside I wanted to be one, to have that freedom to be what they were— teachers, cooks, administrators, or whatever it seemed they wanted to be. I liked their mass, a celebration of faith that didn't require you to speak in tongues or dance in the spirit. I liked the quietness of their beautiful church, and the way the priest broke the bread and you had to say, "Lord I am not worthy to receive you, but only say the word and I shall be healed."

I did not always like them. I remember a time before I went to school there, the time my cousin and I went to see them. I remember the face of the nun in the doorway. Her bright, clear, white complexion and red cheeks. Her head covered and her eyes peering through her wire glasses. I remember my cousin knocking on the door and waiting expectantly. I stood behind her, feeling somewhat apprehensive. I was never sure whether I would stand there long enough to be seen or run and hide before they answered the door. My cousin, who was my age, waited very confidently and patiently. Her patience was a source of comfort for me. We were best friends. I was her opposite—flighty and ready to laugh or giggle at the drop of a hat, or run at the sight of a strange dog. She, on the other hand, always maintained a quiet and calm demeanor, her face expressionless. We looked alike, everyone said. I didn't think so. We both had long hair. We were both thin and sometimes we both seemed thoughtful, but our faces were different. Her Lakotaness was real, mine a mixture of French and Indian. My chin was too pointed and my eyes too expressive.

The day we knocked on the nun's door, my cousin was there at the bidding of an older woman, a relative who was indigent. Her husband had asked her to leave their home, and she did, leaving behind a son. She lived here and there, all alone and always looking hungry, perhaps like Iktomi. I feared somewhere in the back of my mind that I might turn out like her. She stood waiting behind a tall cottonwood tree, hiding. The woman had asked my cousin to ask the nuns for some food, to tell them that we were hungry. We were supposed to say not only that we were hungry but to ask specifically for a "cheese sandwich." I hated cheese sandwiches.

When one of the nuns answered the door, she looked at us. "Yes?" she asked expectantly. I stepped back one step, and my cousin began to speak. "May we have a cheese san-witch?" she asked. I turned red and suddenly felt hot and uncomfortable. I didn't want a cheese sandwich. I wanted to know what was inside the convent. They were mysterious to me, the nuns and the priests that we called *sapų* or 'they that wear black'. I was not Catholic. I had been baptized as an infant by the *ska ų*, meaning 'they that wear white', the Episcopalians. I knew nothing about the nuns. I was curious, and I wanted to know. I would have my chance a few years later to see exactly what was in that convent, but that day when I stood at the door, it was the first time in my life that I had the opportunity to see a nun up close. I was surprised at how young she seemed, how impatient and human she seemed when she abruptly said, "Just a minute," and went back inside. Within a few minutes she came back out with two cold cheese sandwiches. She handed them to us without hesitating and was ready to close the door. My cousin took them and turned away after saying "thank you." I stood there, as if I had seen a ghost. I waited for something terrible to happen to me, but nothing did. I had just encountered something that I had not expected. She was just as human as any of us, that nun who answered that door. "Next time, why don't you cook for them," she said loudly to the woman who stood hiding behind us somewhere. It occurred to me years later that had I felt confident in my ability to speak English, I would have told the nun about her, the woman who had us beg for cheese sandwiches for her. I would have asked the nun whether she felt it was appropriate for a Christian to tell someone who obviously had no food and was hungry to cook for herself. I wanted to pull the nun out of that door, away from that large white house called a "convent," down the neatly graveled road to the place that the woman lived, to the places we all lived. I wanted to show her what it was like out there where we lived, where for some of us, American cheese and white bread were a luxury beyond words. I stood looking at the door after she closed it and left, and I wondered how I could tell her those things, how I could communicate so that she would know the things I wanted her to know, the things I thought she should know about us. "I could not speak English," back then. "Wašicuia owakihi šni."

Off Reservation Blues

Paula Gunn Allen

In the dream I was locked in
stood behind a window
high off the ground.
Wind blew the junipers back and forth
I could see a white-skinned figure
far below tossed among them
looking up at me
the sepia light
the deep green trees
the cold in the teeth of the man
who waved with the trees below
and I tried to speak
through the taller than awake trees
knew I had   to speak
to call
to make him see
me locked so far over his head
my eyes
my voice
caught in the tossing branches
but I could not
sleep wrapped tight around my tongue
my voice caught tight in me
eyes fixed on the spot where he stood
gaze frozen on the trees
blowing back and forth in front of me
dark green whips

night was coming
and I had to speak
raise my hand and hit the glass
I groaned
sound too soft to hear

in wakening again I stand
trying to speak

trees of memory tossing
straining to be free of the holding earth
entranced I stand, staring,
your eyes a pane of glass
your thought a wind whipping my words
like boughs back and forth
you must hear me. I must make you
hear—eyes fixed on the spot,
words flying cold against your teeth—
I groan, sound too soft to hear, I weep,
turn away, smiling softly, draw
my shawl over my face, slide back
against the wall:
so nice to see you again, I say.

If my language is oblique
misunderstandable—
if I confine myself
within demands of imaged time—
I saw true one night:
the keeper and the kept,
saw myself,
how I must
be—not in the forests of *should*—
but actually:
this narrow pass,
this sharpness of tongue,
this blade to cut your heart out
and offer it to the sun
must stay quiet awhile.
Open words, openly said
are not heard.
I hold tightly to your face
beyond the window
awaken myself rather than yet see
that you do not hear me calling you—
even when the wind is warm,
even when the wind is still,
even when the windows are wide open
and not at all above the ground.

¿Qué dice? ¿Qué dice? Child Translators and the Power of Language

Abridged from an article by Antonia Castañeda

Age 7: El doctor/The Doctor

"Dile que no puedo respirar—que se me atora el aire. Dile . . ." How do I say 'atora'?

"Tell your mother that she has to stop and place this hose in her mouth and press this pump or else she will suffocate."

"¿Qué dice? ¿Qué dice?"

He is sitting behind this big desk, and my mother is sitting beside me and holding onto my hand very tightly.

I . . . what does 'suffocate' mean? How do I translate this? I don't have the words.

"¿Qué dice? ¿Qué dice?"

"I . . . uh . . . Dice que . . . uh . . . Dice que si no haces lo que te dice te mueres."

"Dile que cuando me acuesto por la noche que no puedo resollar." 'Resollar,' what does that mean?

Her gasps came out quickly and sounded so awful: a croaking sound that seemed to hurt from deep inside her throat. I sit in front of the big desk remembering, hearing her sounds, and feel again the terror of last night and every time I heard her and could not help. I do not have the words to help her. She will die. And all I could do was sit there and hold her hand and listen to her gasp and gasp for air—for breath that would not reach her, her eyes popping out—and watch her die. She called me her *lengua*, her *voz*. If she dies, it will be my fault.

I tell the doctor she cannot breathe and will die. And he says something I cannot understand about asthmatics and how there is little he can do except give her this pump and that I should be sure to tell her not to panic.

Panic. What does that word mean? How do I say 'panic'?

How does a seven-year-old girl, not yet in the second grade, translate the life and death words *atora, suffocate, resollar, panic*?* How does she explain and interpret words she does not know in either language, while knowing at the same time that her mother's life sits on her tongue and on what she does with the words given her? Where in her seven-year-old knowledge does she find the meaning of words that hold the life or death of the mother who calls her

---

*Respirar 'breathe (freely), catch one's breath'; atorar 'choke'; resollar 'breath deeply'.

"mi lengua"—her tongue—the fleshy, movable organ attached to the floor of the mouth with which words are made? What cultural rites are these in which children become adults long before puberty?

Who are these children who speak in tongues and live in fire? What happens to them as they move through the educational system—the system of which most of us are products, the system to which we send our children, the system that employs us, the system that does violence to our mental integration, and the system that historically has also done violence to our physical selves precisely because we spoke languages other than English?[3] Although many Chicano/Latino children are pushed out of the public educational system in places like Texas and California, they and all children in the United States are steeped in lessons about rugged individualism, democracy, 'American' nationalism, equality, justice, merit, and fair play. What do children of color, children of farmworker families, and other working-class children, whose daily experiences belie the national myths, understand and know about these myths?[4]

Recently, social-science scholars and practitioners—particularly linguists, psychologists, anthropologists, and social workers—have begun to examine and debate issues pertinent to children as translators.[5] Generally, however, these scholars have cast the experience as a recent phenomenon specific to immigrant children and their families. They have centered the debate on the psychological or linguistic 'costs and benefits' to the individual child.

One side argues that translating for parents and family is harmful to the child's psychological development and that, because children play an adult role while they are translating, they may grow up too quickly and resent or lose respect for their parents. This perspective is exemplified by Richard Rodriguez's undernourished *Hunger of Memory*.[6]* Rodriguez accepted and internalized the tenets of a racist, classist society that deemed everything about him—the color of his skin, his language, his physiognomy, and his working-class origins—wrong, unacceptable, and un-American. He internalized these notions and relinquished his Mexican self, choosing education over family, erudite English over Spanish, a 'public' Euro-American life over a 'private' Mexican one. In rejecting his Mexican self, Rodriguez has, in fact, been accepted by Euro-America and has become the darling of certain segments of the white intelligentsia.

The other side of the debate argues that translating can help children develop language skills, and understand American institutions. Lowry Hemphill, a specialist in language development at Harvard University, stated that translating is not necessarily something that should be discouraged, since it is "part and parcel of the whole experience of being an immigrant child. People

---

*A selection from Rodriguez's memoir is reproduced in this volume (part I).

do what they have to do to get by."[7] Ernesto Galarza, whose autobiographical *Barrio Boy* reveals translating as empowering, learned very early—in a remote, mountainous village in Mexico and in a multiethnic, working-class barrio in Sacramento—to see himself in relation to his family, his community, and his class and to understand and interpret the world in terms of power relationships and class differences.[8] Galarza embraced the experience of translating and transformed it into a powerful tool with which to give public voice to the struggle for the rights of industrial workers, including farmworkers, throughout the world. Within that framework, translating was a powerful, positive, and valuable skill to be used and shared with others.

Age 10: La escuela/School

"Dile que venimos con Doña Chelo para averiguar por qué espulsaron a Mariquita."
*"Sí, y dile que . . ."**
The door opens, and the principal comes out, asking, "Who is Mrs. Rodríguez?"
I touch Doña Chelo's arm. She looks at me and steps forward with her hand outstretched.
"We can't have all these Mexican kids disrupting our school."
"¿Qué dice? ¿Qué dice?" Doña Chelo asks.
"If this is Marrría Rodríguez's mother, tell her that her daughter bit the school nurse, and we had to expel her."
"Dile que Mariquita no tiene piojos. Que soy muy limpia—cada noche caliento tinas de agua y baño a todos mis muchachos y los mando muy limpiesitos a la escuela. Y a Mariquita le hago sus trenzas cada mañana. ¿Por qué le echaron todo ese polvo tan apestoso? Dile que la asustaron y la humillaron."
"Doña Chelo says her family is very clean. She heats water every night for baths and sends her children to school clean every day. She braids Mariquita's hair every morning. Why did you pour that ugly powder on her? You scared Mariquita and hurt her."
"Tell her that we do this every year in March when all you kids from the camps start coming in. Tell her that the lice powder is not harmful and that the school nurse tries not to get it in their eyes or mouth. There was no reason for Marrría to cry and scream like she did. And then when the nurse tried to hold her down, she screamed even louder and bit and kicked and hit our poor nurse. Tell her she should send her children to school clean and neat. And she should teach her children to behave, to respect school authorities."
"¿Qué dice? ¿Qué dice? ¿Cuándo puede regresar Mariquita a sus clases? ¿Cómo puede aprender si me la expulsan? Yo no quiero que se queden burros como nosotros, que no nos admitían a las escuelas en Tejas. Dile, Nenita. Dile."†

---

*"Tell him we have come with Doña Chelo to inquire into the reasons they expelled Mariquita." "Yes, and tell him . . ."
†"What is he saying? What is he saying? When can Mariquita return to school? How can she study if they expel her? I do not want her to remain ignorant like us, who were not permitted to attend schools in Texas. Tell him, my little goddaughter, tell him."

*"Les estoy diciendo, Doña Chelo. Les estoy diciendo."**

What did a Tejanita of seven summers know and interpret as she broke through multilayered power differentials to translate for a mother facing racist male creditors, doctors, police, or school authorities? What did a teenage Mexican girl of fifteen understand about sexuality, race, and violence when she had to translate her family's needs to a store owner who made sexual overtures every time she came into the store in the same town where a white man with a hunting rifle came to threaten her brother away from his daughter. . . .† How do these girls and young women assimilate, accept, and/or resist this experience? What do they change, and how are they changed by the act of translating cultures across space, time, and circumstance?

---

*"I am telling them, Doña Chelo. I am telling them."
† *Tejanita:* Texan girl. Two additional child translation narratives depicted in Castañeda's article are not reproduced here.

No Questions Asked

Armand Garnet Ruffo

Gradually you lose your tongue
and hardly notice.
How can you? It doesn't fall from your mouth
and you don't bite it off
and swallow it (if you did you probably wouldn't be here).
The process is subtle. For the longest time
you even keep thinking it's still attached
and continue to use it
to chew or gargle. Tho all the while
you are saying less: Conversations
become a burden,
a portage of words;

in your blunted mouth they become gnarled
and convoluted, so you accede, resign yourself
to this mute fate. Soon
you learn to live without a tongue.
Who needs one anyway, why speak?
You even begin to enjoy your new position
and use it to your advantage.
Your work and play become a silent and private deal,
while everywhere, in the sky, on the ground,
there are raw signs demanding your voice
and you are empty.
Nothing to say.
No excuses required.
No questions asked.

Me Talk Pretty One Day

David Sedaris

At the age of forty-one, I am returning to school and have to think of myself as what my French textbook calls "a true debutant." After paying my tuition, I was issued a student ID, which allows me a discounted entry fee at movie theaters, puppet shows, and Festyland, a far-flung amusement park that advertises with billboards picturing a cartoon stegosaurus sitting in a canoe and eating what appears to be a ham sandwich.

I've moved to Paris with hopes of learning the language. My school is an easy ten-minute walk from my apartment, and on the first day of class I arrived early, watching as the returning students greeted one another in the school lobby. Vacations were recounted, and questions were raised concerning mutual friends with names like Kang and Vlatnya. Regardless of their nationalities, everyone spoke in what sounded to me like excellent French. Some accents were better than others, but the students exhibited an ease and confidence I found intimidating. As an added discomfort, they were all young, attractive, and well dressed, causing me to feel not unlike Pa Kettle trapped backstage after a fashion show.

The first day of class was nerve-racking because I knew I'd be expected to perform. That's the way they do it here—it's everybody into the language pool, sink or swim. The teacher marched in, deeply tanned from a recent vacation, and proceeded to rattle off a series of administrative announcements. I've spent quite a few summers in Normandy, and I took a monthlong French class before leaving New York. I'm not completely in the dark, yet I understood only half of what this woman was saying.

"If you have not *meimslsxp* or *lgpdmurct* by this time, then you should not be in this room. Has everyone *apzkiubjxow*? Everyone? Good, we shall begin." She spread out her lesson plan and sighed, saying, "All right, then, who knows the alphabet?"

It was startling because (a) I hadn't been asked that question in a while and (b) I realized, while laughing, that I myself did *not* know the alphabet. They're the same letters, but in France they're pronounced differently. I know the shape of the alphabet but had no idea what it actually sounded like.

"Ahh." The teacher went to the board and sketched the letter *a*. "Do we have anyone in the room whose first name commences with an *ahh*?"

Two Polish Annas raised their hands, and the teacher instructed them to present themselves by stating their names, nationalities, occupations, and a brief list of things they liked and disliked in this world. The first Anna hailed from an industrial town outside of Warsaw and had front teeth the size of tombstones. She worked as a seamstress, enjoyed quiet times with friends, and hated the mosquito.

"Oh, really," the teacher said. "How very interesting. I thought that everyone loved the mosquito, but here, in front of all the world, you claim to detest him. How is it that we've been blessed with someone as unique and original as you? Tell us, please."

The seamstress did not understand what was being said but knew that this was an occasion for shame. Her rabbity mouth huffed for breath, and she stared down at her lap as though the appropriate comeback were stitched somewhere alongside the zipper of her slacks.

The second Anna learned from the first and claimed to love sunshine and detest lies. It sounded like a translation of one of those Playmate of the Month data sheets, the answers always written in the same loopy handwriting: "Turnons: Mom's famous five-alarm chili! Turnoffs: insecurity and guys who come on too strong!!!!"

The two Polish Annas surely had clear notions of what they loved and hated, but like the rest of us, they were limited in terms of vocabulary, and this made them appear less than sophisticated. The teacher forged on, and we learned that Carlos, the Argentine bandonion player, loved wine, music, and, in his words, "making sex with the womens of the world." Next came a beautiful young Yugoslav who identified herself as an optimist, saying that she loved everything that life had to offer.

The teacher licked her lips, revealing a hint of the saucebox we would later come to know. She crouched low for her attack, placed her hands on the young woman's desk, and leaned close, saying, "Oh yeah? And do you love your little war?"

While the optimist struggled to defend herself, I scrambled to think of an answer to what had obviously become a trick question. How often is one asked what he loves in this world? More to the point, how often is one asked and then publicly ridiculed for his answer? I recalled my mother, flushed with wine, pounding the tabletop late one night, saying, "Love? I love a good steak cooked rare. I love my cat, and I love . . ." My sisters and I leaned forward, waiting to hear our names. "Tums," our mother said. "I love Tums."

The teacher killed some time accusing the Yugoslavian girl of masterminding a program of genocide, and I jotted frantic notes in the margins of my pad. While I can honestly say that I love leafing through medical textbooks devoted to severe dermatological conditions, the hobby is beyond the reach of my French vocabulary, and acting it out would only have invited controversy.

When called upon, I delivered an effortless list of things that I detest: blood sausage, intestinal pâtés, brain pudding. I'd learned these words the hard way. Having given it some thought, I then declared my love for IBM typewriters, the French word for *bruise,* and my electric floor waxer. It was a short list, but still I managed to mispronounce *IBM* and assign the wrong gender to both the floor waxer and the typewriter. The teacher's reaction led me to believe that these mistakes were capital crimes in the country of France.

"Were you always this *palicmkrexis?*" she asked. "Even a *fiuscrzsa ticiwelmun* knows that a typewriter is feminine."

I absorbed as much of her abuse as I could understand, thinking—but not saying—that I find it ridiculous to assign a gender to an inanimate object incapable of disrobing and making an occasional fool of itself. Why refer to Lady Crack Pipe or Good Sir Dishrag when these things could never live up to all that their sex implied?

The teacher proceeded to belittle everyone from German Eva, who hated laziness, to Japanese Yukari, who loved paintbrushes and soap. Italian, Thai, Dutch, Korean, and Chinese—we all left class foolishly believing that the worst was over. She'd shaken us up a little, but surely that was just an act designed to weed out the deadweight. We didn't know it then, but the coming months would teach us what it was like to spend time in the presence of a wild animal, something completely unpredictable. Her temperament was not based on a series of good and bad days but, rather, good and bad moments. We soon learned to dodge chalk and protect our heads and stomachs whenever she approached us with a question. She hadn't yet punched anyone, but it seemed wise to protect ourselves against the inevitable.

Though we were forbidden to speak anything but French, the teacher would occasionally use us to practice any of her five fluent languages.

"I hate you," she said to me one afternoon. Her English was flawless. "I really, really hate you." Call me sensitive, but I couldn't help but take it personally.

After being singled out as a lazy *kfdtinvfm,* I took to spending four hours a night on my homework, putting in even more time whenever we were assigned an essay. I suppose I could have gotten by with less, but I was determined to create some sort of identity for myself: David the hard worker, David the cut-up. We'd have one of those "complete this sentence" exercises, and I'd fool with the thing for hours, invariably settling on something like "A quick run around the lake? I'd love to! Just give me a moment while I strap on my wooden leg." The teacher, through word and action, conveyed the message that if this was my idea of an identity, she wanted nothing to do with it.

My fear and discomfort crept beyond the borders of the classroom and accompanied me out onto the wide boulevards. Stopping for a coffee, asking directions, depositing money in my bank account: these things were out of the question, as they involved having to speak. Before beginning school, there'd been no shutting me up, but now I was convinced that everything I said was wrong. When the phone rang, I ignored it. If someone asked me a question, I pretended to be deaf. I knew my fear was getting the best of me when I started wondering why they don't sell cuts of meat in vending machines.

My only comfort was the knowledge that I was not alone. Huddled in the hallways and making the most of our pathetic French, my fellow students and I engaged in the sort of conversation commonly overheard in refugee camps.

"Sometime me cry alone at night."

"That be common for I, also, but be more strong, you. Much work and someday you talk pretty. People start love you soon. Maybe tomorrow, okay."

Unlike the French class I had taken in New York, here there was no sense of competition. When the teacher poked a shy Korean in the eyelid with a freshly sharpened pencil, we took no comfort in the fact that, unlike Hyeyoon Cho, we all knew the irregular past tense of the verb *to defeat*. In all fairness, the teacher hadn't meant to stab the girl, but neither did she spend much time apologizing, saying only, "Well, you should have been *vkkdyo* more *kdeynfulh*."

Over time it became impossible to believe that any of us would ever improve. Fall arrived and it rained every day, meaning we would now be scolded for the water dripping from our coats and umbrellas. It was mid-October when the teacher singled me out, saying, "Every day spent with you is like having a cesarean section." And it struck me that, for the first time since arriving in France, I could understand every word that someone was saying.

Understanding doesn't mean that you can suddenly speak the language. Far from it. It's a small step, nothing more, yet its rewards are intoxicating and deceptive. The teacher continued her diatribe and I settled back, bathing in the subtle beauty of each new curse and insult.

"You exhaust me with your foolishness and reward my efforts with nothing but pain, do you understand me?"

The world opened up, and it was with great joy that I responded, "I know the thing that you speak exact now. Talk me more, you, plus, please, plus."

The Silence of Polyglots

Julia Kristeva

Not speaking one's mother tongue. Living with resonances and reasoning that are cut off from the body's nocturnal memory, from the bittersweet slumber of childhood. Bearing within oneself like a secret vault, or like a handicapped child—cherished and useless—that language of the past that withers without ever leaving you. You improve your ability with another instrument, as one expresses oneself with algebra or the violin. You can become a virtuoso with this new device that moreover gives you a new body, just as artificial and subli-mated—some say sublime. You have a feeling that the new language is a resur-rection: new skin, new sex. But the illusion bursts when you hear, upon listening to a recording, for instance, that the melody of your voice comes back to you as a peculiar sound, out of nowhere, closer to the old spluttering than to today's code. Your awkwardness has its charm, they say, it is even erotic, according to womanizers, not to be outdone. No one points out your mistakes, so as not to hurt your feelings, and then there are so many, and after all they don't give a damn. One nevertheless lets you know that it is irritating just the same. Occasionally, raising the eyebrows or saying "I beg your pardon?" in quick succession lead you to understand that you will "never be a part of it," that it "is not worth it," that there, at least, one is "not taken in." Being fooled is not what happens to you either. At the most, you are willing to go along, ready for all apprenticeships, at all ages, in order to reach—within that speech of others, imagined as being perfectly assimilated, *some day*—who knows what ideal, beyond the implicit acknowledgment of a disappointment caused by the origin that did not keep its promise.

Thus, between two languages, your realm is silence. By dint of saying things in various ways, one just as trite as the other, just as approximate, one ends up no longer saying them. An internationally known scholar was ironical about his famous polyglotism, saying that he spoke Russian in fifteen languages. As for me I had the feeling that he rejected speech and his slack silence led him, at times, to sing and give rhythm to chanted poems, just in order to say some-thing.

When Hölderlin* became absorbed by Greek (before going back to the sources of German), he dramatically expressed the anesthesia of the person that is snatched up by a foreign language: "A sign, such are we, and of no meaning /

Editor: Friedrich Hölderlin was an eighteenth-century German poet.

Dead to all suffering, and we have almost / Lost our language in a foreign land"
(Mnemosyne).

Stuck within that polymorphic mutism, the foreigner can, instead of saying, attempt doing—house-cleaning, playing tennis, soccer, sailing, sewing, horseback riding, jogging, getting pregnant, what have you. It remains an expenditure, it expends, and it propagates silence even more. Who listens to you? At the most, you are being tolerated. Anyway, do you really want to speak?

Why then did you cut off the maternal source of words? What did you dream up concerning those new people you spoke to in an artificial language, a prosthesis? From your standpoint, were they idealized or scorned? Come, now! Silence has not only been forced upon you, it is within you: a refusal to speak, a fitful sleep riven to an anguish that wants to remain mute, the private property of your proud and mortified discretion, that silence is a harsh light. Nothing to say, nothingness, no one on the horizon. An impervious fullness: cold diamond, secret treasury, carefully protected, out of reach. Saying nothing, nothing needs to be said, nothing can be said. At first, it was a cold war with those of the new idiom, desired and rejecting; then the new language covered you as might a slow tide, a neap tide. It is not the silence of anger that jostles words at the edge of the idea and the mouth; rather, it is the silence that empties the mind and fills the brain with despondency, like the gaze of sorrowful women coiled up in some nonexistent eternity.

From "voz en una cárcel"

Juanita M. Sánchez

my voice is in the prison
of my own history
i never know
am i being too spanish
or not enough english?
. . .
you laugh at my accent
maybe,
maybe just one too many times

From *The Woman Warrior*

Maxine Hong Kingston

Long ago in China, knot-makers tied string into buttons and frogs, and rope into bell pulls. There was one knot so complicated that it blinded the knot-maker. Finally an emperor outlawed this cruel knot, and the nobles could not order it anymore. If I had lived in China, I would have been an outlaw knot-maker.

Maybe that's why my mother cut my tongue. She pushed my tongue up and sliced the frenum. Or maybe she snipped it with a pair of nail scissors. I don't remember her doing it, only her telling me about it, but all during childhood I felt sorry for the baby whose mother waited with scissors or knife in hand for it to cry—and then, when its mouth was wide open like a baby bird's, cut. The Chinese say, "a ready tongue is an evil."

I used to curl up my tongue in front of the mirror and tauten my frenum into a white line, itself as thin as a razor blade. I saw no scars in my mouth. I thought perhaps I had two frena, and she had cut one. I made other children open their mouths so I could compare theirs to mine. I saw perfect pink membranes stretching into precise edges that looked easy enough to cut. Sometimes I feel very proud that my mother committed such a powerful act upon me. At other times I was terrified—the first thing my mother did when she saw me was to cut my tongue.

"Why did you do that to me, Mother?"

"I told you."

"Tell me again."

"I cut it so that you would not be tongue-tied. Your tongue would be able to move in any language. You'll be able to speak languages that are completely different from one another. You'll be able to pronounce anything. Your frenum looked too tight to do those things, so I cut it."

"But isn't 'a ready tongue an evil'?"

"Things are different in this ghost country."

"Did it hurt me? Did I cry and bleed?"

"I don't remember. Probably."

She didn't cut the other children's. When I asked cousins and other Chinese children whether their mothers had cut their tongues loose, they said, "What?"

"Why didn't you cut my brothers' and sisters' tongues?"

"They didn't need it."

"Why not? Were theirs longer than mine?"

"Why don't you quit blabbering and get to work?"

If my mother was not lying she should have cut more, scraped away the rest of the frenum skin, because I have a terrible time talking. Or she should not have cut at all, tampering with my speech. When I went to kindergarten and had to speak English for the first time, I became silent. A dumbness—a shame—still cracks my voice in two, even when I want to say "hello" casually, or ask an easy question in front of the check-out counter, or ask directions of a bus driver. I stand frozen, or I hold up the line with the complete, grammatical sentence that comes squeaking out at impossible length. "What did you say?" says the cab driver, or "Speak up," so I have to perform again, only weaker the second time. A telephone call makes my throat bleed and takes up that day's courage. It spoils my day with self-disgust when I hear my broken voice come skittering out into the open. It makes people wince to hear it. I'm getting better, though. Recently I asked the postman for special issue stamps; I've waited since childhood for postmen to give me some of their own accord. I am making progress, a little every day.

My silence was thickest—total—during the three years I covered my school paintings with black paint. I painted layers of black over houses and flowers and suns, and when I drew on the blackboard, I put a layer of chalk on top. I was making a stage curtain, and it was the moment before the curtain parted or rose. The teachers called my parents to school, and I saw they had been saving my pictures, curling and cracking, all alike and black. The teachers pointed to the pictures and looked serious, talked seriously too, but my parents did not understand English. ("The parents and teachers of criminals were executed," said my father.) My parents took the pictures home. I spread them out (so black and full of possibilities) and pretended the curtains were swinging open, flying up, one after another, sunlight underneath, mighty operas.

During the first silent year I spoke to no one at school, did not ask before going to the lavatory, and flunked kindergarten. My sister also said nothing for three years, silent in the playground and silent at lunch. There were other quiet Chinese girls not of our family, but most of them got over it sooner than we did. I enjoyed the silence. At first it did not occur to me I was supposed to talk or to pass kindergarten. I talked at home and to one or two of the Chinese kids in class. I made motions and even made some jokes. I drank out of a toy saucer when the water spilled out of the cup, and everybody laughed, pointing at me, so I did it some more. I didn't know that Americans didn't drink out of saucers.

I liked the Negro students (Black Ghosts) best because they laughed the loudest and talked to me as if I were a daring talker too. One of the Negro girls had her mother coil braids over her ears Shanghai-style like mine; we were Shanghai twins except that she was covered with black like my paintings.

Two Negro kids enrolled in Chinese school, and the teachers gave them Chinese names. Some Negro kids walked me to school and home, protecting me from the Japanese kids, who hit me and chased me and stuck gum in my ears. The Japanese kids were noisy and tough. They appeared one day in kindergarten, released from concentration camp, which was a tic-tac-toe mark, like barbed wire, on the map.

It was when I found out I had to talk that school became a misery, that the silence became a misery. I did not speak and felt bad each time that I did not speak. I read aloud in first grade, though, and heard the barest whisper with little squeaks come out of my throat. "Louder," said the teacher, who scared the voice away again. The other Chinese girls did not talk either, so I knew the silence had to do with being a Chinese girl.

Reading out loud was easier than speaking because we did not have to make up what to say, but I stopped often, and the teacher would think I'd gone quiet again. I could not understand *I*. The Chinese *I* has seven strokes, intricacies. How could the American *I,* assuredly wearing a hat like the Chinese, have only three strokes, the middle so straight? Was it out of politeness that this writer left off strokes the way a Chinese has to write her own name small and crooked? No, it was not politeness; *I* is a capital and *you* is lower-case. I stared at that middle line and waited so long for its black center to resolve into tight strokes and dots that I forgot to pronounce it. The other troublesome word was *here*, no strong consonant to hang on to, and so flat, when *here* is two mountainous ideographs. The teacher, who had already told me every day how to read *I* and *here*, put me in the low corner under the stairs again, where the noisy boys usually sat.

When my second grade class did a play, the whole class went to the auditorium except the Chinese girls. The teacher, lovely and Hawaiian, should have understood about us, but instead left us behind in the classroom. Our voices were too soft or nonexistent, and our parents never signed the permission slips anyway. They never signed anything unnecessary. We opened the door a crack and peeked out, but closed it again quickly. One of us (not me) won every spelling bee, though.

I remember telling the Hawaiian teacher, "We Chinese can't sing 'land where our fathers died.' " She argued with me about politics, while I meant because of curses. But how can I have that memory when I couldn't talk? My mother says that we, like the ghosts, have no memories.

After American school, we picked up our cigar boxes, in which we had arranged books, brushes and an inkbox neatly, and went to Chinese school, from 5:00 to 7:30 p.m. There we chanted together, voices rising and falling, loud and soft, some boys shouting, everybody reading together, reciting together and not alone with one voice. When we had a memorization test, the teacher let each of us come to his desk and say the lesson to him privately, while the rest of the class practiced copying or tracing. Most of the teachers were men. The boys who were so well behaved in the American school played tricks on them and talked back to them. The girls were not mute. They screamed and yelled during recess, when there were no rules; they had fist-fights. Nobody was afraid of children hurting themselves or of children hurting school property. The glass doors to the red and green balconies with the gold joy symbols were left wide open so that we could run out and climb the fire escapes. We played capture-the-flag in the auditorium, where Sun Yat-sen and Chiang Kai-shek's pictures hung at the back of the stage, the Chinese flag on their left and the American flag on their right. We climbed the teak ceremonial chairs and made flying leaps off the stage. One flag headquarters was behind the glass door and the other on stage right. Our feet drummed on the hollow stage. During recess the teachers locked themselves up in their office with the shelves of books, copybooks, inks from China. They drank tea and warmed their hands at a stove. There was no play supervision. At recess we had the school to ourselves, and also we could roam as far as we could go—downtown, Chinatown stores, home—as long as we returned before the bell rang.

At exactly 7:30 the teacher again picked up the brass bell that sat on his desk and swung it over our heads, while we charged down the stairs, our cheering magnified in the stairwell. Nobody had to line up.

Not all of the children who were silent at American school found voice at Chinese school. One new teacher said each of us had to get up and recite in front of the class, who was to listen. My sister and I memorized the lesson perfectly. We said it to each other at home, one chanting, one listening. The teacher called on my sister to recite first. It was the first time a teacher had called on the second-born to go first. My sister was scared. She glanced at me and looked away; I looked down at my desk. I hoped that she could do it because if she could, then I would have to. She opened her mouth and a voice came out that wasn't a whisper, but it wasn't a proper voice either. I hoped that she would not cry, fear breaking up her voice like twigs underfoot. She sounded as if she were trying to sing through weeping and strangling. She did not pause or stop to end the embarrassment. She kept going until she said the last word, and then she sat down. When it was my turn, the same voice came out, a crippled animal running on broken legs. You could hear splinters in my voice, bones rubbing jagged against one another. I was loud, though. I was glad I didn't whisper. There was one little girl who whispered.

Notes

1. Aldous Huxley, *Point Counter Point* (Normal, Illinois: Dalkey Archive Press, 1996, originally published in 1928), 10.

2. A selection from Alma Villanueva's "Mother May I?" in *Contemporary Chicana Poetry: A Critical Approach to an Emerging Literature*, ed. Marta Ester Sánchez (Berkeley, Los Angeles, and London: University of California Press, 1985), 324.

3. See for two examples: Guadalupe San Miguel, *'Let All of Them Take Heed': Mexican Americans and the Campaign for Educational Equality in Texas, 1910–1981* (Austin: University of Texas Press, 1987); Charles M. Wollenberg, *All Deliberate Speed: Segregation and Exclusion in California Schools, 1855–1975* (Berkeley, Los Angeles, and London: University of California Press, 1978).

4. *Author's note:* For an important discussion of the politics of linguistic domination, and its centrality to the politics and policies of Spanish colonization in Mexico, see Jorge Klor de Alva, "Language, Politics, and Translation: Colonial Discourse and Classic Nahuatl in New Spain," in *The Art of Translation: Voices from the Field,* ed. Rosanna Warren. (Boston: Northeastern University Press, 1989), 143–162.

5. *Editor:* Most recently in the social science literature, children who interpret for their immigrant parents are referred to as language brokers. Two studies report that the many adult-like experiences of children language brokers may accelerate their cognitive and socio-emotional development. For a qualitative study, see Jeff McQuillan and Lucy Tse. "Child language brokering in linguistic minority communities: Effects of cultural interaction, cognition and literacy." *Language & Education* 9 (1995): 195–215. For a quantitative study, see Raymond Buriel, William Pérez; Terri L. De Ment, David V. Chávez, and Virginia R. Morán. "The relationship of language brokering to academic performance, biculturalism, and self-efficacy among Latino adolescents." *Hispanic Journal of Behavioral Sciences* 20, no. 3 (August 1998): 283–297.

6. Richard Rodriguez, *Hunger of Memory: The Education of Richard Rodriguez* (New York: Bantam Books, 1982). *Author's note:* Omission of the accent mark in Rodriguez's surname is consistent with the way he spells his family name.

7. Lowry Hemphill, "For Immigrants' Children, an Adult Role," *New York Times*, August 15, 1991.

8. Ernesto Galarza, *Barrio Boy: The Story of a Boy's Acculturation* (Notre Dame: University of Notre Dame Press, 1971).

[In English] I have no interior language, and without it, interior images—those images through which we assimilate the external world, through which we take it in, love it, make it our own—become blurred too.

—Eva Hoffman

In childhood we are told that our language is wrong. Repeated attacks on our native tongue diminish our sense of self. The attacks continue throughout our lives.

—Gloria Anzaldúa

PART TWO

THE HISTORY OF
SILENCING CHILDREN

Those who steal the words of others develop a deep doubt in the abilities of the others and consider them incompetent. Each time they say their word without hearing the word of those whom they have forbidden to speak, they grow more accustomed to power and acquire a taste for guiding, ordering, and commanding. They can no longer live without having someone to give orders to. Under these circumstances, dialogue is impossible.

—Paulo Freire[1]

I know that it is not the English language that hurts me, but what the oppressors do with it, how they shape it to become a territory that limits and defines, how they make it a weapon that can shame, humiliate, colonize.

—bell hooks

~

Chronology of Events, Court Decisions, and Legislation Affecting Language Minority Children in American Public Education

This chronology summarizes key historical events for the three major groups of language minority students who continue to be negatively affected by the legacy of U.S. public school policy decisions.

The first group, American Indians, had various systems of education in place when the Europeans arrived. For instance, attendance at the Telpuchcalli 'houses of youth' was mandatory for all Aztec males under the age of fifteen. After the fall of Tenochtitlán, Spanish priests reorganized another educational institution, the Calmecac, or school of the Aztec elite, for missionizing purposes. Nahuatl speakers began attending such Catholic schools as early as 1529. The Aztec elite had previously used their own writing system. With the Contact, their youth learned to read in Latin and to use a new writing system, the ABCs, or Roman alphabet. They then appropriated this alphabet to continue to document their lives in Nahuatl,[2] as well as using Spanish for other officially sanctioned purposes. From this time until the present day, whites have sought to educate Indians. By and large, European and later Anglo-American missionaries endeavored to employ the languages of the Indians as a means to offer their allegedly superior spiritual instruction. Their teaching method can be considered a bilingual approach. It is notable that their technique compares favorably to the standard U.S. procedure, English-only teaching, which was used for 250 years to force the Indians to adopt the Anglo-American way of life. The federal government considered off-reservation boarding schools the best place to socialize very young Indian children in the white men's worldview, by separating them from their parents and the "primitive" worldview of their communities. For whites, Indian education was described as a "civilizing" formula to "raise" the aborigine up toward their level. From the Indian point of view, these policies of linguistic decimation and cultural "domestica-tion" were designed to complete the eradication of the first Americans. A brief period of Indian progressive education finally began in 1934, but the govern-ment regressed to past practices in the 1940s. A second fleeting moment of progressive education emerged in 1960s, but it was cut short during the Reagan era. In the twenty-first century, English-only teaching still dominates Indian education.

The second group of language minority students is the descendants of Afri-cans who were enslaved and brought forcibly to the Americas. For over three hundred years, whites considered African Americans to be mere chattel and systematically denied that they were human beings. As slaves, African Ameri-cans were treated as subhuman commodities. Whites granted them less dignity than draft animals. In the South, formal education was systematically denied to them. It was illegal in most Southern states to teach a slave to read. Those who sought formal learning did so under the risk of physical peril. Until after World War I, nine-tenths of all African Americans lived in the Southern states. Free-born African Americans who resided in the Northern states had a better life, although they were burdened by the prevailing American view that they were a lower scale of humanity than the Americans who were the progeny of Euro-peans. The few public schools that were set up for African-American children were, in all cases, less well funded and well structured than white schools. In this setting, African Americans struggled for an education as individuals, as well as in organized ways. During the nineteenth century, nearly one hundred court cases challenged segregation or racial discrimination in schools. African Ameri-cans won a majority of those cases in Northern states. As early as 1855, Massa-chusetts prohibited public school segregation.[3] In the South, the road to desegregated schooling would require one hundred more years of court battles. The battle for equal schooling continues.

The third and largest group of language minority students is Latinos. In this summary, the focus will be on Puerto Rican and Chicano history. The 1848 Treaty of Guadalupe Hidalgo is the first important legal document concerning Chicanos. The treaty was designed to protect the property and civil rights of Mexicans living in the Southwest at the end of the war between the United States and Mexico. In particular it declared that all Mexican citizens (mestizos and American Indians) living in what had been northern Mexico "shall be admitted to the enjoyment of all the rights of citizens of the United States, according to the principles of the Constitution" and shall be "protected in the free enjoyment of their liberty and property, and secured in the free exercise of their religion without restriction." Over thirty-five years before the treaty, Mexico had recognized the full citizenship and equal rights of American Indi-ans and had outlawed its race-based caste system. However, the U.S. Congress weakened the Treaty of Guadalupe Hidalgo before its ratification, by revising article 9, which deals with citizenship rights. In the ensuing years, Anglo-America disregarded the treaty entirely, considering Mexican Americans a conquered people to be subjugated, rather than a group of fellow citizens to embrace. In Texas and elsewhere, Mexicans were denied the right to vote. California's state constitutional convention passed resolutions that ignored the U.S. citizenship of Mexicans. Each state passed retaliatory laws, called "Greaser Laws" in California, to further marginalize Mexicans. Everywhere, they were victims of violence. In short order, Mexican Americans became foreigners in their native land.[4] As Martha Menchaca has convincingly argued, the U.S. legal system, from 1848 to 1947, had accorded privilege to whites and, in the conquered Southwest, instituted new racial restriction policies that violated "the civil rights of Mexicans because under U.S. laws, Indians and 'half-breed Indians' were not considered U.S. citizens." In institutions such as public education, "the inferior treatment of racial minorities" was legitimated.[5] However, as will be shown, the history of Mexican American education in the United States does not end here, as Chicanos and American Indians resisted this onslaught.

Nestled in ostensively tranquil seas, for five hundred years Puerto Ricans have suffered as a colony of two great empires, the Spanish and the American. After Spain ceded the island in 1898, many Puerto Ricans looked with hope to the "Colossal of the North." The Americans, however, viewed Puerto Rico as an island resource to reap profits from, rather than a people to bring into their fold. Given their perspective, it is not surprising that for Anglo-Americans, public education on the island was sustained on a negligible budget and with similar expectations. The colonizers' only passion was Americanizing the native and, in particular, making English the lingua franca, to simplify their administrative concerns. The arrogance of empire is apparent in most Puerto Rican educational relations. Anglo-American attitudes toward Spanish ranged from dismissive to hostile, which was most clearly evidenced in the classroom. English instruction of all educational content was mandated, and by 1907 over four-fifths of all schools held classes in English alone.

Deprivation on the island precipitated the substantial migrations of Puerto Ricans to the Northeastern mainland cities in midcentury. Anglo-American colonialist values did not change once these nominal citizens arrived on the mainland. Puerto Ricans in New York and elsewhere were economic refugees in their own country, and their children attended schools that attested to this. In every U.S. city, these schools were the most severely overcrowded, least resourced, and most poorly staffed, with double sessions, no special classes, and other warehouselike conditions. The empire viewed its colonialized groups, including Puerto Ricans, as less talented, less intelligent, and unmotivated. As

Meyer Weinstein notes, the teachers of these children often viewed them with paternalism, antagonism,* or indifference: "As time went on, I would always take notes and kept a very neat book and pretended to know what was going on in class. . . . The fact that I had not learned anything didn't mean too much to that teacher; she passed me anyway because I was sweet and cooperative."[6] Extremely low rates of academic achievement and correspondingly high drop-out levels followed on this self-fulfilling prophecy.

The most salient aspect in the northeastern cities of the American empire was its shibboleth: To be a real U.S. citizen required speaking English without a trace of a Spanish accent. Puerto Rican teachers, no matter how excellent, were systematically denied permanent positions if they spoke with their community dialect of English. Rather than advancement, the educational issue in the public's mind regarding Puerto Ricans was their so-called language problem. One 1969 report pointed out that the "question of what a non-native speaking child is also a problem. For some, it is anyone whose last name sounds Spanish. For others, it is any pupil who is rated D, E, or F [on a scale] and for still others, it is any pupil who is rated other than A on the scale." The accentedness scale conflates native English ethnic dialect features with features used by second-language learners, since A was characterized as "speaks English, for his age-level, like a native—with no foreign accent or hesitancy due to a foreign language," while F meant "speaks no English."[7]

This appalling attitude was exactly what the 1968 Bilingual Education Act was designed to address. In the ensuing thirty-four years, the structural problems of colonization have not changed, but the act brought about a partial transformation of the way Puerto Rican children and other language minority children across the country were taught. However, in 2002 a new English-first-and-only language federal policy was enacted. This legislation, the "No Child Left Behind" Act, represents a 180-degree policy turn: the word *bilingual* has been completely expunged from federal policy. This act portends grim times for our nation's language minority school children.

1663 Reverend John Eliot publishes the New Testament in the Massachusetts language, with the help of Indian translators and printers.

1775 The U.S. Continental Congress appropriates five hundred dollars to establish Dartmouth College in New Hampshire for the education of Indian children.

1778–1871 The U.S. enters into over 370 treaties with various American Indian nations. More than one hundred include specific provisions for educational facilities.

---

*See Maria Mazziotti Gillan's "Learning Silence," part I.

1819   Congress earmarks ten thousand dollars for religious missions dedicated to Indian education. U.S. efforts for Indian education provide financial support to Protestant and Catholic church missions for several decades.

1839   Stephen R. Riggs finds teaching English to the Sioux "to be very difficult and not producing much apparent fruit," due not to the students' lack of ability, but rather a lack of interest. "Teaching [the Sioux language] Dakota was a different thing. It was their own language." Riggs and a colleague named Pond write a Dakota primer. Pond is convinced that Anglo-American authority over Indians "would depend very much on the correctness and facility" with which their white teachers speak the Indians' languages. Pond noted that "it has often been represented by persons having a superficial knowledge of Indian languages that they are imperfect and defective, and can be made to express but a very limited range of ideas" but that this claim was patently false for the American Indian language with which Pond was most familiar, Dakota.

1849   California Constitution, Article 2, Section 1; New Mexico Organic Law Act, Section 6 (1850); Organic Act of Arizona Constitution (1863)   All three states formally restrict citizenship to whites. Indians were prohibited from obtaining citizenship. Consequently, all Mexicans, whether of partial or full Indian descent, are also denied citizenship.

1850   Spain opens public schools in Puerto Rico for children who cannot afford the fees charged by private schools. They are immediately filled to overcapacity.

1860   Bureau of Indian Affairs opens its first school on the Yakima Indian Reservation. The school was partial payment in exchange for one-third of Washington State.

1868   Fourteenth Amendment to U.S. Constitution creates a uniform citizenship law, granting all citizens the enjoyment of all rights, including the right to vote. It rescinds the rights of states to establish citizenship eligibility. However, Indians, and hence Mexican Americans, are specifically excluded from its protection.

1868   President Grant appoints Peace Commissioners to attempt to bring the Indian wars to an end. The commission concludes that language differences led to misunderstandings and that: "Now, by educating the children of these tribes in the English language these differences would have disappeared, and civilization would have followed at once. . . . Through sameness of language is produced sameness of sentiment, and thought; customs and habits are molded and assimilated in the same way, and thus in time the differences producing trouble would have been gradually obliterated. . . . In the difference of language today lies two-thirds of our trouble. . . . Schools should be established, which [Indian] children should be required to attend; their barbarous dialect should be blotted out and the English language substituted."

1870 *People of California v. de la Guerra* Having been charged with "illegally acting" like a citizen, Pablo de la Guerra, who had previously served as a Santa Barbara district judge, disputes this insult. He appeals his case to the California Supreme Court. By claiming to be white, not Indian, he wins his case. However, other Mexican Americans are not recognized to have this same right.

1871 In a missionary report, a white teacher's experiences in Nebraska are described: "She went on for a year teaching these [Indian student] scholars, which the agent, her especial friend, secured, almost compelling them to attend, and at the end of the year these scholars could read English beautifully, could spell English beautifully, and could write English beautifully, and they did not understand the first word of English."

1872 An Indian agent from Tahlequah, Indian Territory, reports that "The children . . . go to school, and with great labor learn to read and write English, but without understanding the meaning of the words they read and write." On the other hand, because the Cherokee employ their own language, "almost the whole of those Cherokees who do not speak English can read and write the Cherokee by using the characters invented by [the celebrated Cherokee linguist] Sequoyah."

1873 A Quaker named Janney reports on a string of educational successes using Indian languages. Talking about the consequences of developing an orthography for Dakota, Janney writes: "A very small portion of the tribe, so far as I could discover, speak or write the English language, but a large number speak and write their own, and are able to hold correspondence with those who are in Minnesota and Wisconsin." In the same report: "Theirs is a phonetic language, and a smart boy will learn it in three or four weeks; and we have found it far better to instruct them in their own language, and also to teach them English as fast as we can."

1879 Colonel R. H. Pratt launches the infamous Carlisle (Pennsylvania) Boarding School, based on a military regimen. Its inductees are young Indian children who are separated from their parents. Pratt compels complete assimilation and cultural repression. Indian languages are forbidden. An Anglo name is imposed on these children.* They are

---

*See Phil George's "Name Giveaway," part I.

required to wear military uniforms and to cut their hair as whites do. Expressions of time-honored Indian religious and ceremonial culture, as well as traditional foods, are banned.

1880 A correspondent traveling with the U.S. Secretary of the Interior Carl Schurz reports, "Mr. [Stephen R.] Riggs is of the opinion that first teaching the children to read and write in their own language enables them to master English with more ease when they take up that study; and he thinks, also, that a child beginning a four years' course with the study of Dakota would be further advanced in English at the end of the term than one who had not been instructed in Dakota."

1880 *In re Camille* Naturalization Court declares that "half-breed Indians" are not eligible to become naturalized citizens.

1880 The Indian Bureau issues regulations that "all instruction must be in English" in both religious and government schools under threat of loss of government funding.

1881 Missionaries start a newspaper written mostly in the Dakota language named *Iapi Oaye* 'The Word Carrier'. In an editorial it declares: "It is sheer laziness in the teacher to berate his Indian scholars for not understanding English, when he does not understand enough Indian to tell them the meaning of a single one of the sentences he is trying to make them understand properly, though they have no idea of the sense. The teacher with his superior mind, should be able to learn half a dozen languages while these children of darkness are learning one. Even though the teacher's object were only to have them master English, he had better teach it to them in Indian, so they may understand what they are learning."

1884 *Elk v. Wilkens* U.S. Supreme Court rules that Indians were not U.S. citizens.

1885 J. D. C. Atkins, Commissioner of Indian Affairs, states that the languages of American Indian students are a "barbarous dialect" and that "to teach Indian school children their native tongue is practically to exclude English, and to prevent them from acquiring it."

1886 *Iapi Oaye* prospers and expands. It brings out two issues, an all-Dakota edition, and an all-English language edition.

1887 Commissioner Adkins bears further witness: "Every nation is jealous of its own language, and no nation ought to be more so than ours, which approaches nearer than any other nationality to the perfect protection of its people. True Americans all feel that the Constitution, laws, and institutions of the United States, in their adaptation to the wants and requirements of man, are superior to those of any other country; and they should understand that by the spread of the English language will these laws and institutions be more firmly established and widely disseminated. Nothing so surely and perfectly stamps upon an individual a national characteristic as language. . . . [Because the Indians] are in an English-speaking country, they must be taught the language which they must use in transacting business with the people of this country. No unity or community of feeling can be established among different peoples unless they are brought to speak the same language, and thus become imbued with like ideas of duty."

1897 *United States v. Wong Kim Ark* Rules that all U.S. born individuals shall be accorded full rights as citizens—with the explicit exception of American Indians. As a result, this U.S. Supreme Court ruling also indirectly denies U.S. citizenship to Mexican Americans.

1897 *In re Rodríguez* In naturalization court, prosecutors argue that Ricardo Rodríguez cannot apply for citizenship, because by "appearance," he is "of pure Aztec or Indian race." He wins by arguing he was neither Spanish nor Indian.

1890s Observers in the field report that successful missionary teachers learn the tribal language so that they can understand the children and the children can understand them. A Sioux and former Carlisle student, Luther Standing Bear reports: "At that time, teaching amounted to very little. It really did not require a well-educated person to teach on the reservation. The main thing was to teach the children to write their names in English, then came learning the alphabet and how to count. I liked this work very well, and the children were doing splendidly. The first reading books we used had a great many little pictures in them. I would have the children read a line of English, and if they did not understand all they had read, I would explain it to them in Sioux. This made the studies very interesting."

1891 *Iapi Oaye* reprints an article from *The School Journal* declaring the "chief difference between English-speaking and Indian children [is] the need of grinding, drilling, and driving English into them." In the same year in an *Education Review* article, Indian school education is similarly criticized: "Four fifths, if not nine tenths, of the work done is purely mechanical drill. . . . The child reads by rote, he memorizes the combinations in arithmetic, he copies letters and forms, he imitates the actions of his teacher."

1896 *Plessy v. Ferguson* Upholds an 1890 Louisiana law requiring railroads to provide "equal but separate accommodations for the white, and colored races." It thereby sanctions state-imposed segregation. If segregation is seen as "a badge of inferiority," the U.S. Supreme Court holds, that is only because "a race chooses to put that construction upon it."

The ruling becomes the legal foundation of racial segregation in the public schools.

1898 Rules for Indian schools: "All instruction shall be in the English language. Pupils shall be required to converse with employees and each other in English. All school employees must be able to speak English fluently."

1898 The United States prosecutes the Spanish–American War, a month-long conflict against Spain. It acquires territories in the western Pacific and Latin America. Puerto Rico becomes its colony.

1899 *Cumming v. Richmond County Board of Education* The Supreme Court ejects a bid by blacks to force the Augusta Georgia schools to end secondary education for whites until the district restores it for blacks. The ruling, the first school segregation case to reach the U.S. Supreme Court, allows wide disparities in the quality of education provided to blacks and whites in the South.

1901–1928 United States government administers Puerto Rico through a commissioner based in Washington. It provides very limited funding for Puerto Rican public schools while promoting Americanization programs in these schools, and an English-only policy.

1901 Estelle Brown takes the Civil Service Examination expecting "to be tested on my fitness to teach children of a savage race to whom the word education was unknown and who were without knowledge of a written language. No such test was given." She expects questions on tribal history and reservation conditions; she is not even told the tribe she was to teach. In effect, this exam (not unlike contemporary tests for teacher competence) is designed for teachers of mainstream students. This cultural bias excludes many potential Indian teachers, while admitting teachers with little or no knowledge of Indians and Indian education. Low government salaries, plus the rural setting of many Indian schools, means that the Indian school teaching is often the last resort for teachers who cannot find employment elsewhere.

1908 *Berea College v. Kentucky* Upholds Kentucky law prohibiting integrated classes for blacks and whites, in a case brought by a private college with a mixed-race education.

1913 *United States v. Sandoval* New Mexico Supreme Court rules that the Pueblo Indians are savages and therefore have no claim to U.S. citizenship under the Treaty of Guadalupe Hidalgo.

1917 Puerto Rico becomes a U.S. territory, "organized but unincorporated." Puerto Ricans can elect their own legislature and join the United States Army. The commissioner retains power.

1923 Puerto Rico Commissioner Huyle forbids Spanish-only public school newspapers. Only school newspapers that are at least 50 percent English text are permitted.

1926 The progressive Meriam Report on American Indian education recommends the following: ending the curriculum that stresses only Anglo-American cultural values; limiting attendance of nonreservation boarding schools to older children; having younger children attend community schools near home; and the Indian Service's providing youth and parents with tools to adapt both to the white and to the Indian world.

1927 *Gong Lum v. Rice* Affirms a Mississippi school district's right to require a Chinese-American girl to attend a segregated black school, rejecting her bid to attend the school for whites.

1927 California attorney general submits his opinion that Mexican American students are Indians and should be placed under the mandate of de jure segregation from white students.

1929 Navajo Indian children are literally lassoed from horseback and kidnapped by federal officials to be sent to boarding schools where they are forbidden to practice their own traditions or to speak their own language, on pain of whippings or going without food.*

1929 Charles Rhoades, first American Indian to become Commissioner of Indian Affairs, begins to put Meriam Report proposals into practice.

1930 *Independent School District v. Salvatierra* Desegregationists win a partial victory. A Texas judge rules that not all Mexican American students are Indians. Some are "Spanish." The latter group cannot be subject to de jure segregation. The judge does not force the school to desegregate. Moreover, he rules that it is legal to segregate Mexican Americans—on the basis of language.

1930s Beginning of migration of Puerto Ricans to U.S. mainland, mainly to New York City, initiated by professionals and the upper class.

1931 *Álvarez v. Lemon Grove School District* This is the first successful desegregation case won by Mexican Americans. As a local (California) case it cannot be used as a precedent for other statewide or national cases, but it provides the model for the subsequent national education claims to argue that separate classrooms inherently are unequal classrooms. At this time, 90 percent of Texas schools and 85 percent of California schools are segregated by race.

1933 Franklin Roosevelt appoints a longtime Indian-rights advocate, John Collier, as Commissioner of Indian Affairs. Collier promotes sweeping liberalization of Indian education.

---

*See Carole Yazzie-Shaw, "Back in Those Days," part I.

1934 Progressive Indian education begins in earnest during the New Deal period. Children are taught through the medium of their own cultural values while becoming aware of the values of white civilization. Indian Service teachers are taught to be sensitive to Indian culture and to use methods adapted to the unique characteristics and needs of Indian children. Community day schools increase from 132 to 226 and enrollment triples. Military regimentation in the boarding schools is abandoned. Vocational programs are developed to teach skills that will be of use to students if they return to their reservations. Indian schools introduce Indian history, art, and language. A directive is issued that there be no interference with Indian religious life or ceremonial expression.

1935 California legislature passes bill to segregate nonwhite Mexican American students on grounds they are children of "Mongolian parentage," a code word for Indian.

1938 *Gaines v. Canada* This is first challenge to racial discrimination in graduate programs to reach the U.S. Supreme Court. It declares Missouri's failure to provide a law school for blacks to be unconstitutional. The Court finds that the legitimacy of segregated institutions "rests wholly upon the equality" that they offer the separated groups.

1940 United States grants citizenship to Puerto Ricans.

1940s Federal policy reverts to forced assimilation of Indian students. Cross cultural training of Indian schoolteachers ends. During World War II, funding for reservations is cut back. Schools are closed. A 1944 report recommends that students should again attend off-reservation boarding schools, as they had at the turn of the century.

Late 1940s–mid 1950s Massive migration, particularly of rural poor and working classes, from Puerto Rico to New York City. Seventy-five percent of children do not speak English. New York and New Jersey schools with high proportions of Puerto Ricans are severely overcrowded, with split sessions, few special classes. Puerto Rican students who speak English become de facto teacher aides. However, an English-only curriculum is enforced, and Spanish is used only for administrative, "housekeeping" purposes.

1946 *Méndez v. Westminster* De jure segregation is ruled to be illegal. Federal court decision finds that segregating children (not just Mexican Americans) serves no educational purpose.

1948 *Sipuel v. Board of Regents of the University of Oklahoma* Citing the *Gaines* ruling, the Supreme Court directs the University of Oklahoma to provide a legal education to a black student who had been denied entry to its all-white law school. In response, to avoid integrating its graduate school, the state slaps together the minimal semblance of a graduate school for blacks. The high court refuses to overturn Oklahoma's actions.

1948 *Delgado et al. v. Bastrop Independent School District* The Supreme Court rules that segregation of Mexican American students is discriminatory and illegal because it violates the students' Fourteenth Amendment rights.

1940–early 1960s To alleviate teacher shortages, U.S. schools recruit Puerto Rican teachers from the island. However, those who speak English with a Spanish accent cannot become "licensed," and can only be "substitute auxiliary teachers," that is, nonpermanent positions.

1950 *Sweatt v. Painter* The U.S. Supreme Court rules that a hastily contrived law school for blacks in Texas is unconstitutionally inferior. It orders the white law school to admit the black plaintiff.

1950 *McLaurin v. Board of Education of the University of Oklahoma* Strikes down an elaborate set of rules segregating a black student from whites in a graduate education program. Citing harm caused by intangible as well as physical inequalities, the ruling prefigures the end of state-sanctioned segregation.

1952 Puerto Rico becomes a U.S. Commonwealth, a status it retains today.

1954 *Brown v. Board of Education of Topeka* Unanimously declares that segregating elementary and secondary students by race violates black (and hence all racialized) children's constitutional right to equal protection of the law. The opinion arises from cases in four states (Delaware, Kansas, South Carolina, and Virginia). On the same day, the court invalidates school segregation in the District of Columbia on the grounds that it violated the black students' right to due process. The court defers judgment on implementing its rulings.

1955 *Brown v. Board of Education of Topeka* Orders the districts in the original *Brown* cases to make a "prompt and reasonable start toward full compliance." Known as *Brown II*, the ruling obligates local school authorities to overcome obstacles to desegregation "with all deliberate speed." This vague time frame prompts states and school districts to employ delay tactics. The Court also directs federal district judges to oversee the process. But it also stresses that constitutional principles cannot be sacrificed "simply because of disagreement with them."

1957 Yearly reports criticize U.S. mainland schools for the lack of language-appropriate educational and other diagnostic tests for Puerto Rican students. One report states that the "large backlog of retarded language learners . . . is chargeable to the lack of adequate tools for assessing the abilities of non-English speaking pupils."

1958 *Cooper v. Aaron* The Supreme Court rejects a bid by the Little Rock,

Arkansas, district to delay desegregation because of the turmoil that followed a handful of black students desegregating a high school the year before. The justices unanimously rule, "Law and order are not here to be preserved by depriving the Negro children of their constitutional rights." This is a blow to white Southern resistance.

1963 The first Spanish-speaking Puerto Rican substitute auxiliary teacher receives a mainland-teaching license. The no-Spanish-accent requirement remains in force. By 1967 only 125 have received a teaching license. By and large, non–Puerto Rican teachers provide instruction in mainland schools.

1964 *Griffin v. Board of Education* The Supreme Court rules that Prince Edward County, Virginia, one of the districts involved in *Brown*, can no longer avoid integration by keeping its public schools closed, as it had done since 1959. Also affirms a decision blocking tax breaks and tuition grants used to subsidize private schools for whites.

1965 The National Advisory Council on Indian Education is formed. This is a presidential appointed advisory council on Indian education established under Title IX of the Elementary and Secondary Education Act of 1965. The council advises the secretary of education and Congress on funding and administration of programs with respect to which the secretary has jurisdiction, that includes Indian children or adults as participants, or that may benefit Indian children or adults. The council also makes recommendations to the secretary for filling the position of director of Indian education.

1968 *Green v. New Kent County School Board* Declares in a case from Virginia that districts that formerly operated "dual systems" for black and whites have an affirmative duty to eliminate racial discrimination "root and branch." States that districts must promptly dismantle segregation not just in student assignment but also in faculty, staff, transportation, extracurricular activities, and facilities. These become the six "green factors" that are later used by the courts to gauge whether a district has met its obligations to desegregate.

1968 Title VII of the Elementary and Secondary Education Act This legislation, commonly called the Bilingual Education Act, heralds a limited change in the way language-minority children are taught in the United States. It recognizes their needs, promotes greater access to the curriculum, trains educators in the skills they need (such as ESL and bilingual education), and fosters achievement among language minority students. Many opponents, who believe that bilingualism has no place in U.S. public education, will contest it.

1969 *Alexander v. Board of Education* The Supreme Court overturns an appeals court ruling that gave thirty-three Mississippi districts more time to come up with plans to desegregate. The unanimous ruling says districts must end their dual systems for blacks and whites "at once and to operate now and hereafter only unitary schools."

1969 Ralph Nader testifies in Congress that "in any school with Indian students, BIA or public, cultural conflict is inevitable. The student, bringing with him all the values, attitudes, and beliefs that constitute his 'Indianness,' is expected to subordinate that Indianness to the general American standards of the school. The fact that, he, the student, must do all the modifying, all the compromising, seems to say something to him about the relative value of his own culture as opposed to that of the school. . . . It is estimated that for half of the Indians enrolled in federal schools, English is not the first language learned. Yet, when the child enters school, he is expected to function in a totally English-speaking environment. He muddles along in this educational void until he learns to assign meaning to the sounds the teacher makes. By the time he has begun to learn English, he has already fallen well behind in all the basic skill areas. In fact, it appears that his language handicap increases as he moves through school. And although it is no longer official BIA policy to discourage use of native languages, many reports in the hearings indicate the contrary in practice."

1969 *United States v. Montgomery County Board of Education* Upholds the use of numerical quotas to racial balance an Alabama public school faculty.

1969 Senate report 91–501, *Indian Education: A National Tragedy, a National Challenge,* declares: "the dominant policy of the federal government toward the American Indian has been one of coercive assimilation" with "disastrous effects on the education of Indian children."

1970 *Cisneros v. Corpus Christi Independent School District* Mexican Americans are ruled to be an ethnically identifiable minority group and, in terms of desegregation, have rights similar to African Americans. This contradicts the finding of *Ross v. Eckels* (1970), a desegregation case that rules that Mexican Americans are not an identifiable minority group for purposes of desegregation.

1970 *Diana v. State Board of Education, Covarrubias v. San Diego Unified School District* (1971), and *Guadalupe v. Tempe Elementary* (1971) These cases lead to major changes in the grade-level promotion of minority students. All three find that overrepresentation of Mexican Americans in classes for mentally retarded students indicates fundamentally unfair treatment.

1971 *Swann v. Charlotte-Mecklenburg Board of Education* Authorizes mandatory busing, redrawn attendance zones, and the limited use of racial-balance quotas as desegregation tools. Holds that individual schools need not reflect the districtwide racial balance, but that districts bear the burden of proving that any schools that are comprised of students of only one race do not result from discrimination. In one of three related rulings issued the same day, the justices strike down a North Carolina antibusing law that prohibited assignment of students on the basis of race.

1972 *Wright v. Emporia City Council* and *United States v. Scotland Neck Board of Education* In separate rulings issued the same day, the Supreme Court rejects bids to carve out new school districts in Virginia and North Carolina. In both cases, the districts would have had enrollments with a greater ratio of white students than in the desegregated districts they were leaving.

1973 *San Antonio Independent School District v. Rodríguez* The Supreme Court rules that education is not a fundamental constitutional right. Hence school funding systems that are based on local property taxes enabling wealthier districts to provide more funds per student do not violate the Fourteenth Amendment.

1973 A Navaho kindergarten teacher in Arizona is reprimanded on her teacher evaluation for "on several occasions actually having taught Navajo words over the objection of the school's administration." Although her kindergarten students' dominant language is Navajo, Arizona law at that time requires all instruction in public schools to be in English.

1973 *Keyes v. Denver School District No. 1* Three key rulings come out of this case. For the first time, the Court holds a district liable for intentional segregation, even though it had never required separate schools by law. This extends the "affirmative duty" to desegregate to districts beyond the Southern and Mason-Dixon border states. A majority also finds that official discriminatory acts affecting some schools or neighborhoods create a legal presumption that the whole district should desegregate. And the justices hold that Latinos should be counted with blacks in determining whether a school is segregated.

1974 *Milliken v. Bradley* This is the first major restriction imposed on public school desegregation. The 5–4 ruling strikes down a plan to merge the Detroit schools with fifty-three largely white suburban districts. Citing a lack of evidence that those districts were guilty of intentional segregation, it orders a new plan confined to the city, where enrollment had been more than two-thirds black. It thus becomes much harder for courts to order city/suburban desegregation plans to counteract the concentration of minorities in the cities.

1974 *Lau v. Nichols* The U.S. Supreme Court rules that when children arrive in school with little or no knowledge of English, the use of English-only instruction in their education is a violation of their civil rights.

1976 *Pasadena City Board of Education v. Spangler* The U.S. Supreme Court reverses a ruling requiring this California district to adjust attendance zones annually to preserve court-ordered racial status. A lower court had ordered that no school should have a majority of any minority group, a directive with which the district fell out of compliance after one year. On a 6–2 vote, the justices conclude the enrollment shifts stemmed from demographic changes and are not deliberate "segregative acts."

1977 *Milliken v. Bradley* Authorizes courts to require remedial education programs as an antidote to past segregation, in a decision know as *Milliken II*. Upholds a ruling directing Detroit and Michigan to split the cost of programs in four areas: reading, in-service teacher training, student testing, and counseling. This ruling opens the door to broader use of remedial programs and extra funding for racially isolated schools across the country.

1978 *Regents of the University of California v. Allan Bakke* On the basis of Equal Protection Clause of the Fourteenth Amendment, the U.S. Supreme Court rules that a medical school discriminated against a white applicant on the basis of race. Its decision significantly narrows the use of affirmative action in higher education. Admissions procedures could no longer evaluate disadvantaged candidates on different criteria than nonminority candidates, or establish numerical quotas for disadvantaged students. However, Justice Powell rules that universities have the right to select students on many relevant factors, including race, as long as any individual candidate's Fourteen Amendment rights are not violated.

1979 *Columbus Board of Education v. Penick* and *Dayton Board of Education v. Brinkman* Upholds mandatory busing in two districts in Ohio, saying school officials had perpetuated segregation to varying degrees by their actions and inaction since the *Brown* decision. In dissent (future chief justice) Rehnquist says the rulings so blur the line between de jure and de facto segregation that the only way urban districts could avoid court-ordered busing, given residential segregation, was to get rid of neighborhood schools.

1980–1990 Self-determination for American Indian schooling is repeatedly threatened by federal attempts to repeal prior legislation.

1982 *Washington v. Seattle School District No. 1* Strikes down a state antibus-

ing initiative passed by voters, after Seattle voluntarily adopted a desegregation plan involving extensive crosstown busing. A majority of the
justices concludes the initiative was racially motivated.

1982 *Plyer v. Doe* The U.S. Supreme Court rules that Texas cannot exclude
undocumented children from tuition-free enrollment in the state's
public schools, as Texas legislators had attempted to do.

1982 *Crawford v. Board of Education* Upholds an amendment to California's
constitution that prohibited state judges from ordering busing for integration in the absence of a violation of the U.S. Constitution. The
amendment followed a state's Supreme Court order requiring Los
Angeles to desegregate on the grounds that it had been obligated under
the state constitution to attack de facto segregation.

1991 Puerto Ricans declare Spanish the only official language of the island.

1991 *Board of Education of Oklahoma City v. Dowell* Stressing that court
orders to desegregate were designed to be temporary, by a 5–3 vote the
Court states that federal judges should lift desegregation decrees if districts have complied in good faith and remedied past discrimination "as
far as practicable."

1992 *Freeman v. Pitts* The Court authorizes lower courts to relinquish
supervision over some aspects of a district's desegregation-related obligations (such as extracurricular activities), while retaining it in others.
Also judges are granted leeway to consider issues beyond the "green
factors," such as educational quality, in assessing whether districts
should be declared unitary.

1993 Both English and Spanish become official languages of Puerto Rico.

1994 Proposition 187 This referendum is overwhelmingly approved by
California voters. It would have denied to undocumented immigrants
a range of social services, including public education. The electorate
blames immigrants for an economic recession triggered by the end of
the Cold War, but the enmity that Prop. 187 unleashed was fueled by
the imminent "browning of California," when it had become clear that
the politically dominant Anglo-American population would become a
numerical minority. It was immediately struck down in court as unconstitutional, but not bringing racial politics front and center here, and
across the country.

1995 The federal Office of Indian Education is allocated a total fiscal-year
budget of one dollar. Tribal leaders and pan-Indian organization leaders
lobby Congress, hold prayer vigils, and call press conferences to argue
for continued funding. Finally, President Clinton maintains the BIA
and OIE, by vetoing the budget.

1995 *Missouri v. Jenkins* States that an ambitious magnet school plan in

Kansas City aimed at luring suburban whites amounts to judicial over-reach. The 5–4 ruling states that neither the goal of attracting whites, nor the persistence of substandard test scores in the city, justified the plan, which the state had been subsidizing and wanted to end.

1996 *Hopwood v. State of Texas* The Fifth Circuit Court of Appeals claims that the 1978 *Bakke* decision was in fact not a precedent for affirmative action cases. It ruled that it was illegal to use race, ethnicity, or gender in admissions in higher education institutions. This ruling applied to states within its jurisdiction, including Texas, Louisiana, and Mississippi. Other appellate courts, reading the same law, continue to use the *Bakke* precedent, which upholds affirmative action.

1996 Proposition 209 This California referendum prohibits local and state agencies from granting "preferential treatment" to individuals based on their race, ethnicity, or sex in the areas of state contracting, employment, and education. It signals a further retreat from affirmative action. Higher education is most affected by the referendum, which became part of the California state constitution.

1998 Proposition 227 This referendum, which restricts bilingual education and instruction of the native language in California public schools, passes handily. Over one million schoolchildren are affected. As a result, students who do not speak English when they arrive at school must be placed in English-only classrooms after one school year. Proposition 227 becomes the model for other state referenda. In 2000 and 2002 respectively, Arizona (Proposition 203) and Massachusetts (Question 2) pass similar English-only measures, while Colorado voters reject its anti-bilingual education Amendment 31 in 2002.

2002 The "No Child Left Behind" Act This federal legislation reverses thirty-four years of U.S. language policy in public schools. It ends the Bilingual Education Act (1968). Federal funds will continue to support English language learners (ELLs), but the swift and brief teaching of English takes priority over longer-term bilingual academic skill development. Moreover, schools now must make annual English assessments. "Accountability" provisions, such as yearly school evaluations of the percentage of ELLs who are reclassified as fluent in English, will discourage schools from continuing native-language instruction, because failure to show academic progress in English will lead to the loss of federal funds.

2003 *Grutter v. Bollinger* and *Granz v. Bollinger* After twenty-five years, the U.S. Supreme Court returns to the issue of affirmative action in higher education. These rulings dismissed the *Hopwood* appellate court decision. The Court also reaffirmed the *Bakke* precedent, and the right of universities to take racial diversity into account in admissions policies. Schools cannot employ simple formulas that mechanically assign a numeric value to each candidate's race, but they can take race into account (among many other factors) in an individualized evaluation process of each person. The divided rulings indicate that the issue will soon be contested again.

Notes

Quotes were drawn from, and materials adapted from, the following sources. For the history of U.S. public education of American Indians: Jon Reyhner, "American Indian Language Policy and School Success," *The Journal of Educational Issues of Language Minority Students* 12 (Summer 1993): 35–59; Sharon O'Brien, *American Indian Tribal Governments* (Norman: University of Oklahoma Press, 1989), 238–42; and "History and Facts about Indian Education," an American Indian Education Foundation website: www.aiefprograms.org/history_facts/history.html (accessed on October 10, 1998). The editor would like to thank Ralph de Unamuno for his help on this portion of the timeline. For court decisions affecting racial segregation in public education: a sidebar without a byline appearing in *Education Week* 18, no. 28 (March 24, 1999): 27–28, 30. For nineteenth-century legal cases centering on race and citizenship: Martha Menchaca, "Chicano Indianism: A Historical Account of Racial Repression in the United States," *American Anthropologist* 20, no. 3 (1993): 583–603. For legal and legislative rulings affecting Latino education: Antonia Darder, Rodolfo D. Torres, and Henry Gutiérrez, eds., *Latinos and Education: A Critical Reader* (New York: Routledge, 1997); Guadalupe San Miguel Jr. and Richard R. Valencia, "From the Treaty of Guadalupe Hidalgo to Hopwood: The Educational Plight and Struggle of Mexican Americans in the Southwest," *Harvard Educational Review* 68, no. 3 (Fall 1998): 353–412; Guadalupe San Miguel *"Let All of Them Take Heed": Mexican Americans and the Campaign for Educational Equality in Texas, 1910–1981* (Austin: University of Texas Press, 1987); James Crawford "Why Is Bilingual Education So Unpopular with the American Public?" *The Education Policy Studies Brief*, no. 8 (epsl-0302–102-lpru, 2003), website: www.language-policy.org (accessed on September 12, 2003). For Puerto Rican educational history, I drew on Meyer Weinberg, *A Chance to Learn: The History of Race and Education in the United States* (New York: Cambridge University Press, 1977).

1. Paulo Freire, *Pedagogy of the Oppressed* (New York: Seabury Press, 1970), 129.

2. James Lockhart, *The Nahuas after the Conquest: A Social and Cultural History of the Indians of Central Mexico, Sixteenth through Eighteenth Centuries.* (Stanford, CA: Stanford University Press, 1992).

3. Caroline Hendrie, "In Black and White," *Lessons of a Century: A Nation's Schools Come of Age* (Bethesda, MD: Editorial Projects in Education, 2000), 62–79.

4. See, among many other sources, David J. Weber's anthology *Foreigners in Their Native Land: Historical Roots of the Mexican Americans* (Albuquerque: University of New Mexico Press, 1973).

5. Martha Menchaca, "Chicano Indianism: A Historical Account of Racial Repression in the United States," *American Anthropologist* 20, no. 3 (1993): 583–603.

6. Meyer Weinberg, *A Chance to Learn: The History of Race and Education in the United States* (New York: Cambridge University Press, 1977), chapter 6.

7. Weinberg, *A Chance to Learn*, chapter 6.

8. James Baldwin, "If Black English Isn't a Language, Then Tell Me, What Is?" Letter to the editor of the *New York Times*, July 29, 1979. Reprinted in *The Price of a Ticket* (St. Martin's Press).

If you want to really hurt me, talk badly about my language. Ethnic identity is twin skin to linguistic identity, I am my language.

—Gloria Anzaldúa

The brutal truth is that the bulk of the white people in America never had any interest in educating Black people, except as this could serve white purposes. It is not the Black child's language that is in question, it is not his language that is despised: It is his experience. A child cannot be taught by anyone who despises him, and a child cannot afford to be fooled.

—James Baldwin[8]

English is an all-devouring language that has moved across North America like the fabulous plagues of locusts that darkened the sky and devoured even the handles of rakes and hoes. Yet the omnivorous nature of a colonial language is a writer's gift. Raised in the English language, I partake of a mongrel feast.

—Louise Erdrich

PART THREE

THE POTENTIAL AND VULNERABILITY OF MULTILINGUAL CHILDREN

The language in which we are speaking is his before it is mine. How different are the words *home, Christ, ale, master,* on his lips and on mine! I cannot speak or write these words without unrest of spirit. His language, so familiar and so foreign, will always be for me an acquired speech. I have not made or accepted its words. My voice holds them at bay. My soul frets in the shadow of his language.

—Stephen Dedalus
in James Joyce's *A Portrait of the Artist as a Young Man*

Who are these children who speak in tongues and live in fire? What happens to them as they move through the educational system?

—Antonia Castañeda

The Failure to Educate Immigrant Children

Abridged from an article by Guadalupe Valdés

While bilingual education has been a heated topic of debate within the United States in the last decade, the complex issues concerning immigrant children have nonetheless been largely ignored. Discussion about immigrant children has been limited to figuring out either how much of an expense they are to the educational system, as seen with Proposition 187, or how they can be magically mainstreamed into the all-American classroom, as seen with Proposition 227.* In a wonderful, rich article, Guadalupe Valdés presents a compelling report on the complex challenges for immigrant children that have led to many failures of the educational system. Using the experiences of two children whom she followed for seven years, Valdés delineates how twelve-year-old Lilian and thirteen-year-old Elisa were betrayed by an institution that had the power to transform their lives but instead left them waiting for an opportunity that never arrived. These children's accounts illustrate a massive problem that affects many immigrant children. Valdés provides sage advice to help schools better serve its newcomers.

At the beginning of the twenty-first century, one critical issue that concerns the American public is the challenge facing the nation's schools. At center is the increasing diversity of the nation's school populations. This demographic transformation of the student body is primarily a result of the growth in enrollment of immigrant children within the public schools. As a result, yesterday's educational modus operandi does not work in today's schoolrooms. Because of this educational failure, it has become of intense national and local concern. In spite of the politicized nature of the topic, as Guadalupe Valdés illustrates, immigrant children's lives in school, and hence their life expectations, must remain the focus of concerned adults.

Schools are faced with an extraordinary task—to successfully serve the needs of immigrant children while meeting the increasing accountability requirements and rising academic standards required of all public schools. The scores of immigrant children on standardized tests have become the measure of a school's excellence. Yet research studies highlight time and time again that "newly arrived immigrants from non–English-speaking countries encounter serious problems within our educational system" (4). The solution is not simple, but it is clear to linguists and educational researchers: immigrant students

---

*See part II for a chronology of the legal and legislative rulings affecting Latino education.

must develop the kinds of English that are associated with the advanced academic skills needed to benefit fully from quality school instruction. As it is, far too few immigrant children succeed, in spite of their best efforts.

The U.S. public tends to reduce this complex solution to the slogan: "Just teach them English!" Because of the associated politics, the stakes grow higher. And the educator's task has become far more challenging.

Additionally, Valdés stresses the importance of realizing that "in coming to this country and adjusting to American schools, immigrant students and their families travel very long distances. These distances are physical, emotional, and psychological." Education professionals, in their focus on teaching methods and test scores, often overlook this. Recognizing the impact of such distances, Valdés opens an important window not only onto what "some of the distances between homes and schools, countries and cultures involve, but what it means for youngsters to arrive at school without knowing English" (4).

To this end, Valdés describes the painful experiences of two middle school students—Lilian and Elisa—over a seven-year period. Valdés uses "their lives and experiences as a lens" through which she "examines both the policy and instructional dilemmas that surround the education of immigrant children in this country" (4). Lilian and Elisa are young adults now with much diminished life possibilities. Their lives reflect the lost life potential of many immigrant children, and failed promise of U.S. public education today.

Lilian and Elisa had similar backgrounds. Both came from rural Latin America. Their close-knit traditional families were economically disadvantaged. However, both girls arrived at school with solid educational backgrounds. In Spanish, Lilian and Elisa both read and "wrote quite competently—that is, words were properly segmented" and what they "wrote expressed real meaning" (6). Moreover, both children were eager to build upon these educational foundations. Their single challenge was to master English well enough to be able to fully immerse themselves into school. It was very clear to Valdés, as she observed them in their middle school classrooms, that both girls attacked this challenge with gusto and earnestness. However, the urban environment they encountered proved to be endlessly different from that of their home countries.

As children, they readily expressed their feelings of displacement and homesickness in a childlike manner. Lilian, for example, "was very homesick . . . and she missed the smells of her village as well as her friends" (5). Unfortunately, the educational environment the girls stepped into was not ready to help them deal with these psychological issues.

Moreover "as is also the case at other schools in which population shifts have rapidly changed the composition of the student body," the middle school they attended was unprepared to meet the demands placed "on the staff and on the curriculum that had not been anticipated" (5). The English-as-a-second-language (ESL) classrooms they were placed in were overcrowded. Few ESL teachers or materials were available to Lilian and Elisa. Many of their peers, as beginning English learners, were assigned to so-called 'sheltered' classrooms, which are not recommended for students at their lowest level of mastery. These classes are designed for intermediate level students.

Other schools across the U.S. share these structural constraints. However, the biggest problem was one that most affected these children: their teachers could not relate to their academic and psychological needs. Most teachers "could predict few of the problems their new students would encounter. Most knew little about poverty. They had little notion of why working-class immigrant parents might not be able to make midday appointments with their children's teachers. They suspected disinterest, apathy, and even antagonism and were baffled and troubled by the failure of these parents to 'care' about their children" (5).

"The new students, on the other hand, did not quite yet know how to be American middle school students. . . . They were not sure why being in band or in chorus or in the computer club might be important. They frequently confused teachers' friendly demeanor with permissiveness, and they quickly found themselves in trouble. They understood little of what went on around them and often became discouraged and disinterested" (5).

In her observations of the teaching in ESL classrooms, Valdés found that the "activities carried out in the classroom were generally not communicative in nature and work focused almost exclusively around copying vocabulary lists and copying sentences" (7). Using these so-called worksheets kills valuable instructional time, and squanders student motivation and energy. Another signal of educator problems was that "mainstream English teachers . . . were especially reluctant to have even highly proficient English-speaking immigrant students in their classes and preferred them to be placed in the ESL sequence. They worried particularly about the 'errors' that were still present in these students' English language production." Frankly, the teachers were concerned "about their own ability to work with such youngsters effectively" (6).

In the end, two schools existed in one facility: one that effectively cultivated its mainstream students, while the other merely warehoused its newcomers. "English-language learners interacted only with each other and with teachers who taught their classes" (7). For those children, no matter how motivated, acquiring adequate language skills became an impossible task under these circumstances since "no group activities involving collaboration took place, . . . very little practice of oral English went on in the classroom, . . . no instruction in reading was provided, and the only reading materials available to students were story books" for preschool "children and the Barnell-Loft series of readers designed for special education students who are native speakers of English" (9).

At their school, Lilian and Elisa's teachers were also unaware of the dilemmas that both of these girls' mothers faced. Sonia, Lilian's mother, came from a world in which poor village people do not have much social mobility. So "it was hard for Sonia to understand how going to school might really make a difference in her children's lives." Besides working and taking care of the household, Sonia also "felt guilty because she was letting her children down, because she did not know how to help them, and because she did not have time to go to school and learn English" (10).

Magda, Elisa's mother, also cleaned houses, worked nights in a factory, and cared for an elderly man on the weekends. To put food on the table, she hardly saw her children. Although Magda tried to get as much information to help her children as possible, she was still misinformed in many aspects, such as the quality of Elisa's ESL classes. Moreover, Magda developed only "superficial sophistication" of U.S. society. She did not realize that "she knew only a little about how American life worked" (11).

As a result of these three concerns—that teachers did not understand the problems immigrant students were to face, knew very little about poverty, and held damaging misconceptions about their students' parents—the girls were not offered crucial instrumental support and had no way of knowing "how to be American middle school students," so they became "discouraged and disinterested" in school (5). They lacked the means to voice their needs. And no adult addressed the real dilemma: their teachers lacked the training, sometimes even awareness, to provide the extra help that the girls desperately needed. The students found it almost impossible to learn the rules of a system entirely different from their home, and that had so many complications on different levels. Faced with this tremendous task, Lilian and Elisa felt inferior and inadequate in the classroom everyday surroundings. As a result, they were not aided in school. In fact, the U.S. educational system injured them.

"Today, almost seven years after the study began, a lot has happened in the lives" of the two girls. "Lilian did not finish high school. Like her middle school, the high school that she attended was carefully divided into two schools. Lilian was in the ESL track, where she once again had several periods of instruction focusing on English vocabulary, English structure, and English reading. Her subject matter classes were remedial, taught in slow and simplified English, and aimed at students who, like her, had had very little exposure to academic content in the middle years. Lilian was bored, frequently absent, and while" she was docile and cooperative in class, was "still completely uninterested in school" (11). The motivated child who at 12, when given articles in English to read, had eagerly applied "her word attack skills in Spanish in order to read in English," and "was able to hypothesize what the articles were about," "what they probably said on the basis of her real-world knowledge" (6) was gone. Sadly, this motivated learner would never return.

Elisa, on the other hand, acquired a lot of English. She had become a native speaker—but not of Standard English. Still, she had a hard time escaping from the 'ESL ghetto'. This is the place where many immigrant children are trapped, held captive by the LEP (Limited English Proficient) or ELL (English Language Learner) institutional labels that haunt them. This 'ESL ghetto' does not allow them to realize their full academic potential, thereby limiting their life possibilities.

After two years of high school, during which Elisa enrolled in all mainstream classes, her family "moved to the Miami area, where once again, she was enrolled exclusively in mainstream classes. Elisa took ACTs and SATs and prepared for college. In September, she took the regular English placement test at a local community college, intending to enroll in a few courses at a time" while she continued to work. "Unfortunately, Elisa was not permitted to register for classes. Apparently, non-English-background students cannot be placed in the writing sequence using the regular-English placement test. Because Elisa's test revealed that she is not "really" a native English speaker. . . . The tiny flaws in English that did not prevent her from maintaining a C + average in high school were . . . unacceptable to community college teachers. . . . She was told that, in order to enroll, she will need to take the ESL placement test and register for ESL writing instead" (12).

"The school experiences of Elisa and Lilian, their successes and their failures, have much to tell us about the lives that immigrant children live. They also have much to offer us as we debate policies about the design of educational programs, about teacher preparation, about testing, and most important, about the role of English in the education of newly arrived children" (12).

"Part of the difficulty is that most policymakers and members of the public have little information about what actually happens in schools." In spite of this lack of familiarity with the classroom reality, "however, far-reaching decisions are often made about immigrant children, about how they should be educated, and about which language should be used in their education. In the current context in which anti-immigrant sentiment is at an all-time high, newly arrived children are routinely accused by the general public of not wanting to learn English and of failing to profit from the education that the state is giving them at great cost" (13). Of course, the reality is that the education provided for these children is very poor. These children are not responsible for, nor can they correct, their educational circumstances.

"What is evident from observations of Lilian and Elisa is that simply" having students fill out endless sets of photocopied fill-in-the-blank English language exercises, and "memorize vocabulary may not result in the outcomes that the children themselves, their families, or the public is expecting." In order "to prepare these students to succeed in school in subject matter courses that are taught in English, a clear and unambiguous set of language learning objectives must be put forward." This must be done "in spite of existing uncertainties about the process of second-language acquisition and in spite of debates about best methods and practices" (14).*

In the classroom setting, students who are learning the English language should be guided to achieve three goals:

(a) Use English to communicate in social settings. This is necessary, but it is far from sufficient. Moreover, students should also
(b) Use English in socially and culturally appropriate ways. This includes using English to become students who can build on their knowledge bases. Most importantly, they should
(c) Use English in all academic content areas to succeed academically (14).

This means schools and teachers must give these students the classroom opportunity and academic tools to build their capacity to express themselves in English as they are able to do with their Spanish or other home languages. They should be able to do a myriad of things with English; for example, learn to choose from among language varieties, read and get the meaning of texts, express their feelings, and find the humor in situations.

"There is much that we already know about the kinds of English language proficiencies that students must develop in order to succeed in school." Lily Wong Fillmore has demonstrated "that in order to participate in the life and work of schools and to learn academic subject matter, immigrant students must develop two fundamental skills in English:

(a) They must be able to comprehend the spoken language of their teachers as they explain and present instruction
(b) They must comprehend the language of textbooks from which they are expected to learn" (14).[1]

The experiences of Lilian and Elisa mirrored what other immigrant children run into in school. They have the same kind of struggles, including not only inadequate second language teaching methods, but also poor instruction in core subjects. Moreover, their teachers tend not to motivate them. Nor do they recognize the psychological circumstances that confront these children.

---

*For a summary of language acquisition processes, refer to Snow's article "The Four Spokes of the Second Language Learning Wheel," in part V.

Overtly or tacitly, some teachers cast doubt on their students' potential. And they may hold misconceptions about immigrant parents. This lack of understanding compounds the immigrants' disadvantaged socioeconomic status and cultural distance.

Despair among the immigrant children grows when they find themselves trapped in an educational situation without hope. Once students were placed within dysfunctional ESL programs, they rarely found the opportunity to get out. These children need more opportunities and alternative programs. Now, with the English-only, anti-bilingual-education movement taking hold in many communities across the nation, these children and their parents end up with fewer options. The consequences are the same—immigrant children are relegated to inadequately trained teachers working in ill-equipped classrooms. These children wind up having to fend for themselves, most often doing a poor job of it. Their classroom experience is a trial—not a source of resources and growth—that they must cope with on the basis of little familiarity. Their potential for educational success is jeopardized by these shortcomings—and to add insult to injury—they are unfairly compared to monolingual standards.

Valdés believes that while the task at hand is difficult, a workable solution to this problem can be formulated. Her analysis of the prior policies to deal with the second language acquisition of immigrant children shows that such plans have been inefficient for various reasons. For one, some current and previously attempted proposals have focused extensively on the science of teaching. Such a focus ignores the importance of the student's role within the learning process. Other policies have completely disregarded the sociocultural and psychological factors that have a tremendous impact on the educational performance of these students.

Second-language instruction for immigrant children must emanate, in Valdés's view, from the critical understanding that language is more than correct pronunciation, memorization of vocabulary, and practice of grammatical forms. At its very core, language is the opportunity for self-expression through the discovery of new ideas and experiences. Students will be able to generate deeper personal interest in mastering English—when they realize that this knowledge holds for them the opportunity to make themselves heard and be taken notice of. Once students understand that their fears, dreams, and observations can be voiced in this new language and be understood as well as validated, they will be comfortable with their schooling. When this happens, immigrant students in our schools will have a brighter future.[2]

From *36 Children*

Herbert Kohl

One day Ralph cursed at Michael and unexpectedly things came together for me. Michael was reading and stumbled several times. Ralph scornfully called out, "What's the matter, Psyches, going to pieces again?" The class broke up and I jumped on that word "psyches."

"Ralph, what does *psyches* mean?"

An embarrassed silence.

"Do you know how to spell it?"

Alvin volunteered. "S-i-k-e-s."

"Where do you think the word came from? Why did everybody laugh when you said it, Ralph?"

"You know, Mr. Kohl, it means like crazy or something."

"Why? How do words get to mean what they do?"

Samuel looked up at me and said: "Mr. Kohl, now you're asking questions like Alvin. There aren't any answers, you know that."

"But there are. Sometimes by asking Alvin's kind of questions you discover the most unexpected things. Look."

I wrote *Psyche*, then *Cupid*, on the blackboard.

"That's how *psyche* is spelled. It looks strange in English, but the word doesn't come from English. It's Greek. There's a letter in the Greek alphabet that comes out *psi* in English. This is the way *psyche* looks in Greek."

Some of the children spontaneously took out their notebooks and copied the Greek.

"The word *psyche* has a long history. *Psyche* means mind or soul for the Greeks, but it was also the name of a lovely woman who had the misfortune to fall in love with Cupid, the son of Venus, the jealous Greek goddess of love . . ."

The children listened, enchanted by the myth, fascinated by the weaving of the meaning of *psyche* into the fabric of the story, and the character, Mind, playing tricks on itself, almost destroying its most valuable possessions through its perverse curiosity. Grace said in amazement:

"Mr. Kohl, they told the story and said things about the mind at the same time. What do you call that?"

"*Myth* is what the Greeks called it."

Sam was roused.

"Then what happened? What about the history of the word?"

"I don't know too much, but look at the words in English that come from *Cupid* and *Psyche*."

I cited *psychological, psychic, psychotic, psychodrama, psychosomatic, cupidity*—the children copied them unasked, demanded the meanings. They were obviously excited.

Leaping ahead, Alvin shouted: "You mean words change? People didn't always speak this way? Then how come the reader says there's a right way to talk and a wrong way?"

"There's a right way now, and that only means that's how most people would like to talk now, and how people write now."

Charles jumped out of his desk and spoke for the first time during the year.

"You mean one day the way we talk—you know, with words like *cool* and *dig* and *sound*—may be all right?"

"Uh huh. Language is alive, it's always changing, only sometimes it changes so slowly that we can't tell."

Neomia caught on.

"Mr. Kohl, is that why our reader sounds so old-fashioned?"

And Ralph.

"Mr. Kohl, when I called Michael *psyches*, was I creating something new?"

Someone spoke for the class.

"Mr. Kohl, can't we study the language we're talking about instead of spelling and grammar? They won't be any good when language changes anyway."

We could and did. That day we began what had to be called for my conservative plan book "vocabulary," and "an enrichment activity." Actually it was the study of language and myth, of the origins and history of words, of their changing uses and functions in human life. We began simply with the words *language* and *alphabet*, the former from the Latin for tongue and the latter from the first two letters of the Greek alphabet. Seeing the origin of *alphabet* and the relationship of *cupidity* to Cupid and *psychological* to Psyche had a particularly magical effect upon the children. They found it easy to master and acquire words that would have seemed senseless and tedious to memorize. Words like *psychic* and *psychosomatic* didn't seem arbitrary and impenetrable, capable of being learned only painfully by rote. Rather they existed in a context, through a striking tale that easily accrued associations and depth. After a week the children learned the new words, asked to be tested on them, and demanded more.

"Vocabulary" became a fixed point in each week's work as we went from Cupid and Psyche to Tantalus, the Sirens, and the Odyssey and the linguistic riches that it contains. We talked of Venus and Adonis and spent a week on first *Pan* and *panic, pan-American*, then *pandemonium*, and finally on *demonic* and *demons* and *devils*. We studied *logos, philos, anthropos, pathos,* and their derivatives. I spun the web of *mythos* about language and its origins. I went to German (*kindergarten*), Polynesian (*taboo*), or Arabic (*assassin*), showing what a motley open-ended fabric English (and for that matter any living language) is. The range of times and peoples that contributed to the growth of today's American English impressed me no less than it did the class. It drove me to research language and its origins; to reexplore myth and the dim origins of man's culture; and to invent ways of sharing my discoveries with the children.

The children took my words seriously and went a step further. Not content to be fed solely words that grew from sources that I, the teacher, presented, they asked for words that fitted unnamed and partially articulated concepts they had, or situations they couldn't adequately describe.

"Mr. Kohl, what do you call it when a person repeats that same thing over and over again and can't stop?"

"What is it called when something is funny and serious at the same time?"

"What do you call a person who brags and thinks he's big but is really weak inside?"

"Mr. Kohl, is there a word that says that something has more than one meaning?"

The class became word-hungry and concept-hungry, concerned with discovering the "right" word to use at a given time to express a specific thought. I was struck by the difference of this notion of rightness and "the right way" to speak and write from the way children are supposed to be taught in school. They are supposed to acquire correct usage, right grammar and spelling, the right meaning of a word, and the right way to write a sentence. Achievement and I.Q. tests give incomplete sentences and the child is instructed to fill in the "right" word. Many teachers correct children's writing on the basis of a canon of formal rightness without bothering to ask what the children's words mean. I did the same thing myself.

I noticed that the children frequently said that they were bad at their friends, or their parents, or some teacher who angered them. They insisted upon describing a certain type of anger as "being bad at," and I kept telling them that it was wrong because "to be bad at" someone doesn't exist in English. And in a way I was "right"; it didn't exist, nor did the concept it was trying to express exist in English as I spoke and wrote it. But the children did mean "to be bad at," and meant something very specific by it. "To be bad" is a way of defying authority and expressing anger at the same time, as indicating one's own strength and independence. The use of "bad" here is ironical and often admiring. One child explained to me that down South a "bad nigger" was one who was strong enough and brave enough to be defiant of the white man's demands no matter how much everyone else gave in. Only later did I discover Bessie Smith in J. C. Johnson's "Black Mountain Blues," using "bad" in the same way as the kids:

Back on Black Mountain a child would smack your face
Back on Black Mountain a child would smack your face
Babies cry for liquor and all the birds sing bass

Black Mountain people are bad as they can be
Black Mountain people are bad as they can be
They uses gun powder just to sweeten their tea.*

I think that before we talked about language and myth the children, if they thought about it at all, felt that most words were either arbitrary labels pinned on things and concepts the way names seem to be pinned onto babies, or indicators of connections amongst these labels. These "labels" probably represented the way the adult world capriciously decided to name things. I doubt whether the children ever thought of adults as having received language from yet other adults even more remote in time. My pupils must have found the language of their teachers strange and arbitrary indeed. The "right" language of school texts and middle-class teachers must have seemed threatening and totalitarian, especially since the only living words the children knew and used were the words they used on the streets, words teachers continually told them were "wrong" and "incorrect."

The ideas that words were complex phenomena with long and compelling histories was never presented to the children. I doubt many teachers entertained it. The canons of the schools pretend that a small preselected segment of the language of the moment is an eternally correct and all-inclusive form. This form is embodied in basic word lists and controlled vocabulary readers, as if the mastering of the language consists of learning a list of fifty or a hundred words by rote. The use of language in human life is continually avoided or ignored, as if it poses too great a threat to "correctness" and "rightness." No wonder then that the children showed so persistently and ingeniously how much they feared and avoided the language of the schools.

Later in the semester I taught the class a lesson on naming, a topic that seems deceptively simple yet minimally encompasses history, psychology, sociology, and anthropology. I put everybody's full name on the blackboard, including my own, and asked the class how people got names. The answer was, naturally, from their parents who made the choice—but not the full choice, it emerged, when Michael remembered that his parents' surnames came from their parents. Then how far back can you go? The children thought and Grace raised a delicate question. If the names go back through the generations how come her

*Lines from "Black Mountain Blues," words and music by J. C. Johnson, reprinted with the kind permission of the Songwriters Guild of America. All rights reserved.

name wasn't African since her ancestors must have been? In answer I told the class about my own name—Kohl, changed from Cohen, changed from Okun, changed from something lost in the darkness of history; one change to identify the family as Jewish, one change to deny it. Then I returned to the question of slave names and the destruction of part of the children's African heritage that the withholding of African names implied.

Neomia said that she knew of someone who changed his name because he wanted to start a new life, and Sam told the class that his brother called himself John X because X meant unknown and his original African name was unknown. We talked of people who named their children after famous men and of others who gave exotic names. From there the discussion went on to the naming of animals—pets, wild animals, racehorses; things—boats, houses, dolls; and places. The class knew by that time in the school year that one doesn't talk of words in isolation from human lives and history, and by then I had begun to know what to teach.

The emphasis on language and words opened the children to the whole process of verbal communication. Things that they had been struggling to express, or worse, had felt only they in their isolation thought about, became social, shareable. Speaking of things, of inferiority and ambiguity, or irony and obsession, brought relief, and perhaps for the first time gave the children a sense that there were meaningful human creations that one could discover in a classroom.

Yet not all concepts have been verbalized, and the children frequently talked of having feelings and desires that no words I gave them expressed adequately. They had to create new words, or develop new forms of expression to communicate, and that can neither be taught nor done upon command. We could go to the frontier, however, and speak about the blues, about being bad or hip or cool—about how certain ways of living or historical times created the need for new words. We talked about the nuclear age, the smallness of the modern world, the jargon of democracy and communism, integration and segregation. The children looked in awe at *Finnegans Wake* and Joyce's monumental attempt to forge a new language; they listened to Bob Dylan, recorded the words of soul songs and classical blues, read poetry. We started out talking about words and ended up with life itself. The children opened up and began to display a fearless curiosity about the world.

I sense that I've jumped ahead too quickly, for the whole thing happened slowly, almost imperceptibly. There were days of despair throughout the whole year, and I never learned how to line the class up at three o'clock. There were days when Alvin was a brilliant inspiring pupil at ten and the most unbearable, uncontrollable nuisance at eleven thirty; when after a good lesson some children would turn angry and hostile, or lose interest in everything. There were small fights and hostilities, adjustments and readjustments in the children's relationships to each other and to me. I had to enlarge my vision as a human being, learn that if the complex and contradictory nature of life is allowed to come forth in the classroom, there are times when it will do so with a vengeance.

Today's Deficit Thinking about the Education of Minority Students

Abridged from a chapter by Richard R. Valencia and Daniel G. Solórzano

Reforms within the American educational system have come about through litigation, protest, and legislation. Some have been extremely important, such as the court case of Brown v. Board of Education *and legislation such as* Title IX *(1972). Despite these kinds of measures that have sought to eradicate blatant discriminatory practices, there is still a prevalent form of thought that continues to hinder the potential of minority students within the educational system—deficit thinking. For a full understanding of the significance and prevalence of this ideology, which is harmful to the well-being of minority students, it is important to discuss how its different rationales ''have worked their way into the broader context of American social thought regarding race, ethnic, gender and class relations.'' Valencia and Solórzano point out that this ideology not only persists in contemporary educational thought and practice, ''but by all indicators it continues to gain ground'' in the twenty-first century (160).*

We may believe that our point of view regarding education is entirely rational, but everyone's thinking is based on certain, most often unconsidered assumptions. Valencia and Solórzano point out that identifying these unspoken assumptions—namely, our ideology about education—is inherently difficult to undertake, because of the nature of ideology. The ideological premise in question is that marginalized children—particularly language minority students— suffer from personal deficits that explain their continued abysmal educational success rate. This is part of a centuries-old, most often unspoken presupposition, which continues to underlie many current forms of educational thought and practice. An earlier form of this premise, now easily dismissed, was never questioned at an earlier time. This notorious rationale accounted for why these children did poorly in school using "genetic bases as explanations of human behavior, particularly racial/ethnic differences in intelligence" (160). The genetic-based view of educational deficits of marginalized students was prevalent in the first half of the twentieth century. When the genetic rationale fell out of favor, however, the premise wasn't discarded. Instead, other rationales were added to maintain the false premise.

"Contemporary deficit thinking views draw from the culture of poverty paradigm" (160) which purports to explain the educational predicament of students of color from low socioeconomic backgrounds, on account primarily that they are poor, and presumably they lack the incentives to better themselves. Lastly, so-called "cultural and accumulated environmental deficits continue to be embraced by some modern day deficit thinkers" (160) as the cause of poor education performance among children living in poverty. In fact, these so-called deficits are fabricated concepts that are promoted and sustained by deficit thinkers. This particular form of deficit thinking strategically blames the culture and environment of the home and family for these students' so-called educability deficit. Together, these three kinds of deficit thinking divert attention from the institutional factors contributing to the marginalized student's predicament. They justify the classroom situation, blaming the children for a situation they did not create. Whether its rationale is genetics, poverty, culture and language, or home environment, the end result is that the deficit ideology defrauds marginalized students.

"Inferior Genes, Inferior Intelligence: Neohereditarianism" (160). The idea of hereditarianism is that inferior genes generate intellectual deficits of groups—not individuals. It was first introduced into educational institutions in the 1920s with standardized tests, namely IQ testing. Two things were alleged with the development of such tests. The explicit claim was that intelligence could reliably be measured. The unstated expectation was that so-called 'native' differences in the intelligence levels would confirm the then self-evident differences among the so-called races. At this time, the two groups being compared to the apparently superior Euro-American were African Americans and recently arrived immigrants from southern and eastern Europe. A sequence of flawed inferences justified this racist view. The obvious group disparities in test scores were immediately and uncritically attributed to different levels of intelligence. Such differences were believed to arise directly from superior or inferior genes. Since this foregone conclusion had apparently been scientifically ascertained by standardized IQ tests, the prevalent racist bias of the time was ratified: humankind ranged on a hierarchy of genetic quality that placed Americans of northern Europe extraction at its apex, and all other races below them.

There were four fundamental problems with this line of thinking, including the premises that intelligence could be reduced to a single linear scale, that the tests devised actually sampled the inherent intelligence of individuals, and that intelligence so conceived was not randomly distributed across the planet, but just happened to pattern with the social groupings of people of the time. A further methodological criticism was that it rested on "the assumption of equivalent or comparable [test taker] experiences and backgrounds" (182). The scientists conducting these trials attributed the outcomes of the tests solely to race. They failed to realize that many factors, including language differences (non-English speakers were administered the test in English), life experience, culture, as well as previous formal and informal education, were responsible for the group differences observed in their results. These now obvious factors determined the scores that people would register in these primitive examinations. However, the scores were uncritically assumed to reflect different levels of native intelligence. Since, the test results corroborated deep-seated public prejudices, the public overlooked such criticisms for fifty years.

These prejudices were given a strong public impetus with Arthur Jensen's 1969 monograph: "How much can we boost IQ and scholastic achievement?" In this controversial work, Jensen "conjectured that the lower performance of black children—compared to whites—on intelligence tests was mostly due to genetic influences" (161). On this speculation, he theorized two levels of educability, low and high. From this supposition, Jensen recommended unequal schooling to accommodate such apparent differences in intelligence. Jensen went farther, suggesting that the curriculum for black students should concentrate on lower-level skills, because these children were genetically unable to master higher-level cognitive skills. "Jensen argued that educational attempts to boost disadvantaged children's IQs have been misdirected," and therefore the schools should focus on teaching them lower-level "concrete and specific skills" (167).

Jensen's monograph set off public debates. However, the public heard, by and large, only that his statistics were somewhat shaky. This was not the worst failing of Jensen's work.

Valencia and Solórzano summarize many scholars' criticisms of each of Jensen's suppositions. Among them, his figure for in-group intelligence heritability was criticized as far too large (a coefficient of roughly .80). Worse still, his figure for between-group intelligence heritability was conjecture, because the studies required to establish it had not been undertaken. As for the basis of Jensen's recommendations for differential schooling, Valencia and Solórzano note that it "came under fire by several scholars," because among other things, he took for granted that high/low educational abilities could be rendered statistically into independent factors. The authors conclude "although Jensen had the benefits of modern day statistical tools and an advanced knowledge base of human genetics," the core of his "analysis followed the tradition of the 1920s genetic pathology model" (169).

Even today, the genetic basis for deficit thinking has vocal advocates, and many silent followers. "One of the most sustained treatises on genetic pathology deficit thinking ever published," *The Bell Curve: Intelligence and Class Structure in American Life,* became a 1994 best-seller. The authors of this ponderous academic book, Richard J. Herrnstein and Charles Murray, declare that "cognitive differentiation among Americans . . . has resulted in a bifurcated society" (174). They divides people into two extremes: a "cognitive elite," with IQs over 120; and a "very dull" group with IQs of less than 75. Herrnstein and Murray further asserted that the cognitive elite acted in good ways, and the very dull behaved otherwise. This cognitive elite graduated from high school, got prestigious jobs, earned lots of money. Very dull people tend to drop out of high school, be unemployed, get divorced more often, bring children into the world outside of marriage, and depend on welfare. They tend to be bad parents. They are also more likely to be criminals, discourteous people, and bad citizens (174). In other words, being on the "smart" side of the IQ scale makes one more likely to be a nice person with "socially desirable behavior," while falling on the dull end predisposes one to being a nasty person with "socially undesirable behavior."

The Bell Curve had many of the same problems as Jensen's earlier work. Valencia and Solórzano catalog four types of criticisms: a "reliance on the old, now thoroughly debunked pseudo-scientific hereditarianism of the 1920s," partial reliance on "disreputable neohereditarianism," and a "misleading" use of statistics, all of which were marshaled to promote a "biased" political agenda (179). They provide a set of scathing quotes by leading scholars, including the book is "a chilly synthesis of the work of disreputable race theorists and eccentric eugenicists . . . some of Murray and Herrnstein's substantive arguments rely on questionable data and hotly contested scholarship, produced by academics whose ideological biases are pronounced. To this extent, important portions of the book must be treated with skepticism" (Rosen and Lane 1995, quoted on page 178).

In spite of such withering criticism, neohereditarianism has not been vanquished. To arm us against further assaults, Valencia and Solórzano provide a standard to measure the soundness of all future neohereditarian claims. To provide real evidence that two groups possess differential intellectual capabilities, any would-be hereditarian must compare members of the groups who share *"very similar linguistic, cultural, developmental and educational experiences.* Critics of the hereditarian position would argue that this fundamental assumption is *never met.* If a basic assumption of the theory is not valid, then the framework is scientifically indefensible" (181, emphasis in original).

⌒

"Blaming the Victim, Blaming the Poor: the Underclass" (183). While the most repulsive undercurrent of racism feeds the genetics rationale for deficit thinking in education, other rationales exist which reflect prejudice in more subtle ways. One powerful rationale constructs a particular view of the marginalized: that low educability is due to poverty. This justification of the plight of marginalized students assumes that certain maladaptive activities of poor parents are passed on to their children, which predisposes the children to replicate such

behavior. The so-called "culture of poverty" is presumably a common set of survival strategies (including disdain for public education) that are purported to exist among certain groups of people, all of whom are in the grip of privation.

The critique of the concept is predictable: it fails to acknowledge the similarity among these people—they are economically oppressed. Since it is difficult to speak in the U.S. about socioeconomic classes, cultural is made to play proxy for class. In spite of the criticism, this misleading concept is still popular, again because it reaffirms societal prejudices about poor people.[3] In the 1950s, the culture of poverty ostensibly explained the economic plight of marginalized people as a consequence of their culture. In the 1990s, the terminology changed, but the idea remained. Now people in the "underclass" purportedly uphold a culture that keeps them in desperate straits. These lines of thinking reinforce the view that such people cannot or do not want to flee their wretchedness. Sadly, their children are doomed to poverty. And public schooling cannot alter their fate.

Valencia and Solórzano point out that by the late 1980s, politicians and the mass media widely disseminated the concept of the underclass. For example, "the political presidential campaigns in 1988" focused much attention "on the attitudinal and behavioral aspects of the underclass that allegedly were at odds with mainstream values and behaviors" (183). In this manner, in the public's mind, to be part of the underclass not only means being dreadfully poor—which is true—but also means being deviant and inferior. This move validates prejudices about the poor, as it exonerates the privileged classes of all responsibility for the socioeconomic system that benefits them—at the expense of the poor.

Let us think again about the concept of the underclass. What is the cause of poverty? This is both a very challenging sociological and classic ethical query. However, in its deficit thinking formulation, a simplistic answer is given. The notion of the underclass presumes that poverty is due first and foremost to personal behavior, while paying minimal attention to the economic system that perpetuates inequity. It is unfair to presume that the poor are poor mostly because they are too dim or indifferent to avoid their plight. Moreover, the children of the poor are not to blame for their dilemma. To presume that poverty is strictly a matter of personal behavior allows us to blame the children of "people who do not behave in accordance with so-called social norms as measured by such variables as crime rates, welfare dependency, joblessness, teenage pregnancy and child abuse. . . . Suffice it to say, it is here—in the behavioral-based conceptions of the underclass—which deficit thinking is most likely to arise. The ideologically conservative explanation of the underclass phenomenon [lies] in the life-style and allegedly self-sustaining culture of this socially and economically isolated group" (184).

Valencia and Solórzano point out four interrelated issues (which are passed over in most discussions of the underclass) that undercut the claim that individuals are dependent on an ill-fated subculture. First, the strength of the underclass concept is diminished when one acknowledges that social behavior is shaped by external societal factors, as well as personal motivation. Given two students with equivalent talent and incentive, the one whose basic life needs are not met is much less favored to attain a higher education. Second, adding the role of white racism to the formulation of the underclass is crucial. People of color have for centuries been wrongly racialized, stigmatized and denied equal rights and privileges in U.S. society. Even today, real equal opportunity is still a dream; it does not exist in the inner city. Third, discussing socioeconomic structure—class and capitalism—brings to light the significant impact of economics, which is vital to understand poverty. Adding economics to the equation permits a far more thorough explanation for why people remain poor for long periods of time, in spite of their best efforts. People in the underclass are economically disadvantaged. Very recently, their always-restricted employment opportunities, which are most vulnerable to cyclic economic downturns, have been even further reduced as a consequence of increased inner-city segregation, the end of U.S. industrial growth leading to massive national economic restructuring, and escalating globalization—not increased laziness. Finally, the validity of the underclass premise can be further scrutinized when the consequence of its use is noted: it perpetuates the myth of the blameworthy lazy poor. To reproach the poor allows the privileged sectors of U.S. society to ignore how the great majority of poor people actively seek to change their situation, and strive for their children's future. As used in most discussions, the concept of the underclass blames the disadvantaged for the external structural problems of the society they inhabit. The educational ideology of deficit thinking compounds the problems that poor children face, by adding insult to injury. The concrete origins of the supposed underclass are primarily a matter of labor market inequalities, and "institutional racism in the creation, maintenance and domination" of marginalized people (186).

" 'Inadequate' Parents, Home and Child" (189). Educational deficit thinking is a flexible and destructive ideology. It rationalizes educational inequity of groups of students—not individuals—in several ways. Certain kinds of students fail school, as preordained by their genes. Or, those same students have been socialized into a 'culture of poverty' that predisposes them to a bad education as part of their life in the 'underclass'. A third expression of this ideology blames the educational disappointment of these children on the supposed inadequacies of their parents and home environments. How odd that these same students are readily labeled with different social pathologies, at once genetic and then cultural, while structural inequities within and across school districts are always ignored in the various formulations of the ideology.* Like all ideologies, deficit thinking makes so much common sense, that people tend to disregard any criticisms. Still, it attacks the families of marginalized children. Valencia and Solórzano point to three targets of this third type of deficit thinking: parental value and involvement in education; cognitive socialization and competence of families; and, the creation of the so-called at-risk family and child. Defining the points of origin of these three areas will elucidate how deficit thinking has managed to persist, despite being roundly criticized by social researchers and advocates of marginalized students time and again.

"One aspect of deficit thinking that fails to die is the major myth that low-income parents of color typically do not value the importance of education, that they fail to inculcate such a value in their children, and that they seldom participate—through parental involvement activities—in the education of their offspring" (190). History has shown otherwise. To take one marginalized group as an example, Mexican American family goals and values have always centered on education. Their "quest for equal educational opportunity and participation in their children's schooling is so rich" that their struggle for better education can be formulated in "five historical and contemporary processes" (190–191). These processes include parental and community efforts in the area of litigation (such as *Méndez v. Westminster* (1946)), where cases concerning the improvement of their children's education have been taken to court, despite hardships, to correct an injustice. There have also been great accomplishments carried out by the work of advocacy organizations such as the League of United Latin American Citizens, stalwart protectors of students' rights. Additionally, individual scholar activists such as George I. Sánchez have dedicated their professional careers to bettering the educational opportunities of children of color. Moreover, the Chicano community as a whole has also rallied around political demonstrations such as high school "blow-outs," that is student walkouts,† hunger strikes, and recent sustained political campaigns

---

Editor: These structural differences include significant school site disparities: in teacher preparation and experience (inner-city schools end up with the poorest quality overall), in local school district per student budget allocation, in school size (for example, number of children per school, square foot per child, square foot play area per school—for which, again, schools of racialized minorities are the largest and most crowded and ill-kept), in ratio of textbook to child, in age of textbooks, in ratio of library books to child, in accessibility of libraries, and in a hundred other factors that over and again disadvantage these children.
†Most memorably in 1968, 10,000 Mexican-American students from East Los Angeles, California, demonstrated against the inferior education that the Los Angeles School District provided for them. This form of protest continues. In an eighteen-month period, the *Los Angeles Times* carried six reports of Mexican-American demonstrations for better public education (4/16/98, 7/12/98, 7/19/98, 8/30/98, 4/25/99, 10/22/99).

against Proposition 187 and Proposition 227, for the sake of protecting the future of their children. Finally, there has been the enactment of legislation, such as the 1981 Texas Bilingual Education Law, intended to better the educational opportunities of language minority students.

Despite such examples of Mexican parental involvement in educational matters, the long-standing deficit-thinking belief shifts "blame from structural problems in schools to the shoulders of Latino parents, who are expected to carry the exclusive burden of school success for their children" (191). Educators and citizens should recognize that the power of deficit thinking is greatest when it is taken for granted and not questioned, because it injures each child by propagating stereotypes. Valencia and Solórzano state that these stereotypes now extend beyond the off-the-cuff response of the proverbial man-in-the-street. Since the 1960s they have appeared in academic literature. This literature highlights "the 'culturally deprived' or 'culturally disadvantaged' family, home, and child." By targeting marginalized populations, certain intellectuals claim, "the unique environment of a given subculture may not provide the prerequisite learnings or general acculturation essential to school success or to optimal life development" (192). To rebut this spiteful line of reasoning, it must be stressed that low-income parents of color understand very well that educational achievement is one key to success for their children. In point of fact, immigrant parents very often uproot their families specifically to afford for their children the opportunities of life and education in the U.S. These very same parents place an exceedingly high value on education, having staked their own lives as collateral for the sake of their children, and yet from the point of view of this version of deficit thinking, these parents are unconcerned about their children's education.

For example, Valencia, Henderson and Rankin (1985) have demonstrated many of the positive home life experiences, which were once believed to only occur in middle-class homes, take place in low-income homes as well. These include Mexican American mothers who (like parents of other marginalized students) exhibit "high educational aspirations for their children, positive reinforcement for intellectual behavior, read regularly to their offspring," and expose "their children to a variety of learning experiences outside the home."[4] This and many other studies reveal that children of low-income homes do not either lack the values or the behavior which could erroneously characterize them as having low interest in education.

Deficit thinking is so pervasive that it must be contested explicitly: All children (irrespective of race, marginalization, or immigrant status) have the same educational potential that is automatically allocated to middle-class Euro-American children.

In spite of evidence that marginalized children live in home environments where their educational progress is a priority, deficit thinking still manages to sabotage their aspirations by representing them as "at-risk" children. Valencia and Solórzano quote from a major critique of the notion: "The new term, *at risk*, is a resurrected metaphor of the *cultural deprivation* and *culturally disadvantaged* terms used with great frequency in the 1960s (Sleeter, 1995 foreword). As such, the construct of at risk is a 'retooled [social construction] for the 1990s, placing yet another repressive label on an ever widening group of young people and their families'" (Swadener 1995, quoted on page 197). "The discourse of 'children at risk' deflects attention away from injustices perpetuated and institutionalized by the dominant society and again frames oppressed communities and homes as lacking in the cultural and moral resources for advancement" (Sleeter 1995, quoted on page 197).

This construct was born as part of "a major strategy utilized by legislators and policymakers in their attempts to understand and solve the secondary school dropout problem—particularly among low-income racial/ethnic minority students" (195). It is used to identify characteristics of students who are predisposed to dropping out, for example, those students who are overage for their grade level, or those with failing grades. The at-risk label "is now entrenched in the educational literature as well as in the talk of educators and policymakers" (195). "Part of the problem with the concept is that it tends to overlook any strengths and promise of the student so-labeled, while drawing attention to the presumed shortcomings of the individual, . . . particularly alleged shortcomings rooted in familial and economic backgrounds of students" (196). Valencia and Solórzano state that the 'at risk' concept is a form of "deficit thinking in that the notion pays little, if any, attention to how schools are institutionally" responsible for sustaining "ways that exclude students from learning. . . . The idea blames the victim," as do the other rationalizations stemming from the deficit thinking ideology (196). Millions of language minority and other, marginalized students are affected.

"In sum, deficit thinking is alive and well in the contemporary period. A strong case can be made that the genetic pathology thesis, culture of poverty model, and cultural and accumulated environmental deficit models have, and are, growing in currency. What is most disturbing, [Valencia and Solórzano] feel, is the apparent pervasiveness among the general public of such beliefs held toward minority groups" (198). The powerful ideology of deficit thinking controls much of U.S. educational thinking and practice. The public continues to set policy with "little knowledge and understanding of the many problems the poor and certain racial/ethnic minority groups have in attaining equitable and useful schooling" (199). When we blame the impoverished student, the student of color, the immigrant student, and the language minority student for the structural failings of the U.S. public school system, America's privileged folk have renounced any personal responsibility for these children's plight, which is a result of blatant structural inequities that they built into, and continue to maintain, within the institution. Only by recognizing the three faces of this discriminatory ideology can we curb its massive power, which robs millions of students of their full potential—our nation's intellectual resources—each day that school is in session.

Academic Ignorance and Black Intelligence

William Labov

Why do children in the inner-city schools, blacks, Latinos, poor whites, Asian Americans, American Indians, and (of course) immigrants show such low educational achievement? In U.S. society, three distinct responses are heard. Richard Herrnstein, author of The Bell Curve, *maintains the position that heredity is substantially more important than environment in determining intelligence, as measured by IQ tests. Many sociologists, anthropologists, economists, educators, and a few psychologists take issue with that viewpoint.* Many researchers maintain that environmental factors, rather than any genetic deficit, explain the poor performance of lower-class inner-city children.*

A third position held by linguists and many anthropologists locates the problem not in the children but in the relations between them and the school system. This position holds that inner-city children do not necessarily have inferior mothers, language, or experience but that the language, family style, and ways of living of inner-city children are significantly different from the standard culture of the classroom and that this difference is not always properly understood by teachers and psychologists. Linguists believe that we must begin to adapt our school system to the language and learning styles of the majority in inner-city schools. They argue that everyone has the right to learn the standard languages and culture in reading and writing (and speaking, if they are so inclined); but this is the end result, not the beginning of the educational process. They do not believe that the standard language is the only medium in which teaching and learning can take place or that the first step in education is to convert all first-graders to replicas of white middle-class suburban children.

William Labov, professor of linguistics at the University of Pennsylvania, past president of the Linguistic Society of America, member of the National Academy of Science, and principal architect of the field of sociolinguistics, or as he prefers, empirical linguistics, states that

> *This article grew out of my own attempt to state the linguistic position on these issues in 1968. While psychologists are obviously divided, linguists find (somewhat to their own surprise) that they all agree. My own statement here is based on research carried out in South Central Harlem from 1965 to 1968 by a team of two white and two black investigators. [Labov's exemplary research has continued to break ground in the ensuing thirty years.] Our aim was to describe the differences between the standard English of the classroom and the vernacular language used by members of the street culture. We carried out long-term participant-observation with a number of black adolescent peer groups: the Jets, the Cobras, the Thunderbirds, the Aces, the Oscar*

---

*One such critique is Valencia and Solórzano's, in the previous selection.

Brothers. Their dialect will be referred to below as the Black English Vernacular (BEV). It is a remarkably consistent grammar, essentially the same as that found in other cities: Detroit, Chicago, Philadelphia, Washington, San Francisco, Los Angeles, New Orleans. It is important to note that this Black English Vernacular is only a small part of what might be called "Black English." Black Americans do not, of course, speak a single dialect, but a wide range of language forms that cover the continuum between this vernacular and the most formal literary English.—W. L.

In the [1960s], a great deal of federally sponsored research [was] devoted to the educational problems of children in ghetto schools. To account for the poor performance of children in these schools, educational psychologists have tried to discover what kind of disadvantage or defect the children are suffering from. The viewpoint which has been widely accepted and used as the basis for large-scale intervention programs is that the children show a cultural *deficit* as a result of an impoverished environment in their early years. A great deal of attention has been given to language. In this area, the deficit theory appears as the notion of *verbal deprivation*: black children from the ghetto area are said to receive little verbal stimulation, to hear very little well-formed language, and as a result are impoverished in their means of verbal expression. It is said that they cannot speak complete sentences, do not know the names of common objects, cannot form concepts or convey logical thoughts.

Unfortunately, these notions are based upon the work of educational psychologists who know very little about language and even less about black children. The concept of verbal deprivation has no basis in social reality; in fact, black children in the urban ghettos receive a great deal of verbal stimulation, hear more well-formed sentences than middle-class children, and participate fully in a highly verbal culture; they have the same basic vocabulary, possess the same capacity for conceptual learning, and use the same logic as anyone else who learns to speak and understand English. The myth of verbal deprivation is particularly dangerous because it diverts the attention from real defects of our educational system to imaginary defects of the child; and as we shall see, it leads its sponsors inevitably to the hypothesis of the genetic inferiority of black children, which the verbal-deprivation theory was designed to avoid.

The deficit theory attempts to account for a number of facts that are known to all of us: that black children in the central urban ghettos do badly on all school subjects, including arithmetic and reading. In reading, they average more than two years behind the national norm. Furthermore, this lag is cumulative, so that they do worse comparatively in the fifth grade than in the first grade. The information available suggests that this bad performance is correlated most closely with socioeconomic status. Segregated ethnic groups, however, seem to do worse than others: in particular, Indian, Mexican-American, and black children.

We are obviously dealing with the effects of the caste system of American society—essentially a "color-marking" system. Everyone recognizes this. The question is, By what mechanism does the color bar prevent children from learning to read? One answer is the notion of *cultural deprivation* put forward by Martin Deutsch and others: the black children are said to lack the favorable factors in their home environment which enable middle-class children to do well in school. These factors involve the development, through verbal interaction with adults, of various cognitive skills, including the ability to reason abstractly, to speak fluently, and to focus upon long-range goals. In their publications, the psychologists Deutsch, Irwin Katz, and Arthur Jensen also recognize broader social factors. However, the deficit theory does not focus upon the interaction of the black child with white society so much as on his failure to interact with his mother at home. In the literature we find very little direct observation of verbal interaction in the black home: most typically, the investigators ask the child if he has dinner with his parents, and if he engages in dinner-table conversation with them. He is also asked whether his family takes him on trips to museums and other cultural activities. This slender thread of evidence is used to explain and interpret the large body of tests carried out in the laboratory and in the school.

The most extreme view which proceeds from this orientation—and one that is now being widely accepted—is that lower-class black children have no language at all. Some educational psychologists first draw from the writings of the British social psychologist Basil Bernstein the idea that "much of lower-class language consists of a kind of incidental 'emotional accompaniment' to action here and now." Bernstein's views are filtered through a strong bias against all forms of working-class behavior, so that he sees middle-class language as superior in every respect—as "more abstract, and necessarily somewhat more flexible, detailed and subtle." One can proceed through a range of such views until one comes to the practical program of Carl Bereiter, Siegfried Engelmann, and their associates. Bereiter's program for an academically oriented preschool is based upon the premise that black children must have a language which they can learn, and their empirical findings that these children come to school without such a language. In his work with four-year-old black children from Urbana, Illinois, Bereiter reports that their communication was by gestures, "single words," and "a series of badly connected words or phrases," such as *They mine* and *Me got juice*. He reports that black children could not ask questions, that "without exaggerating . . . these four-year-olds could make no statements of any kind." Furthermore, when these children were asked, "Where is the book?" they did not know enough to look at the table where the book was lying in order to answer. Thus Bereiter concludes that the children's speech forms are nothing more than a series of emotional cries, and he decides to treat them "as if the children had no language at all." He identifies their speech with his interpretation of Bernstein's restricted code: "The language of culturally deprived children . . . is not merely an underdeveloped version of standard English, but is a basically non-logical mode of expressive behavior." The basic program of his preschool is to teach them a new language devised by Engelmann, which consists of a limited series of questions and answers such as *Where is the squirrel? / The squirrel is in the tree.* The children will not be punished if they use their vernacular speech on the playground, but they will not be allowed to use it in the schoolroom. If they should answer the question "Where is the squirrel?" with the illogical vernacular form "In the tree," they will be reprehended by various means and made to say, "The squirrel is in the tree."

Linguists and psycholinguists who have worked with black children are likely to dismiss this view of their language as utter nonsense. Yet there is no reason to reject Bereiter's observations as spurious: they were certainly not made up. On the contrary they give us a very clear view of the behavior of student and teacher which can be duplicated in any classroom. Our own research is done outside the schools, in situations where adults are not the dominant force, but on many occasions we have been asked to help analyze the results of research into verbal deprivation in such test situations.

Here, for example, is a complete interview with a black boy, one of hundreds carried out in a New York City school. The boy enters a room where there is a large, friendly white interviewer, who puts on the table in front of him a block or a fire engine, and says, "Tell me everything you can about this!" Twelve seconds of silence ensue. The interviewer tries again:

ADULT: What would you say it looks like?
              [8 seconds of silence]
CHILD: A spaceship.
ADULT: Hmmmmm.
              [13 seconds of silence]
CHILD: Like a je-et.
              [12 seconds of silence]
              Like a plane.
              [20 seconds of silence]
ADULT: What color is it?
CHILD: Orange.
              [2 seconds]

An' whi-ite.
[2 seconds]
An' green.
[6 seconds of silence]
ADULT: An' what could you use it for?
[8 seconds of silence]
CHILD: A je-et.
[6 seconds of silence]
ADULT: If you had two of them, what would you do with them?
[6 seconds of silence]
CHILD: Give one to some-body.
ADULT: Hmmm. Who do you think would like to have it?
[10 seconds of silence]
CHILD: Cla-rence.
ADULT: Mm. Where do you think we could get another one of these?
CHILD: At the store.
ADULT: Oh-ka-ay!

We have here the same kind of defensive, monosyllabic behavior which is reported in Bereiter's work. What is the situation that produces it? The child is in an asymmetrical situation where anything he says can, literally, be held against him. He has learned a number of devices to *avoid* saying anything in this situation, and he works very hard to achieve this end.

If one takes this interview as a measure of the verbal capacity of the child, it must be as his capacity to defend himself in a hostile and threatening situation. But unfortunately, thousands of such interviews are used as evidence of the child's total verbal capacity, or more simply his verbality: it is argued that this lack of "verbality" *explains* his poor performance in school.

The verbal behavior which is shown by the child in the test situation quoted above is not the result of ineptness of the interviewer. It is rather the result of regular sociolinguistic factors operating upon adult and child in this asymmetrical situation. In our work in urban ghetto areas, we have often encountered such behavior. For over a year Clarence Robins had worked with the Thunderbirds, a group of boys ten to twelve years old who were the dominant pre-adolescent group in a low-income project in Harlem. We then decided to interview a few younger brothers of the Thunderbirds, eight to nine years old. But our old approach didn't work. Here is an extract from the interview between Clarence and eight-year-old Leon L.:

CR: What if you saw somebody kickin' somebody else on the ground, or was using a stick, what would you do if you saw that?

LEON:	Mmmm.
CR:	If it was supposed to be a fair fight—
LEON:	I don' know.
CR:	You don' know? Would you do anything? . . . huh? I can't hear you.
LEON:	No.
CR:	Did you ever see somebody get beat up real bad?
LEON:	. . . Nope???
CR:	Well—uh did you ever get into a fight with a guy?
LEON:	Nope.
CR:	That was bigger than you?
LEON:	Nope.
CR:	You never been in a fight?
LEON:	Nope.
CR:	Nobody ever pick on you?
LEON:	Nope.
CR:	Nobody ever hit you?
LEON:	Nope.
CR:	How come?
LEON:	Ah 'on' know.
CR:	Didn't you ever hit somebody?
LEON:	Nope.
CR:	[*incredulous*] You never hit nobody?
LEON:	Mhm.
CR:	Aww, ba-a-a-be, you ain't gonna tell me that.

This nonverbal behavior occurs in a relatively *favorable* context for adult-child interaction, since the adult is a black man raised in Harlem, who knows this particular neighborhood and these boys very well. He is a skilled interviewer who has obtained a very high level of verbal response with techniques developed for a different age level, and has an extraordinary advantage over most teachers or experimenters in these respects. But even his skills and personality are ineffective in breaking down the social constraints that prevail here.

When we reviewed the record of this interview with Leon, we decided to use it as a test of our own knowledge of the sociolinguistic factors which control speech. We made the following changes in the social situation; in the next interview with Leon, Clarence:

1. Brought along a supply of potato chips, changing the "interview" into something more in the nature of a party.
2. Brought along Leon's best friend, eight-year-old Gregory.

3. Reduced the height imbalance. When Clarence got down on the floor of Leon's room, he dropped from 6 feet, 2 inches to 3 feet, 6 inches.
4. Introduced taboo words and taboo topics, and proved to Leon's surprise that one can say anything into our microphone without any fear of retaliation. It did not hit or bite back. The result of these changes is a striking difference in the volume and style of speech.

[The tape is punctuated throughout by the sound of potato chips.]

CR:	Is there anybody who says, "Your momma drink pee"?
⎰ LEON:	*[rapidly and breathlessly]* Yee-ah!
⎱ GREG:	Yup.
LEON:	And your father eat doo-doo for breakfas'!
CR:	Ohhh! *[laughs]*
LEON:	And they say your father—your father eat doo-doo for dinner!
GREG:	When they sound on me, I say "C.B.M."
CR:	What that mean?
⎰ LEON:	Congo booger-snatch! *[laughs]*
⎱ GREG:	Congo booger-snatcher! *[laughs]*
GREG:	And sometimes I'll curse with "B.B."
CR:	What that?
GREG:	Oh, that's a "M.B.B." Black boy. *[Leon crunching on potato chips]*
GREG:	'Merican Black Boy.
CR:	Oh.
GREG:	Anyway, 'Mericans is same like white people, right?
LEON:	And they talk about Allah.
CR:	Oh, yeah?
GREG:	Yeah.
CR:	What they say about Allah?
⎰ LEON:	Allah—Allah is God.
⎱ GREG:	Allah—
CR:	And what else?
LEON:	I don' know the res'.
GREG:	Allah i—Allah is God, Allah is the only God, Allah—
LEON:	Allah is the *son* of God.
GREG:	But can he make magic?
LEON:	Nope.
GREG:	I know who can make magic?
CR:	Who can?
LEON:	The God, the real one.
CR:	Who can make magic?
GREG:	The son of po'—(CR: Hm?) I'm sayin' the po'k chop God! He only a po'k chop God! *[Leon chuckles]*

The "nonverbal" Leon is now competing actively for the floor; Gregory and Leon talk to each other as much as they do to the interviewer. The monosyllabic speaker who had nothing to say about anything and could not remember what he did yesterday has disappeared. Instead, we have two boys who have so much to say that they keep interrupting each other, who seem to have no difficulty in using the English language to express themselves.

One can now transfer this demonstration of the sociolinguistic control of speech to other test situations, including IQ and reading tests in school. It should be immediately apparent that none of the standard tests will come anywhere near measuring Leon's verbal capacity. On these tests he will show up as very much the monosyllabic, inept, ignorant, bumbling child of our first interview. The teacher has far less ability than Clarence Robins to elicit speech from this child; Clarence knows the community, the things that Leon has been doing, and the things that Leon would like to talk about. But the power relationships in a one-to-one confrontation between adult and child are too asymmetrical. This does not mean that some black children will not talk a great deal when alone with an adult, or that an adult cannot get close to any child. It means that the social situation is the most powerful determinant of verbal behavior and that an adult must enter into the right social relation with a child if he wants to find out what a child can do. This is just what many teachers cannot do.

The view of the black speech community which we obtain from our work in the ghetto areas is precisely the opposite from that reported by Deutsch, Engelmann, and Bereiter. We see a child bathed in verbal stimulation from morning to night. We see many speech events which depend upon the competitive exhibitions of verbal skills: singing, sounding, toasts, rifting, louding—a whole range of activities in which the individual gains status through his use of language. We see the younger child trying to acquire these skills from older children—hanging around on the outskirts of the older peer groups, and imitating this behavior. We see, however, no connection between verbal skill at the speech events characteristic of the street culture and success in the schoolroom; which says something about classrooms rather than about a child's language.

There are undoubtedly many verbal skills which children from ghetto areas must learn in order to do well in school, and some of these are indeed characteristic of middle-class verbal behavior. Precision in spelling, practice in handling abstract symbols, the ability to state explicitly the meaning of words, and a richer knowledge of the Latinate vocabulary may all be useful acquisitions. But is it true that *all* of the middle-class verbal habits are functional and desirable in school? Before we impose middle-class verbal style upon children from other cultural groups, we should find out how much of it is useful for the main work of analyzing and generalizing, and how much is merely stylistic—or even dysfunctional. In high school and college, middle-class children spontaneously complicate their syntax to the point that instructors despair of getting them to make their language simpler and clearer.

Our work in the speech community makes it painfully obvious that in many ways working-class speakers are more effective narrators, reasoners, and debaters than many middle-class speakers, who temporize, qualify, and lose their argument in a mass of irrelevant detail. Many academic writers try to rid themselves of the part of middle-class style that is empty pretension, and keep the part necessary for precision. But the average middle-class speaker that we encounter makes no such effort; he is enmeshed in verbiage, the victim of sociolinguistic factors beyond his control.

I will not attempt to support this argument here with systematic quantitative evidence, although it is possible to develop measures which show how far middle-class speakers can wander from the point. I would like to contrast two speakers dealing with roughly the same topic: matters of belief. The first is Larry H., a fifteen-year-old core member of another group, the Jets. Larry is being interviewed here by John Lewis, our participant-observer among adolescents in South Central Harlem.

> JL: What happens to you after you die? Do you know?
>
> LARRY: Yeah, I know. (What?) After they put you in the ground, your body turns into—ah—bones, an' *shit*.
>
> JL: What happens to your spirit?
>
> LARRY: Your spirit—soon as you die, your spirit leaves you. (And where does the spirit go?) Well, it all depends. (On what?) You know, like some people say if you're good an' shit, your spirit goin' t'heaven . . . 'n' if you bad, your spirit goin' to hell. Well, *bullshit!* Your spirit goin' to hell anyway, good or bad.
>
> JL: Why?
>
> LARRY: Why? I'll tell you why. 'Cause, you see, doesn' nobody really know that it's a God, y'know, 'cause, I mean I have seen black gods, pink gods, white gods, all color gods, and don't nobody know it's really a God. An' when they be sayin' if you good, you goin' t'heaven, tha's *bullshit*, 'cause you ain't goin' to no heaven, 'cause it ain't no heaven for you to go to.

Larry is a gifted speaker of the Black English vernacular (BEV) as opposed to standard English (SE). His grammar shows a high concentration of such characteristic BEV forms as negative inversion [*don't nobody know*], negative concord [*you ain't goin' to no heaven*], invariant *be* [*when they be sayin'*], dummy *it* for SE *there* [*it ain't no heaven*], optional copula deletion [*if you're good . . . if you bad*], and full forms of auxiliaries [*I have seen*]. The only SE influence in this passage is the one case of *doesn't* instead of the invariant *don't* of BEV. Larry also provides a paradigmatic example of the rhetorical style of BEV: he can sum up a complex argument in a few words, and the full force of his opinions comes through without qualification or reservation. He is eminently quotable, and his interviews give us a great many concise statements of the BEV point of view. One can almost say that Larry speaks the BEV culture.

It is the logical form of this passage which is of particular interest here. Larry presents a complex set of interdependent propositions which can be explicated by setting out the SE equivalents in linear order. The basic argument is to deny the twin propositions:

(A) If you are good,
(B) then your spirit will go to heaven.

(not A) If you are bad,
(C) then your spirit will go to hell.

Larry denies (B), and allows that if (A) or (not A) is true, (C) will follow. His argument may be outlined:

1. Everyone has a different idea of what God is like.
2. Therefore nobody really knows that God exists.
3. If there is a heaven, it was made by God.
4. If God doesn't exist, he couldn't have made heaven.
5. Therefore heaven does not exist.
6. You can't go somewhere that doesn't exist.
7. (not B) Therefore you can't go to heaven.
8. (C) Therefore you are going to hell.

This hypothetical argument is not carried on at a high level of seriousness. It is a game played with ideas as counters, in which opponents use a wide variety of verbal devices to win. There is no personal commitment to any of these propositions, and no reluctance to strengthen one's argument by bending the rules of logic as in the (2, 4) sequence. But if the opponent invokes the rules of logic, they hold. In John Lewis' interviews, he often makes this move, and the force of his argument is always acknowledged and countered within the rules of logic.

> JL: Well, if there's no heaven, how could there be a hell?
>
> LARRY: I mean—ye-eah. Well, let me tell you, it ain't no hell, 'cause this is hell right here, y'know! (This is hell?) Yeah, this is hell right here!

Larry's answer is quick, ingenious, and decisive. The application of the (3-4-5) argument to hell is denied, since hell is here, and therefore conclusion (not B) stands. These are not ready-made or preconceived opinions, but new propositions devised to win the logical argument in the game being played. The reader will note the speed and precision of Larry's mental operations. He does not wander, or insert meaningless verbiage. It is often said that the nonstandard vernacular is not suited for dealing with abstract or hypothetical questions, but in fact, speakers of BEV take great delight in exercising their wit and logic on the most improbable and problematical matters. Despite the fact that Larry H. does not believe in God, and has just denied all knowledge of him, John Lewis advances the following hypothetical question:

> JL: . . . But, just say that there is a God, what color is he? White or black?
>
> LARRY: Well, if it is a God . . . I wouldn' know what color, I couldn' say—couldn' nobody say what—
>
> JL: But now, jus' suppose there was a God—
>
> LARRY: Unless'n they say . . .
>
> JL: No, I was jus' sayin' jus' suppose there is a God, would he be white or black?
>
> LARRY: . . . He'd be white, man.
>
> JL: Why?
>
> LARRY: Why? I'll tell you why. 'Cause the average whitey out here got everything, you dig? And the nigger ain't got *shit*, y'know? Y'unnerstan'? So—um—for—in order for *that* to happen, you know it ain't no black God that's doin' that *bullshit*.

No one can hear Larry's answer to this question without being convinced of being in the presence of a skilled speaker with great "verbal presence of mind," who can use the English language expertly for many purposes.

Let us now turn to the second speaker, an upper-middle-class, college-educated black man being interviewed by Clarence Robins in our survey of adults in South Central Harlem.

> CR: Do you know of anything that someone can do, to have someone who has passed on visit him in a dream?

CHARLES: Well, I even heard my parents say that there is such a thing as something in dreams, some things like that, and sometimes dreams do come true. I have personally never had a dream come true. I've never dreamt that somebody was dying and they actually died (Mhm), or that I was going to have ten dollars the next day and somehow I got ten dollars in my pocket. (Mhm.) I don't particularly believe in that, I don't think it's true. I do feel, though, that there is such a thing as—ah—witchcraft. I do feel that in certain cultures there is such a thing as witchcraft, or some sort of *science* of witchcraft; I don't think that it's just a matter of believing hard enough that there is such a thing as witchcraft. I do believe that there is such a thing that a person can put himself in a state of *mind* (Mhm), or that—er—something could be given them to intoxicate them in a certain—to a certain frame of mind—that—that could actually be considered witchcraft.

Charles M. is obviously a "good speaker" who strikes the listener as well-educated, intelligent, and sincere. He is a likable and attractive person—the kind of person that middle-class listeners rate very high on a scale of "job suitability" and equally high as a potential friend. His language is more moderate and tempered than Larry's; he makes every effort to qualify his opinions, and seems anxious to avoid any misstatements or overstatements. From these qualities emerges the primary characteristic of this passage—its *verbosity*. Words multiply, some modifying and qualifying, others repeating or padding the main argument. The first half of this extract is a response to the initial question on dreams, basically:

1. Some people say that dreams sometimes come true.
2. I have never had a dream come true.
3. Therefore I don't believe (1).

This much of Charles M.'s response is well directed to the point of the question. He then volunteers a statement of his beliefs about witchcraft which shows the difficulty of middle-class speakers who (a) want to express a belief in something but (b) want to show themselves as judicious, rational, and free from superstitions. The basic proposition can be stated simply in five words:

But I believe in witchcraft.

However, the idea is enlarged to exactly one hundred words, and it is difficult to see what else is being said. The vacuity of this passage becomes more evident if we remove repetitions, fashionable words, and stylistic decorations:

But I believe in witchcraft.
I don't think witchcraft is just a belief.
A person can put himself or be put in a state of mind that is witchcraft.

Without the extra verbiage and the OK words like *science, culture* and *intoxicate*, Charles M. appears as something less than a first-rate thinker. The initial impression of him as a good speaker is simply our long-conditioned reaction to middle-class verbosity: we know that people who use these stylistic devices are educated people, and we are inclined to credit them with saying something intelligent.

Let us now examine Bereiter's own data on the verbal behavior of the black children he dealt with. The expressions *They mine* and *Me got juice* are cited as examples of a language which lacks the means for expressing logical relations—in this case characterized as "a series of badly connected words." In the case of *They mine*, it is apparent that Bereiter confuses the notions of logic and explicitness. We know that there are many languages of the world which do not have a present copula, and which conjoin subject and predicate complement without a verb. Russian, Hungarian, and Arabic may be foreign, but they are not by the same token illogical. In the case of black English we are not dealing with even this superficial grammatical difference, but rather with a low-level rule which carries contraction one step further to delete single consonants representing the verbs *is, have,* or *will*. We have yet to find any children who do not sometimes use the full forms of *is* or *will*, even though they may frequently delete it.

   The deletion of the *is* or *are* in black English is not the result of erratic or illogical behavior: it follows the same regular rules as standard English contraction. Wherever standard English can contract, black children use either the contracted form or (more commonly) the deleted zero form. Thus *They mine* corresponds to standard English *They're mine*, not to the full form *They are mine*. On the other hand, no such deletion is possible in positions where standard English cannot contract: just as one cannot say *That's what they're* in standard English, *That's what they* is equally impossible in the vernacular we are considering. The appropriate use of the deletion rule, like the contraction rule, requires a deep and intimate knowledge of English grammar and phonology. Such knowledge is not available for conscious inspection by native speakers: the rules we have worked out for standard contraction have never appeared in any grammar, and are certainly not a part of the conscious knowledge of any standard English speakers. Nevertheless, the adult or child who uses these rules must have formed at some level of psychological organization clear concepts of tense marker, verb phrase, rule ordering, sentence embedding, pronoun, and many other grammatical categories which are essential parts of any logical system.

Bereiter's reaction to the sentence *Me got juice* is even more puzzling. If Bereiter believes that *Me got juice* is not a logical expression, it can only be that he interprets the use of the objective pronoun *me* as representing a difference in logical relationship to the verb; that the child is in fact saying that "the juice got him" rather than "he got the juice"! If on the other hand the child means "I got juice," then this sentence form shows only that he has not learned the formal rules for the use of the subjective form *I* and oblique form *me*.

Bereiter shows even more profound ignorance of the rules of discourse and of syntax when he rejects "In the tree" as an illogical or badly formed answer to "Where is the squirrel?" Such elliptical answers are of course used by everyone, and they show the appropriate deletion of subject and main verb, leaving the locative which is questioned by *wh* + *there*. The reply *In the tree* demonstrates that the listener has been attentive to and apprehended the syntax of the speaker. Whatever formal structure we wish to write for expressions such as *Yes* or *Home* or *In the tree*, it is obvious that they cannot be interpreted without knowing the structure of the question which preceded them, and that they presuppose an understanding of the syntax of the question. Thus if you ask me, "Where is the squirrel?" it is necessary for me to understand the sentence from an underlying form which would otherwise have produced *The squirrel is there*. If the child had answered *The tree*, or *Squirrel the tree*, or *The in tree*, we would then assume that he did not understand the syntax of the full form, *The squirrel is in the tree*. Given the data that Bereiter presents, we cannot conclude that the child has no grammar, but only that the investigator does not understand the rules of grammar. It does not necessarily do any harm to use the full form *The squirrel is in the tree*, if one wants to make fully explicit the rules of grammar which the child has internalized. Much of logical analysis consists of making explicit just that kind of internalized rule. But it is hard to believe that any good can come from a program which begins with so many misconceptions about the input data. Bereiter and Engelmann believe that in teaching the child to say *The squirrel is in the tree* or *This is a box* and *This is not a box*, they are teaching him an entirely new language, whereas in fact they are only teaching him to produce slightly different forms of the language he already has.

If there is a failure of logic involved here, it is surely in the approach of the verbal-deprivation theorists, rather than in the mental abilities of the children concerned. We can isolate six distinct steps in the reasoning which has led to programs such as those of Deutsch, Bereiter, and Engelmann:

1. The lower-class child's verbal response to a formal and threatening situation is used to demonstrate his lack of verbal capacity, or verbal deficit.

2. This verbal deficit is declared to be a major cause of the lower-class child's poor performance in school.

3. Since middle-class children do better in school, middle-class speech habits are said to be necessary for learning.

4. Class and ethnic differences in grammatical form are equated with differences in the capacity for logical analysis.

5. Teaching the child to mimic certain formal speech patterns used by middle-class teachers is seen as teaching him to think logically.

6. Children who learn these formal speech patterns are then said to be thinking logically, and it is predicated that they will do much better in reading and arithmetic in the years to follow.

This article has proved that numbers (1) and (2) at least are wrong. However, it is not too naive to ask, What is wrong with being wrong? We have already conceded that black children need help in analyzing language into its surface components, and in being more explicit. But there are, in fact, serious and damaging consequences of the verbal-deprivation theory. These may be considered under two headings: (a) the theoretical bias and (b) the consequences of failure.

It is widely recognized that the teacher's attitude toward the child is an important factor in the latter's success or failure. The work of Robert Rosenthal on "self-fulfilling prophecies" shows that the progress of children in the early grades can be dramatically affected by a single random labeling of certain children as "intellectual bloomers." When the everyday language of black children is stigmatized as "not a language at all" and "not possessing the means for logical thought," the effect of such a labeling is repeated many times during each day of the school year. Every time that a child uses a form of BEV without the copula or with negative concord, he will be labeling himself for the teacher's benefit as "illogical," as a "nonconceptual thinker." This notion gives teachers a ready-made, theoretical basis for the prejudice they may already feel against the lower-class black child and his language. When they hear him say *I don't want none* or *They mine*, they will be hearing, through the bias provided by the verbal-deprivation theory, not an English dialect different from theirs, but the primitive mentality of the savage mind.

But what if the teacher succeeds in training the child to use the new language consistently? The verbal deprivation theory holds that this will lead to a whole chain of successes in school, and that the child will be drawn away from the vernacular culture into the middle-class world. Undoubtedly this will happen with a few isolated individuals, just as it happens in every school system today for a few children. But we are concerned not with the few but the many, and for the majority of black children the distance between them and the school is bound to widen under this approach.

The essential fallacy of the verbal-deprivation theory lies in tracing the educational failure of the child to his personal deficiencies. At present, these deficiencies are said to be caused by his home environment. It is traditional to explain a child's failure in school by his inadequacy; but when failure reaches such massive proportions, it seems necessary to look at the social and cultural obstacles to learning and the inability of the school to adjust to the social situation.

The second area in which the verbal-deprivation theory is doing serious harm to our educational system is in the consequences of this failure and the reaction to it. [When an educational program fails which is built on the assumption that the student—not the school—exhibits deficiencies, the interpretation of the failure] which we receive will be from the same educational psychologists who designed this program. The fault will be found, not in the data, the theory, or the methods used, but rather in the children who have failed to respond to the opportunities offered them. When black children fail to show the significant advance which the deprivation theory predicts, it will be further proof of the profound gulf which separates their mental processes from those of civilized, middle-class mankind. [. . . For example, some prominent figures associated with Operation Head Start reacted to its shortcomings] by saying that intervention did not take place early enough. Bettye M. Caldwell notes that

> the research literature of the last decade dealing with social-class differences has made abundantly clear that all parents are not qualified to provide even the basic essentials of physical and psychological care to their children.

[Some deficit theorists are now moving away from genetic justifications for their findings, and have begun to fill the literature with reflections on] "long-standing patterns of parental deficit." "There is, perhaps unfortunately," writes Caldwell, "no literacy test for motherhood." Failing such eugenic measures, she has proposed "educationally oriented day care for culturally deprived children between six months and three years of age." The children are returned home each evening to "maintain primary emotional relationships with their own families," but during the day they are removed "hopefully to prevent the deceleration in rate of development which seems to occur in many deprived children around the age of two to three years."

There are others who feel that even the best of the intervention programs will not help the black child no matter when they are applied—that we are faced once again with the "inevitable hypothesis" of the genetic inferiority of the black people. Arthur Jensen, for example, argues that the verbal-deprivation theorists have been given every opportunity to prove their case and have failed. This opinion forms part of the argument leading to his overall conclusion that the "preponderance of the evidence is . . . less consistent with a strictly environmental hypothesis than with the genetic hypothesis."[5]

Jensen argues that the middle-class white population is differentiated from the working-class white and black population in the ability for "cognitive or conceptual learning," which Jensen calls Level II intelligence as against mere "associative learning," or Level I intelligence.* Thus Jensen found that one group of middle-class children were helped by their concept-forming ability to recall twenty familiar objects that could be classified into four categories: animals, furniture, clothing, or foods. Lower-class black children did just as well as middle-class children with a miscellaneous set, but showed no improvement with objects that could be so organized.

[Linguists can readily offer evidence from language acquisition process of human children to dispute the observation on free recall that Jensen mentions to support his prejudice.] In the earliest stages of language learning, [all] children acquire "selectional restrictions" in their use of words. For example, they learn that some verbs take ANIMATE subjects, but others only INANIMATE ones: thus we say *The machine breaks* but not *John breaks*; *The paper tears* but not *George tears*. A speaker of English must master such subtle categories as the things which *break*, like *boards, glasses,* and *ropes*; things which *tear*, like *shirts, paper,* and *skin*; things which *snap*, like *buttons, potato chips,* and *plastic*, and other categories which *smash, crumple,* or *go bust*.

In studies of Samoan children, Keith Kernan has shown that similar rules are learned reliably long before the grammatical particles that mark tense, number, and so on. The experimentation on free recall that Jensen reports ignores such abilities, and defines intelligence as a particular way of answering a particular kind of question within a narrow cultural framework. Recent work of anthropologists in other cultures is beginning to make some headway in discovering how our tests bias the results so as to make normally intelligent people look stupid. Michael Cole and his associates gave the same kind of free recall tests to Kpelle speakers in Liberia. Those who had not been to school—children or adults—could only remember eight or ten out of the twenty and showed no "clustering" according to categories, no matter how long the trials went on. Yet one simple change in the test method produced a surprising change. The interviewer took each of the objects to be remembered and held it over a chair: one chair for each category, or just one chair for all categories. Suddenly the Kpelle subjects showed a dramatic improvement, remembered

---

*Valencia and Solórzano discuss Jensen's work, part III.

seventeen to eighteen objects, and matched American subjects in both recall and the amount of clustering by categories. We do not understand this effect, for we are only beginning to discover the subtle biases built in our test methods which prevent people from using the abilities that they display in their language and in everyday life.

~

Linguists are in an excellent position to demonstrate the fallacies of the verbal-deprivation theory. All linguists agree that nonstandard dialects are highly structured systems; they do not see these dialects as accumulations of errors caused by the failure of their speakers to master standard English. When linguists hear black children saying *He crazy* or *Her my friend* they do not hear a "primitive language." Nor do they believe that the speech of working-class people is merely a form of emotional expression, incapable of relating logical thought. Linguists therefore condemn with a single voice Bereiter's view that the vernacular can be disregarded.

There is no reason to believe that any nonstandard vernacular is in itself an obstacle to learning. The chief problem is ignorance of language on the part of all concerned. Our job as linguists is to remedy this ignorance: Bereiter and Engelmann want to reinforce it and justify it. Teachers are now being told to ignore the language of black children as unworthy of attention and useless for learning. They are being taught to hear every natural utterance of the child as evidence of his mental inferiority. As linguists we are unanimous in condemning this view as bad observation, bad theory, and bad practice.

That educational psychology should be strongly influenced by a theory so false to the facts of language is unfortunate; but that children should be the victims of this ignorance is intolerable. If linguists can contribute some of their valuable knowledge and energy toward exposing the fallacies of the verbal-deprivation theory, we will have done a great deal to justify the support that society has given to basic research in our field.[6]

Beginning Where the Children Are

Abridged from an article by Luis Moll and Norma González

Luis Moll and Norma González contest the commonly unexamined assumption that language minority children enter the classroom with little or no knowledge. People—not only teachers—who come into contact with marginalized children often view them as lacking truly valuable understanding. But children don't arrive at the school doors without any understanding or knowledge. The families of these children provide them with strategies for interaction and survival within society. Moll and González claim that the teacher must find ways to integrate and build on this knowledge base, these funds of knowledge, for the most beneficial education. The funds-of-knowledge method that they advocate requires teachers to seek out parents' knowledge: the kinds of knowledge, and the kinds of strategies for interacting with society, that parents provide for their children. In short, the teacher should become personally acquainted with the social and cultural background of these children. With a better understanding of the parents' actual knowledge—the occupational skills, styles of interaction, and social strategies—teachers can truly "begin where the students are" and build school knowledge and academic skills on the foundations that minority children's parents provide. The optimal way to learn about a child's funds of knowledge is for teachers to go into the households as ethnographers and get to know the experiences the families have endured. Even if this is not practically possible, teachers should reach out to learn about such home knowledges so that such information can be integrated into the classroom curriculum. Teachers must actively build a bridge between home and school.

As a teacher, it is important to recognize and build on the knowledge and culture that children bring to the classroom, rather than unconsciously assuming that a child arrives at the school doors as an empty vessel, bereft of knowledge. By using a child's culture and knowledge as tools and resources, the teacher is best able to help children develop further learning. Ideally, teachers should have knowledge of their students' cultural experiences, but two common problems prevent this. The first problem consists of the negative expectations that are maintained by teachers about students of different cultural and linguistic backgrounds. By not examining and questioning social stereotypes, teachers hinder the education of the nonmainstream and working-class children by failing to take into account the circumstances in which their families live. After her experience changed her mind, one teacher recalled her initial pessimism by saying, "I did not realize it at the time, but I used to believe that my students had limited opportunities in life. I thought that poverty was the root of many of their problems, and that this was something too big for me to change as a teacher" (104–105). This teacher had set expectations according to negative stereotypes about socioeconomic classes and gave up on her students without giving them a fair and equal chance at success.

The second issue is understanding what "culture" really means. The popular definition of culture is characterized by such elements as: "dances, food, language, folklore, ethnic heritage festivals, and international potlucks. Although these affirmations are undoubtedly positive in fostering tolerance, there is an unspoken assumption of a normative and clearly defined culture 'out there' that may not take into account the everyday lived experiences of students and their families" (90).

Moll and González address the importance of teachers taking into account the knowledge that students have gained through their families their own personal and cultural experiences. Once teachers acknowledge their students' prior experiences and knowledge, they make their teaching more relevant by incorporating the students' funds of knowledge into their lessons.

The term *funds of knowledge* had previously been used by Carlos Vélez-Ibáñez, and by James Greenberg, who defined as "reservoirs of accumulated knowledge and strategies for survival that households possess" (90).[7] Every household contains funds of knowledge that help the family function and interact with society as well as form social networks.

In the best of worlds, teachers employ the tools of anthropologists and visit, come to know personally, participate in, and analyze their students' actual households. The teachers enter their students' communities to observe how households "function as part of a wider economy and how family members obtain and distribute their material and intellectual resources through strategic social ties or networks or through other adaptive arrangements" (93). Through social networks families help one another find jobs, take care of children, and provide other informative factors for survival. The teachers take field notes, write personal journals, and hand out surveys to gather information and obtain a sense of the funds of knowledge of each household. After in-home observations, they come together in study groups to discuss their findings. By discovering the funds of knowledge of households and communities, the teachers were able to create new teaching modules that used knowledge that children immediately would recognize as significant in their lives.

As part of funds of knowledge, social networks transmit knowledge across households. Social networks serve as a source of social capital. James Coleman defines it as follows: "What I mean by social capital in the raising of children is the norms, the social networks, and the relationships between adults and children that are of value for the child's growing up" (105). Social capital serves as a resource that can be utilized to make connections between the family, community, and school. A teacher who knows about the child's home-based social capital used it to structure educational experiences which are both culturally sensitive and tailored to the needs of the children. For example, Coleman associates a decrease in the drop-out rate within some schools he studied to the incorporation of family social capital (funds of knowledge) in the curriculum.

Teachers become aware of the funds of knowledge of the families by observing family household activities and learning about their work. One family, observed by Moll and González, provides an example of the extensive funds of knowledge that can be tapped for educational advantage from an inquiry into the social networks and social capital working within a household.

The Zavala family is part of the urban working class. Mr. Zavala is referred to as an entrepreneur, who builds and owns some apartments. At age seventeen, he joined the Army and throughout his life had various jobs ranging from cable installer, repairman, and painter. Everyone in the family is involved in the economic sector of society, not just Mr. Zavala. His son, Juan, who is in sixth grade, has his own bike shop in his backyard. His daughters, Carmen and Conchita, also participate by selling candies brought from trips to Mexico to their friends.

The Zavala family is part of a larger social network. For example, Mr. Zavala's brothers and sisters rent houses from other family members, and his children go to their uncle, who is a junior high school teacher, for help with their homework. In the Zavala family, education is very important. Reading and writing are very crucial and each individual does it for different reasons. Mr. Zavala reads and writes, but mostly on issues concerning his work. Mrs. Zavala also writes, as it involves the well-being of her children. Both are involved in the school by participating in the PTA, helping in trips, workshops, and preparing food for school events. At home, they help with homework and acknowledge its importance. They also take the children to the library.

It is obvious the Zavala family have accumulated vast amounts of knowledge through their daily actions, experiences, jobs, expertise, interests, and concerns. Moll and González state that "people must teach and learn new knowledge and skills to deal with a changing reality. . . . These households, then as should be obvious, are not socially or intellectually barren: they contain knowledge; people use reading and writing; they mobilize social relationships, and they teach and they learn." Upon discarding the commonplace presumption that children speaking other languages and living in homes structured by different cultures lack any school-worthy knowledge, "one learns not only about the extent of knowledge found among these working-class households but about the special importance of the social and cultural world, and of social relations, in the development of knowledge" (97–98).

Many teachers unthinkingly assume that children from immigrant, ethnic, or working-class origins lack the ability to learn as much and as quickly as mainstream children, and do not have "worthwhile knowledge and experiences" (98). As a result of actually going into the students' homes to experience these home environments, most teachers were overwhelmed by the circumstances that their students and families have overcome. Their stereotypes were dismantled as they became more familiar with the households and their backgrounds. Moll and González mention that some teachers were "struck by the sheer survival of the households against seemingly overwhelming odds. Others were astonished at the sacrifices the households made in order to gain a better education for their children. They all found parents who were engineers, teachers, and small business owners in Mexico, who pulled up stakes and now work in jobs far below their capabilities in order to obtain a 'better life and education' for their children" (98).

Many teachers, who worked with Moll and González, built social relationships with the families as a result of the funds of knowledge project. The teachers were invited to Mexican family celebrations such as *quinceañeras*.* "Teachers became a part of the families' social networks, signaling that relationships of *confianza* 'mutual trust' had developed" (98). With *confianza* in turn, parents participated fully in their children's classroom education. They became more comfortable visiting the school and asking questions. In Moll and González's study, teachers began incorporating funds of knowledge found within the household into their lesson plans. After witnessing the funds of knowledge of a household that regularly participated in trans-border activities in northern Mexico, one teacher "discovered that her student commonly returned from these trips with candy to sell. Elaborating on this student's marketing skills, an integrated unit was spun around various aspects of candy and the selling of candy" (99).

The teachers who participated in Moll and González's study spoke about their previous stereotypes and the change of outlook that they underwent. One teacher mentioned earlier, spoke of her change in perspective: "This fatalistic obsession of mine has slowly melted away as I have gotten to know my students and their families. I believe this transformation is the most important one I have made. Its ramifications have reached far beyond the classroom" (105).

By visiting the homes and learning more about them she realized that her negative outlook about children who come from poor immigrant and language minority families was completely false. She was able to recognize the children's real potential and saw the value and importance of the home knowledge that their families provide. She also realized the terrible consequences of her pri-

---

Quinceañera 'Mexican celebration of a girl's fifteenth birthday'.

vately held reduction of her students' educational chances. Having seen the richness of their funds of knowledge, this teacher was able to find ways to enrich the educational experience for everyone in the classroom.

The teachers who challenged themselves gained a very concrete sense of their students' cultural background. They learned to disregard stereotypes as they got to know their students as individuals; not tokens of a foreign and misunderstood culture. Moreover, by using the funds of knowledge of the child, the classroom becomes a comfortable space where the parents, teachers, community, and students become active members in a successful educational process, one where learning and experience are simultaneously cultivated in both hearts and minds.

Excerpt from "Translating Translation: Finding the Beginning"

Alberto Alvaro Ríos

Linguists, by using electrodes on the vocal cords, have been able to demonstrate that English has tenser vowels than, for example, Spanish. The body itself speaks a language differently, so that moving from one language to another is more than translating words. It's getting the body ready as well. It's getting the heart ready along with the mind.

I've been intrigued by this information. It addresses the physicality of language in a way that perhaps surprises us. In this sense, we forget that words aren't simply what they mean—they are also physical acts.

I often talk about the duality of language using the metaphor of binoculars, how by using two lenses one might see something better, closer, with more detail. That apparatus, the binoculars, are of course physically clumsy—as is the learning of two languages, and all the signage and so on that this entails—they're clumsy, but once put to the eyes a new world in that moment opens up to us. And it's not a new world at all—it's the same world, but simply better seen, and therefore better understood.

We try to do what people want, but they have to know what they're asking for. That search for understanding is often itself a search for, and an act of, translation as well.

Several years ago I was doing an Artists in the Schools residency at the high school in Eloy, Arizona. Two memorable events occurred. The first was among a group of gifted students: a fire alarm rang, but nobody got up. We were having such a good time, nobody seemed willing to stop. One student said, "It's probably fake anyway. Couldn't we just send someone out to check?"

That was nice, but something else occurred on the same day, a Thursday. I was also working with a group of—what to call them, what were they called? Non-gifted students? In this class, there was an attentive group of four or five students in front, but in back and to the sides students were in various states of engagement, the most active of which was a poker game.

The students were Mexican and Chicano, mostly, migrant worker children,

157

and those not being entirely attentive were comprised mostly of *cholos*.*
Cholos are what Pachucos used to be. The young men, in particular, have a
uniform: chino pants, black belt, thick, black shoes, two T-shirts—a regular
one over a thin-strapped one—and a hair net.

The hair net by itself is interesting, and to an outsider perhaps effeminate.
But there were many reasons for a hair net. These boys' older brothers often
worked, for example, in fast-food restaurants, and had to wear nets. And a net,
it was a show of attitude—you took your net off when the important things
happened. School was not that.

In working with these students, I was also faced with a substitute teacher,
who had no ideas on how to control the class and who was very glad that I
was the one standing up in front.

The week went its own way, with me talking and reading, the students in
front responding, and the others playing cards and throwing pencils. But I
know this classroom, and that was the thing. I also understood what happened
next.

On this Thursday of the week, one of the boys in back got up, starting
walking his walk to the front, ostensibly to sharpen a pencil, but he kind of
hung around me at the desk. I was done for the day, and everyone was working, or supposed to be working, on a writing assignment.

"Hey, *ese*," he said to me, with a small pointing of the right hand.

"Hey," I say.

He nodded his head. "You really like this poetry shit," he asked.

"Yes," I said.

And then he followed with the very best thing I could have hoped for. "So,
how many fights you had?"

In that moment I knew exactly what he was asking me. He was trying to
understand, to make some bridge, to make some sense for himself. It was a
moment I won't forget. Whatever I answered doesn't finally matter. He had
already found some kind of answer in his question.

He was looking for an equation, for something to understand. And he said it
in the best way he could.

Language is more than what we say—it's also how we say it, and whether
or not we even understand what we are saying. Language is manners, then,
well-said or not; language is the attempt to understand as much as the understanding itself. It is the how as much as the what, form as much as content,
intent as much as words.

**Editor: cholo* 'Chicano gang member', *pachuco* 'Chicano youth of the 1930–1940s who both
Anglo-American and Mexican societies disaffected.'

These are the lateral muscles and physical directions of language that translation often fails to use. I had to be able to hear what this young man was asking me, whether or not I was prepared. It was another vocabulary altogether, yet filled with familiar words.

But maybe that's all right. Maybe that's exactly what keeps a computer or a book from doing the job. Maybe that's what keeps us human, and engaged, and necessary.

How many fights have I had? he asked.

Just one, I said, like you.

Notes

1. Lily Wong Fillmore, "Language Minority Students and School Participation: What Kind of English Is Needed?" *Journal of Education* 164, no. 2 (1982): 143–56.

2. For Guadalupe Valdés's full discussion of these children, see her *Learning and Not Learning English: Latino Students in American Schools* (New York: Teachers College Press, 2001).

3. *Editor:* The notion of the culture of poverty was given legitimacy in Michael Harrington's highly regarded and widely discussed liberal exposé of U.S. poverty, class, and race: *The Other America* (New York: Macmillan, 1962).

4. Richard R. Valencia, R.W. Henderson, and R.J. Rankin, "Family Status, Family Constellations and Home Environment Variable as Predictors of Cognitive Performance of Mexican American Children," *Journal of Educational Psychology* 77 (1985): 193.

5. Arthur Jensen, "How Much Can We Boost IQ and Scholastic Achievement?" *Harvard Educational Review* 39, no. 1 (1969): 1–123.

6. For William Labov's classic article on this topic, see "The Logic of Nonstandard English," which first appeared in *Georgetown Monographs on Language and Linguistics* 22 (1969): 1–22, 26–31, and has been reprinted many times.

7. Carlos Vélez-Ibáñez, "Networks of Exchange among Mexicans in the U.S. and Mexico: Local Level Mediating and International Transformations," *Urban Anthropology* 17, no. 1 (1988): 27–51; and James B. Greenberg, "Historical Constitution, Social Distribution, and Transmission," paper presented at the Annual Meeting of the Society for Applied Anthropology, 1989.

8. Gustavo Pérez Firmat, "Dedication," in *Los Atrevidos: An Anthology of Cuban-American Writers,* ed. Carolina Hospital (Princeton: Ediciones Ellas, 1988), 159.

The fact that I
am writing to you
in English
already falsifies what I
wanted to tell you.
My subject:
how to explain to you that I
don't belong to English
though I belong nowhere else.

—Gustavo Pérez Firmat[8]

This is the oppressor's language yet I need it to talk to you.

—Adrienne Rich, "The Burning of Paper Instead of Children"

PART FOUR

MOTHER TONGUE

I cling to my culture because it is my memory, and what is a poet
without memory? I cling to my culture because it is my skin,
because it is my heart, because it is my voice, because it breathes
my mother's mother's mother into me. My culture is the genesis
and the center of my writing, the most authentic space I have to
write from. I am blind without the lenses of my culture.

—Benjamin Alire Sáenz

Elena

Pat Mora

My Spanish isn't enough.
I remember how I'd smile
listening to my little ones,
understanding every word they'd say,
their jokes, their songs, their plots.
    *Vamos a pedirle dulces a mamá. Vamos.**
But that was in Mexico.
Now my children go to Amercian high schools.
They speak English. At night they sit around
the kitchen table, laugh with one another.
I stand by the stove and feel dumb, alone.
I bought a book to learn English.
My husband frowned, drank more beer.
My oldest said, "*Mamá*, he doesn't want you
to be smarter than he is." I'm forty,
embarrassed at mispronouncing words,
embarrassed at the laughter of my children,
the grocer, the mailman. Sometimes I take
my English book and lock myself in the bathroom,
say the thick words softly,
for if I stop trying, I will be deaf
when my children need my help.

---

*'Let's ask mama for some candy. Let's go.'

From *Healing Earthquakes*

Jimmy Santiago Baca

Pórtate bien,
behave yourself, you always said to me.
I behaved myself
when others were warm in winter
and I stood out in the cold.
I behaved myself when others had full plates
and I stared at them hungrily,
never speaking out of turn,
existing in a shell of good white behavior
with my heart a wet-feathered
bird growing but never able to crack out of the shell.
Behaving like a good boy,
my behavior shattered
by outsiders who came
to my village one day
insulting my grandpa because he couldn't speak
                    English
                    English—
the invader's sword
the oppressor's language—
that hurled me into profound despair
that day Grandpa and I walked into the farm office
for a loan and this man didn't give my grandpa
an application because he was stupid, he said,
because he was ignorant and inferior,
and that moment
cut me in two torturous pieces
screaming my grandpa was a lovely man
that this government farm office clerk was a rude beast—
            and I saw my grandpa's eyes go dark
            with wound-hurts, regret, remorse
            that his grandchild would witness
        him humiliated
and the apricot tree in his soul
was buried

was cut down
using English language as an ax,
and he hung from that dead tree
like a noosed-up Mexican
racist vigilantes strung up ten years earlier
for no other reason than that he was different,
than that they didn't understand
his sacred soul, his loving heart,
his prayers and his songs,
Your words, *Pórtate bien*,
resonate in me,
and I obey in my integrity, my kindness, my courage,
as I am born again in the suffering of my people,
in our freedom, our beauty, our dual-faced,
dual-cultured, two-songed soul
and two-hearted
    ancient culture,
    me porto bien, Grandpa,
        your memory
        leafing my heart
        like the sweetly fragrant sage.

    . . .

the scene with its wooden floor,
my shoes scraping sand grains that had blown in,
the hot sun warming my face,
    and me standing in a room later
    by myself,
after the farm-aid man turned us down
and I knew our sheep were going to die,
knew Grandfather's heart was going to die,
that moment
    opened a wound in my heart
    and in the wound the scene replays itself
    a hundred times,
    the grief, the hurt, the confusion
    that day changed my life forever,
    made me a man, made me understand
    that because Grandfather couldn't speak
English,

his heart died that day,
and when I turned and walked out the door
onto Main Street again,
    squinting my eyes at the whirling dust,
    the world was never the same
    because it was the first time
    I had ever witnessed racism,
    how it killed people's dreams, and during all of it
    my grandfather said, *Pórtate bien, mijo,*
    behave yourself, my son, *Pórtate bien.*

Mother Tongue

Amy Tan

I am not a scholar of English or literature. I cannot give you much more than personal opinions on the English language and its variations in this country or others.

I am a writer. And by that definition, I am someone who has always loved language. I am fascinated by language in daily life. I spend a great deal of my time thinking about the power of language—the way it can evoke an emotion, a visual image, a complex idea, or a simple truth. Language is the tool of my trade. And I use them all—all the Englishes I grew up with.

Recently, I was made keenly aware of the different Englishes I do use. I was giving a talk to a large group of people, the same talk I had already given to half a dozen other groups. The nature of the talk was about my writing, my life, and my book, *The Joy Luck Club*. The talk was going along well enough, until I remembered one major difference that made the whole talk sound wrong. My mother was in the room. And it was perhaps the first time she had heard me give a lengthy speech, using the kind of English I have never used with her. I was saying things like, "The intersection of memory upon imagination" and "There is an aspect of my fiction that relates to thus-and-thus"—a speech filled with carefully wrought grammatical phrases, burdened, it suddenly seemed to me, with nominalized forms, past perfect tenses, conditional phrases, all the forms of standard English that I had learned in school and through books, the forms of English I did not use at home with my mother.

Just last week, I was walking down the street with my mother, and I again found myself conscious of the English I was using, the English I do use with her. We were talking about the price of new and used furniture and I heard myself saying this: "Not waste money that way." My husband was with us as well, and he didn't notice any switch in my English. And then I realized why. It's because over the twenty years we've been together I've often used that same kind of English with him, and sometimes he even uses it with me. It has become our language of intimacy, a different sort of English that relates to family talk, the language I grew up with.

So you'll have some idea of what this family talk I heard sounds like, I'll quote what my mother said during a recent conversation which I videotaped and then transcribed. During this conversation, my mother was talking about a political gangster in Shanghai who had the same last name as her family's, Du, and how the gangster in his early years wanted to be adopted by her family, which was rich by comparison. Later, the gangster became more powerful, far richer than my mother's family, and one day showed up at my mother's wedding to pay his respects. Here's what she said in part:

"Du Yusong having business like fruit stand. Like off the street kind. He is Du like Du Zong—but not Tsung-ming Island people. The local people call putong, the river east side, he belong to that side local people. That man want to ask Du Zong father take him in like become own family. Du Zong father wasn't look down on him, but didn't take seriously, until that man big like become a mafia. Now important person, very hard to inviting him. Chinese way, came only to show respect, don't stay for dinner. Respect for making big celebration, he shows up. Mean gives lots of respect. Chinese custom. Chinese social life that way. If too important won't have to stay too long. He come to my wedding. I didn't see, I heard it. I gone to boy's side, they have YMCA dinner. Chinese age I was nineteen."

You should know that my mother's expressive command of English belies how much she actually understands. She reads the *Forbes* report, listens to *Wall Street Week*, converses daily with her stockbroker, reads all of Shirley MacLaine's books with ease—all kinds of things I can't begin to understand. Yet some of my friends tell me they understand 50 percent of what my mother says. Some say they understand 80 to 90 percent. Some say they understand none of it, as if she were speaking pure Chinese. But to me, my mother's English is perfectly clear, perfectly natural. It's my mother tongue. Her language, as I hear it, is vivid, direct, full of observation and imagery. That was the language that helped shape the way I saw things, expressed things, made sense of the world.

Lately, I've been giving more thought to the kind of English my mother speaks. Like others, I have described it to people as "broken" or "fractured" English. But I wince when I say that. It has always bothered me that I can think of no way to describe it other than "broken," as if it were damaged and needed to be fixed, as if it lacked a certain wholeness and soundness. I've heard other terms used, "limited English," for example. But they seem just as bad, as if everything is limited, including people's perceptions of the limited English speaker.

I know this for a fact, because when I was growing up, my mother's "limited" English limited *my* perception of her. I was ashamed of her English. I believed that her English reflected the quality of what she had to say. That is, because she expressed them imperfectly her thoughts were imperfect. And I had plenty of empirical evidence to support me: the fact that people in department stores, at banks, and at restaurants did not take her seriously, did not give her good service, pretended not to understand her, or even acted as if they did not hear her.

My mother has long realized the limitations of her English as well. When I was fifteen, she used to have me call people on the phone to pretend I was she. In this guise, I was forced to ask for information or even to complain and yell at people who had been rude to her. One time it was a call to her stockbroker in New York. She had cashed out her small portfolio and it just so happened we were going to go to New York the next week, our very first trip outside California. I had to get on the phone and say in an adolescent voice that was not very convincing, "This is Mrs. Tan."

And my mother was standing in the back whispering loudly, "Why he don't send me check, already two weeks late. So mad he lie to me, losing me money."

And then I said in perfect English, "Yes. I'm getting rather concerned. You had agreed to send the check two weeks ago, but it hasn't arrived."

Then she began to talk more loudly. "What he want, I come to New York tell him front of his boss, you cheating me?" And I was trying to calm her down, make her be quiet, while telling the stockbroker, "I can't tolerate any more excuses. If I don't receive the check immediately, I am going to have to speak to your manager when I'm in New York next week." And sure enough, the following week there we were in front of this astonished stockbroker, and I was sitting there red-faced and quiet, and my mother, the real Mrs. Tan, was shouting at his boss in her impeccable broken English.

We used a similar routine just five days ago, for a situation that was far less humorous. My mother had gone to the hospital for an appointment, to find out about a benign brain tumor a CAT scan had revealed a month ago. She said she had spoken very good English, her best English, no mistakes. Still, she said, the hospital did not apologize when they said they had lost the CAT scan and she had come for nothing. She said they did not seem to have any sympathy when she told them she was anxious to know the exact diagnosis, since her husband and son had both died of brain tumors. She said they would not give her any more information until the next time and she would have to make another appointment for that. So she said she would not leave until the doctor called her daughter. She wouldn't budge. And when the doctor finally called her daughter, me, who spoke in perfect English—lo and behold—we had assurances the CAT scan would be found, promises that a conference call on Monday would be held, and apologies for any suffering my mother had gone through for a most regrettable mistake.

I think my mother's English almost had an effect on limiting my possibilities in life as well. Sociologists and linguists probably will tell you that a person's developing language skills are more influenced by peers. But I do think that the language spoken in the family, especially in immigrant families which are more insular, plays a large role in shaping the language of the child. And I believe that it affected my results on achievement tests, IQ tests, and the SAT. While my English skills were never judged as poor, compared to math, English could not be considered my strong suit. In grade school I did moderately well, getting perhaps B's, sometimes B-pluses, in English and scoring perhaps in the sixtieth or seventieth percentile on achievement tests. But those scores were not good enough to override the opinion that my true abilities lay in math and science, because in those areas I achieved A's and scored in the ninetieth percentile or higher.

This was understandable. Math is precise; there is only one correct answer. Whereas, for me at least, the answers on English tests were always a judgment call, a matter of opinion and personal experience. Those tests were constructed around items like fill-in-the-blank sentence completion, such as, "Even though Tom was _____, Mary thought he was _____." And the correct answer always seemed to be the most bland combinations of thoughts, for example, "Even though Tom was shy, Mary thought he was charming," with the grammatical structure "even though" limiting the correct answer to some sort of semantic opposites, so you wouldn't get answers like, "Even though Tom was foolish, Mary thought he was ridiculous." Well, according to my mother, there were very few limitations as to what Tom could have been and what Mary might have thought of him. So I never did well on tests like that.

The same was true with word analogies, pairs of words in which you were supposed to find some sort of logical, semantic relationship—for example, "*Sunset* is to *nightfall* as _____ is to _____." And here you would be presented with a list of four possible pairs, one of which showed the same kind of relationship: *red* is to *stoplight*, *bus* is to *arrival*, *chills* is to *fever*, *yawn* is to *boring*. Well, I could never think that way. I knew what the tests were asking, but I could not block out of my mind the images already created by the first pair, "*sunset* is to *nightfall*"—and I would see a burst of colors against a darkening sky, the moon rising, the lowering of a curtain of stars. And all the other pairs of words—red, bus, stoplight, boring—just threw up a mass of confusing images, making it impossible for me to sort out something as logical as saying: "A sunset precedes nightfall" is the same as "a chill precedes a fever." The only way I would have gotten that answer right would have been to imagine an associative situation, for example, my being disobedient and staying out past sunset, catching a chill at night, which turns into feverish pneumonia as punishment, which indeed did happen to me.

I have been thinking about all this lately, about my mother's English, about achievement tests. Because lately I've been asked, as a writer, why there are not more Asian Americans represented in American literature. Why are there few Asian Americans enrolled in creative writing programs? Why do so many Chinese students go into engineering? Well, these are broad sociological questions I can't begin to answer. But I have noticed in surveys—in fact, just last week—that Asian students, as a whole, always do significantly better on math achievement tests than in English. And this makes me think that there are other Asian-American students whose English spoken in the home might also be described as "broken" or "limited." And perhaps they also have teachers who are steering them away from writing and into math and science, which is what happened to me.

Fortunately, I happen to be rebellious in nature and enjoy the challenge of disproving assumptions made about me. I became an English major my first year in college, after being enrolled as pre-med. I started writing nonfiction as a freelancer the week after I was told by my former boss that writing was my worst skill and I should hone my talents toward account management.

But it wasn't until 1985 that I finally began to write fiction. And at first I wrote using what I thought to be wittily crafted sentences, sentences that would finally prove I had mastery over the English language. Here's an example from the first draft of a story that later made its way into *The Joy Luck Club*, but without this line: "That was my mental quandary in its nascent state." A terrible line, which I can barely pronounce.

Fortunately, for reasons I won't get into today, I later decided I should envision a reader for the stories I would write. And the reader I decided upon was my mother, because these were stories about mothers. So with this reader in mind—and in fact she did read my early drafts—I began to write stories using all the Englishes I grew up with: the English I spoke to my mother, which for lack of a better term might be described as "simple"; the English she used with me, which for lack of a better term might be described as "broken"; my translation of her Chinese, which could certainly be described as "watered down"; and what I imagined to be her translation of her Chinese if she could speak in perfect English, her internal language, and for that I sought to preserve the essence, but neither an English nor a Chinese structure. I wanted to capture what language ability tests can never reveal: her intent, her passion, her imagery, the rhythms of her speech and the nature of her thoughts.

Apart from what any critic had to say about my writing, I knew I had succeeded where it counted when my mother finished reading my book and gave me her verdict: "So easy to read."

Lakota Words

Delphine Red Shirt

I grew up in a time before the old ways disappeared completely and the new ways emerged in their place. I think of it as a time just before sunrise when the morning dew clings to you and as the sun rises, the dew dries before your eyes. If I had had time-lapse photography, I could have watched it dry molecule by molecule, the way I now watch the old ways disappear.

I watched them disappear with my maternal grandfather. I saw Kah-kah die and take with him words that will never be used again. Kah-kah used words to depict a way of life that has forever disappeared. Our way of life was tied to our language, the way we addressed each other: brother, sister, father, mother, grandfather, grandmother, uncle, aunt, and cousin; the way in which we described our emotions, both publicly and privately; the way we described a smile, a wave, or a Lakota mannerism; the way my mother could describe a person with one word, a word that says everything and nothing, that creates an image which you both appreciate and dread. "Oh, I know people like that," you would say.

I now watch my mother—she too is battered by time—drying up like the dew right before my eyes. She too will take with her words that her father used, words that were used in the daily course of life, before English, its sterile sounds and double meanings, invaded our world and our language. In Lakota, when you say something, it can be taken literally. In English you can say something and mean the opposite, or you can be sarcastic and biting. In Lakota when you say something, it is taken as truth unless, of course, you are a liar. *Owewak'ąk'ą s'a*, they would say about you. 'She lies'. They would never say it to you to your face. They would listen to you as if you spoke the truth, but they would know that you are a liar and would have already known that before you began to speak, and everything you say is taken in light of that truth. In Lakota everything is black or white, unpleasant or pleasant, indirect or direct, disrespectful or respectful. In English the nuances are many, and they can be overwhelming to one whose native language is not English.

I remember struggling well into my adult life with the pronunciation of certain English words. The three years I spent in a government school on the reservation prepared me for nothing more than a mediocre understanding of English. In those early years, my tongue tripped over it. I spoke it flatly and without emotion. I could not adjust my voice to its tone and pitch, and I hated it. I learned defensively to say "I don't know" as slowly and deliberately as possible. I used those three words to answer any and all questions: "I don't know." Then, one day in great irritation and frustration, my older brother lashed out at me, "Don't ever again say 'I don't know'." He said angrily in Lakota, *Slolya yelo*, meaning 'You know, I know you know'. That contrary part of me, that part of me that knows that I should defer to an older brother in respect said, slowly and deliberately, in Lakota, *Slolwaye śni*, which means 'Know these things I do not', literally translated.

There are words in Lakota that are used to describe things in our language which have been a part of our lives since time began: words like *cạte, ableza*, and *olowạ*, which respectively mean 'heart', 'perception', and 'song'. These are words that we say with eloquence. *Mi cạte*, we say, 'my heart', and *mi cạte ataya*, 'with my whole heart', or *mi cạte ụ okihisniya*, meaning 'my heart is not in it'. All of our emotions—happiness, joy, excitement, sadness, anger, malice, sorrow, and even love—are expressed using the word *cạte*, 'the heart'.

It is a word that contains all that we are as a people. It expresses our longings. We say *Cạte awacịya*, meaning 'My heart longs for it'. Literally translated it means 'My heart lacks it, therefore I long for it'. Of all the words using *cạte*, I prefer *cạte t'ịza*, a word that I've heard Kah-kah and Mom-mah use over and over again. It means, literally, 'heart that is firm', or simply, 'to have courage, to be courageous'. *Cạtemat'ịza*, they would say. 'My heart is firm'. They were right; they did have courage, great courage, to be able to live as they did, to lose the things they loved—their language and the old ways—and to guard what they had by retaining what they could with their hearts firm and strong.

In the same way, we are a people that say *ableza ye!* in the feminine voice, which means 'try to see it, perceive it'. Or we say *awableza*, which means 'see it clearly, be alert for it'. In a similar way we say *amableza*, or 'you see those things in me, you perceive those things in me'. The word *olowan* means 'song'. These are the words that we say with eloquence. My grandfather and mother are eloquent in Lakota. In English my grandfather refused to speak more than he needed to. My mother accepts English as something that is necessary to know in order to get by in the world, but her language of choice, the one she enjoys, is Lakota. "*Malak'ota*," she would say. 'I am Lakota'. In English she might say *furnitures* when she meant to use the word *furniture*, just as my grandfather would declare to his lessees who leased his reservation land, "You helpa me, I helpa you, and we helpa we." They did not use English unless it was necessary, and because of their rejection of English, I had to learn both.

In a conversation, my mother utters the old words effortlessly, words that I have to repeat silently to myself, my tongue and throat adjusting to the guttural, to the tone, and to the feeling that I could never speak it as smoothly as she did. I quietly jot down the old words, afraid sometimes to ask her what they mean, afraid that I would lose her confidence in me if I did ask. She

believes that I know and will remember all the words I have heard spoken in
her home, all the words that she and her father have used to depict a life that I
will never know. I am tempted to say, "Slolwaye śni, slolwaye śni, slolwaye
śni," or 'I don't know, I don't know, I don't know'.

One day she told me, "They are bringing the language back. They are
teaching it again," she said. I wait for the "but," the qualifier that one who is
knowledgeable about these things always says when speaking to one who is less
knowledgeable. I know my mother, and I wait for her to finish her observation. She is *ksapa* or 'wise' in the old traditional sense, and she refuses to move
in either direction, as acceptor or rejector of this new movement to preserve
the language. "*As*," meaning 'but', she continues, "some of the people
involved in reviving the language are those who learned it from the dictionary.
If you notice they say "*d*" when they mean to say "*l*." They confuse the dialects," meaning the Dakota dialect with the Lakota dialect. She said that there
are some who know the old language and can speak it precisely. She does not
include herself among them.

I remember once she told me, "The waśicu's religion is weak. He only prays
on Sunday." "Kiksuya ye," she said. "You remember that." Mom-mah said
our religion is strong, and she said if you believe it, it is even stronger. "Wacek-
iya ye," she said. "You pray, like we pray, every day. Every moment we
remember to, we pray." I remember hearing her early in the morning.
"Kableza acą," as 'the sun rises', after she puts on a pot of tea, she prays.

Her prayers reach far beyond time and space. She prays with her old words
spoken calmly and confidently. Her words sound like the word *onomatopoeia*,
repeated over and over. Onomatopoeia, onomatopoeia, onomatopoeia. She
prays, "T'ųkaśila, ųśųlapiye. Awąųyąkapi ye. Taku ecųk'ų pi hena ųkisakib
mani ye. T'ųkaśila, mi cįca kį tuktektel ųpi kį hena awąwicakyąka ye. Ąpetu wą
lecel ųkinażį pi kį le nitawa. Mititakuye oyas'į." Her prayer translated means,
'Grandfather, pity us. Look upon us with mercy. Whatever we do, walk beside
us. Grandfather, my children, watch over them wherever they are. For this day
in which we stand belongs to you. For all of my relatives, I pray'.

I know if I looked in upon her as she prays in the quiet kitchen while her
tea brews on the gas stove, her posture would be humble: her hands demurely
set in her wide deep lap, her head bowed and tilted slightly. Her posture belies
the nature of her prayers. She is not humble. She is the earth itself perpetuating
life even as death is all around her. Even as everything breaks down and things
fall apart, she stays constant.

Her prayers remain the same. Each morning before anyone else awakens,
she makes sure that her gentle persistent prayers are heard. She makes sure that
"T'ųkaśila," 'Grandfather', as He awakens the world this and every morning,
is reminded of her presence. In the old language, she reminds Him that we are

still here, that the language He gave to us is still spoken in gratitude. She prays always for life for others, and for pity for herself, she who sits like a mountain each day, unmovable and unchanging. I have heard that whatever you wish or pray for others, you will get. I see this truth in her. She prays for life for others, and while those she prays for each morning, each moment of every day, die, she lives.

When I hear her speak the language the way it should be spoken, I want to speak like her. I want to be like her. I want to remember the old words, the sound of my own name as it was given to me, "Ḣoka Wị he miye," 'Badger Woman, that is who I am'. I want to write down the old words, the fond way she refers to her *tiwahe*, her family. She calls her brothers by their honored names: she calls a younger brother *misų*; she calls an older brother *tiblo*. She is the only female in a family of five men. *Wịyą Ișnala* is her Indian name. 'Only Woman'. That is who she is in Kah-kah's family.

I am not as confident as she is, and I do not use these words to describe my younger brother and my older brother. It is not that I have forgotten; I have not learned how to be comfortable using these words the way she does. "Ate," she calls her father. "Ina mitąwa kị he," she says of her mother. She knows her relatives twice removed, "taku kiciyapi," or 'the way they are related'. I try to write down what she tells me. "Wicotakuye hena slolkiya ye," she tells me. 'Know who your relatives are'. She considers that knowledge important so that bloodlines are kept pure, because it was considered taboo to marry a relative, no matter how distant. These were the things she wanted me to know.

She wanted me to know who my cousins were. I would call a female cousin *cep'ąši*. I would call my male cousin *šiceši*. I have heard her use these words fondly. I have heard her honor her relatives with these names, embracing her female cousins. *T'ożą* she calls her nieces, and *t'oška*, she says to her nephews. I try to be like her, to carry around all the things that the old way and the old language require that I remember: the things I need to know to keep myself together, to keep myself from falling apart. I want to remain constant like her. I want to remember to pray, to remember to sit in a humble way while deep inside my strength is like the earth. I try to be more patient than she is—the way she says she waits for dawn to pray, "każążą aye cąyą," meaning 'as the light appears at dawn'. I know that unless I write the things I want to remem- ber—the old words and my connection to those around me through them—I will forget, and the sun will rise and these things that she told me to remember, "Kiksuya ye," will dry up, molecule by molecule.

Immigrants

Pat Mora

wrap their babies in the American flag,
feed them mashed hot dogs and apple pie,
name them Bill and Daisy,
buy them blonde dolls that blink blue
eyes or a football and tiny cleats
before the baby can even walk,
speak to them in thick English,
      hallo, babee, hallo,
whisper in Spanish or Polish
when the babies sleep, whisper
in a dark parent bed, that dark
parent fear, "Will they like
our boy, our girl, our fine american
boy, our fine american girl?"

My Hawai'i

Nana Veary

'Ea mai Hawai'i Nui Ākea,
'Ea mai loko, mai loko mai o ka pō
Puka mai ka moku, ka 'āina
Ka lālani 'āina o Nu'umea. . . .

Then rose Hawai'i from the space of time
Arose from inside, from the inner darkness,
Then appeared the island, the land
The row of the islands of Nu'umea. . . .

So chanted Ka'upena Wong on March 12, 1988, at my 80th birthday. At a large gathering in my daughter's home, his deep and haunting voice called to the present our Hawaiian past. There was power in this ancient genealogical chant, as if the entire past of my family, of the entire Hawaiian race, were called into the room. The opening lines of this chant, as given by the historian Kahakuika-moana, recount the origin of each of the Hawaiian islands. They tell of the ancestral beings connected with each island, their peopling by the first Hawaiians, and the generations that came after them.

During Ka'upena's chant, every member of my family cried, from my daughters and grandchildren to my great-grandchildren, the youngest of whom was only six months old. The young ones cried audibly, their parents wept silently, but all of us cried, moved by some deep force. I understood the chant and my family's place in the genealogy, but no one else did. Yet we were all moved to tears by the same force.

Counting my long-deceased mother, whose presence I felt strongly, there were five generations of us in the room. The last time I heard that chant I was about seven years old. I remembered my mother performing that chant, and I heard her voice in Ka'upena's that day. When it was over, I looked around at all the different people gathered—old Hawaiians and little children, community leaders and movie stars, businessmen and young people looking like punk rockers. I smiled, realizing that here, in 1988, we were celebrating our heritage in the form of a great-grandmother's birthday, united by a common thread that reached back to the very beginnings of Hawai'i.

I am pure Hawaiian and grew up in a Hawai'i of another era, a place that was entirely different from what we know today. Life was simpler and its rhythm was more natural. I was lucky to be taught and raised according to the old Hawaiian ways. My Hawaiian upbringing, the influence of my parents and grandparents, has sustained me through a long life that has spanned most of the 20th century. In my 80 years, I have managed to combine the life of a modern-day householder with the wanderings of a spiritual seeker. I raised three children, became grandmother to ten and great-grandmother to eight, studied with a *kahuna* (Hawaiian teacher), meditated with a guru, climbed Mount Fuji, studied metaphysics, prayed as a Christian, and sat long hours in Zen meditation, all in my search for truth.

Finally, after years of searching, I have come home. I hope to share my journey with you. I should warn you, however, that I skip the details of my personal life and offer you, instead, the truths that I treasure as I reflect upon my life.

I was born in 1908 on O'ahu and was raised as the foster daughter of a pure Hawaiian mother and a Scots father. Both spoke fluent Hawaiian. He was an atheist; she was a devout Christian who felt a reverence for life and an appreciation for nature that were mainstays of Hawaiian culture. I was named Hannah Lihilihipuamelekule, after the marigolds in my grandmother's garden. Lihilihipuamelekule means 'the lacy petals of the marigold blossoms'.

From the beginning, I was a loner, an orphan. My natural father died while my mother was pregnant with me. My birth was registered under Kualaku, the name of my foster mother's husband. My mother's foster mother took care of both of us. When I was four and a half years old, my mother died, and my foster grandmother took over raising me. From this point on in the story, I shall refer to her as my mother.

In the old Hawaiian culture, if someone, especially a young person, said, "I want that baby," there were no *ifs, ands,* or *buts.* You got that baby, even if you were a stranger. That is the Hawaiian *'ohana* (family) style, the *hānai* method of childrearing. There was no such thing as an unwanted baby. Every child was loved. So it was that my foster mother, Mary, said she wanted me and became my mother upon the early death of my natural mother.

I grew up in Pālama, near downtown Honolulu on the island of O'ahu. Throughout my childhood, the influence of my grandparents was strong. They were, like the older Hawaiians of their day, extremely dignified and spiritually aware. My grandfather was a fisherman and a *kahuna kālaiwa'a*, a canoe-builder. He and my grandmother lived at the entrance to Pearl Harbor in a fishing village called Pu'uloa. We looked forward to visiting them every weekend in their little grass hut.

One day while I was there, children of the village who had been playing in front of the house called out to my grandmother, *"Ē kupuna, he malihini kēia e hō'ea maila."* Grandmother, there is a stranger coming. My grandmother responded, *"Ke hiki mai ka malihini, kāhea mai ia'u."* When he arrives, call me.

When he arrived, the children called, *"Ē kupuna, ua hō'ea maila."* He has arrived. My grandmother came, stood on the *lānai*, and said to the stranger, *"Ē komo mai, kipa mai e pā'ina."* Come in and dine.

While they were eating, I sat on the floor of the *lānai* to eavesdrop. When he was through eating, the visitor thanked my grandmother, and she came forward with a little *puniu*, a coconut dish with salt in it. She extended her hand, and he picked three lumps of salt, put them in his mouth, and went off. When the stranger left, I asked my grandmother if she knew him.

"'A 'ore" she said. *"He malihini ho'i."* No, he was a *malihini*. When I asked her why she fed him, she got angry, ordered me to sit on the floor in front of her, and said, "I want you to remember these words for as long as you live, and never forget them: *'A'ole au i hānai aku nei i ke kanaka; akā hānai aku nei au i ka 'uhane a ke Akua i loko ona."* I was not feeding the man; I was entertaining the spirit of God within him.

I was six years old when this happened, and I have never forgotten my grandmother's words. This practice of honoring the other was so much a part of the culture that it needed no name. Today we call it the "aloha spirit," but to the Hawaiians of old it was inherent and natural. They lived it. To feed a stranger passing by—that is pure aloha. Today we have to be taught it because we are so far removed from the Hawaiian culture. And we have given it a name.

"Alo" means the bosom, the center of the universe. *"Hā"* is the breath of God. The word is imbued with a great deal of power. I do not use the word casually. Aloha is a feeling, a recognition of the divine. It is not just a word or greeting. When you say "aloha" to someone, you are conveying or bestowing this feeling.

In the Hawai'i of my childhood, this feeling bonded the entire community. The whole village was your family; their sorrows became yours and yours, theirs. We felt we were all related and could not help loving one another. As a child, I called our neighbors "uncle" or *tūtū* or "auntie," a practice still observed by Hawaiian families today. We called it a calabash relationship, a word derived from the tradition we had of always sharing a great big calabash of *poi* that everybody dipped into, strangers and all. Eating from the same bowl, the same calabash—that is aloha.

In most written accounts of old Hawai'i, this inherent spirit of giving and respect is overshadowed by stories of warring chiefs and human sacrifice. In every culture, from Asia to Christendom to our 20th century America in Vietnam and Central America, the warlike aspect of human nature has reared its head and claimed its toll in lives. The Hawaiians were no different. Led by the royalty and chiefs, they did, indeed, wage war.

Yet the underlying nature of the Hawaiian has always been gentle and strong in spirituality. These qualities were inherent in their culture, expressed in their everyday lives—in how they greeted strangers and revered their gods, in how they gave away everything, from food to land and even children. When the villagers went fishing, they distributed their catch all along the coast as long as the fish would last. When those of the neighboring village went fishing, they did the same. The fishing code for the Hawaiians was and still is: Don't take what you want; take only what you need. When there is excess, throw it back or give it away.

When people visited my grandparents, they went home with cooked taro or *poi* and a jar full of *limu* 'seaweed' and salt, dried fish or dried *he'e* 'octopus'. Pearl Harbor in those days had lobsters and was even noted for oysters with pearls. When ships were drydocked, the Hawaiians picked the *pipipi* 'mollusks' from the bottom of the ship. In the gardens grew bananas and avocados and guava, which we bartered or gave away. From the land and sea came an abundance that was shared and appreciated.

My grandmother's words about feeding the stranger expressed the basic Hawaiian ethic—a firm belief in human spirituality. Although the Hawaiians felt that their *'aumākua* (personal spirits or family guardians) were forms outside of themselves, they also felt their presence within. The word itself, meaning 'my father', encouraged this awareness. It was an unconscious knowing that prompted them to honor and respect "something" within people—the human spirit. So they treated even strangers with reverence. My Hawaiian relatives used to say, *"'A 'ole 'oe e 'ike i nā po'opo'o o ha'i."* In other words, "Don't judge others. You don't know their spiritual background."

Rich in metaphor, the Hawaiian language was melodious and graceful like the people. The Hawaiians said, *"He nane kā 'olelo."* The language is a riddle. Before the missionaries came and converted the language into the written word, the Hawaiians used figures of speech in language that was like poetry.

I was fortunate to be taught to speak Hawaiian in the old way. My mother taught me to speak the language softly, without saying anything negative or elaborating. "Leave the details out," she said, "and speak softly." We learned that way because my grandparents were stubborn. They did not want to change the Hawaiian language, so they spoke in idioms. All the ancient chants are in idioms, but today there is virtually nobody, not even those fluent in Hawaiian, who speaks that way.

∼

One day at my grandparents', I was watching my grandmother quilting on the *lānai* while my grandfather raked leaves in the yard. My grandmother said to me, "I don't hear the rake. Go to the railing and see what your grandfather is doing." I saw him leaning on the rake, looking at a group of girls passing by. I reported this to my grandmother.

After awhile, she went up behind him and said softly, *"Ē nānā ana 'oe iā wai?"* Who are you looking at? Startled, he said, *"Ē nānā ana ho'i au, i ka māla pua e mā'alo ala."* I was looking at a garden of flowers passing by.

Thus their daily conversations mingled poetry and metaphors in beautiful imagery. Another time, when my grandfather and I were walking along the beach, a little boy came running after us, saying, *"Ē kupuna, kali mai ia'u."* Grandfather, wait for me! Finally he caught up with us and walked along until he said, *"Ē kupuna, make wai 'ia au."* Grandfather, I am thirsty. Grandfather said, *"He pūnāwai kau i ka lewa,"* figuratively referring to a coconut as a fountain of water hanging in the air. The little boy understood the metaphor and, without a word, climbed a nearby coconut tree, gathered some coconuts, broke them open, and drank happily of their water.

This use of the language vanished long ago. Hawaiians today speak the missionary language, a literal type of Hawaiian. The riddle is gone. This is tragic, for when you lose the language, you lose your identity. In all my trips around the world during the 1950s, I found that Hawai'i was the only place where the native language is no longer spoken. When you land in Japan, Japanese is spoken. When you land in France, French is spoken. The Hawaiians have nothing, nothing but aloha, and even that they have to re-learn.

Sometime around 1930, we lived briefly on Maui. A Hawaiian girl that I knew invited me to visit her parents up in Kula. When we arrived, I said *"Hui! 'Auhea ka po'e o kēia hale?"* Where are the people of this house? The man who came out, the father, said in English, "Come up, come up!" I remember that so well: I spoke in Hawaiian to him, and he answered me in English. His wife came out and said, *"Komo mai."* Then she said in English, "Eat!" They were pure Hawaiians, but even way back in the 1930s they could not speak Hawaiian. It is sad because the language is beautiful, and what has been lost can never be replaced.

~

Chief Wachuseh

José Antonio Burciaga

I first heard the word *wachuseh* before I started school and learned English. For me, the word had always been Spanish. "This is better than wachuseh," my father would say in Spanish and I would be impressed because he reserved the word for only the best. He never told me what it meant, but I knew. Wachuseh was a mythical Indian chief, perhaps an Aztec emperor, or at least the Indian chief on the red covers of school writing tablets. I could visualize him, tall, muscular, toasted brown with an Aztec feathered head dress, the epitome of perfection.

Eventually, I came to decode and recognize that wachuseh came from the question "What did you say?" But by then the four-word question had become so engraved in my mind that to this day, an Indian chief comes to mind when I hear it. Wachuseh became a word meaning something that was better than anything anyone could say.

Wachuseh has been a common and popular phrase among immigrants to this country. It's often used as a question when someone doesn't understand English or the concept of what is being said in English. The phrase may have originated from English speakers who could not understand the accented speech of an immigrant. It's also popular among many Afro-Americans and effectively expressed as "whachusay?" when questioning or disbelieving a statement.

I love words such as wachuseh as much as the people who use them. The significance of such compressed words goes beyond their original meaning to say even more. Born into a bicultural and bilingual world, I have experienced the birth of new words, new worlds, ideas that came from two languages and two cultures, words that changed meanings and power. So many other cultures and languages from Black English to Yiddish have contributed to the evolution and enrichment of the English language. These words enriched because they gave birth to a new world of ideas from a combination of cultures, ideas that were lacking a name until then.

Chutzpah filled a void in the English language; there was nothing in our slang like it. The introduction of *macho* into the English language was another such idea, even though the English definition has a more negative connotation than the Spanish, where the term can be as innocent as its basic literal definition of 'male'. In Mexican Spanish it's *huevos*, in peninsular Spanish it's *cojones* for 'balls'. Some Mexican or Chicano ideas have no English words. To call someone a *pendejo* in Spanish is not the same as calling him or her stupid or even *estúpido* or *estúpida*.

My father had a vocabulary of Spanish words that to this day are not found in popular Spanish language dictionaries. He was born into a poor, migrant farm working family in a community of people that still used ancient words that some found improper and backwards but are to be found in Miguel Cervantes's classic *Don Quixote*. My father commonly used words such as *minjurne* for mixture, or *cachibaches* for junk. I would hear them without knowing their definition but I knew exactly what he meant when talking within a specific context. Some words were archaic, others were a combination of English and Spanish. And though he knew the 'standard' Spanish of 'educated' people, he also worked, lived, laughed and cried with words that were more expressive and indigenous to the border than standard Spanish.

Translation

Rhina Espaillat

Cousins from home are practicing their English,
picking out what they can, slippery vowels
queasy in their ears, stiff consonants
bristling like Saxon spears too tightly massed
for the leisurely tongues of my home town.

They frame laborious greetings to our neighbors;
try learning names, fail, try again, give up,
hug then and laugh instead, with slow blushes.
Their gestures shed echoes of morning bells,
unfold narrow streets around them like gossip.

They watch us, gleaning with expert kindness
every crumb of good will dropped in our haste
from ritual to ritual; they like the pancakes,
smile at strangers, poke country fingers
between the toes of our city roses.

Their eyes want to know if I think in this
difficult noise, how well I remember
the quiet music our grandmother spoke
in her tin-roofed kitchen, how love can work
in a language without diminutives.

What words in any language but the wind's
could name this land as I've learned it by campfire?
I want to feed them the dusty sweetness
of American roads cleaving huge spaces,
wheatfield clean and smooth as a mother's apron.

I want to tell them the goodness of people
who seldom touch, who bring covered dishes
to the bereaved in embarrassed silence,
who teach me daily that all dialogue
is reverie, is hearsay, is translation.

~

Bilingual Cognates

José Antonio Burciaga

Bilingual Love Poem

Your sonrisa is a sunrise
that was reaped from your smile
sowed from a semilla
into the sol of your soul
with an ardent pasión,
passion ardiente,
sizzling in a mar de amar
where more is amor,
in a sea of sí
filled with the sal of salt
in the saliva of the saliva
that gives sed but is never sad.

Two tongues that come together
is not a French kiss
but bilingual love.*

A cognate is a word related to another through derivation, borrowing or
descent. From one language to another, I suppose they become bilingual cognates if not bloopers. Like in the poem above, there are Spanish and English
words that look alike or sound alike:

- Vincent Price has been known as "beans and rice" or vice versa.
- El Benny Lechero was actually a short serial movie character in the fifties
  known as "The Vanishing Shadow."
- Somewhere in the Southwest there was a teacher who thought his Chicano kids were calling him "Cool Arrow" when in reality they were calling him a *culero*, an insult.†
- Two Chicanos were dining at a fashionable restaurant and one of them
  says to the other, "This is the best *gabacho (gazpacho)* soup I've ever tasted."‡

Sonrisa 'smile', *semilla* 'seed', *pasión* 'passion', *ardiente* 'ardent', *mar de amar* 'sea of love', *amor*
'love', *sí* 'yes', *sed* 'thirst'.
†*Culero* is derived from *culo* 'anus'.
‡*Gabacho* is a derogatory term for Anglo-American.

- My mother once called her comadre and her German-born husband answered. "Lucina is not in," he said in perfect Spanish, "she is out buying *grocerías*." (*Grocerías* are coarse, vulgar statements and acts.)
- One morning our friend Muggins called and my Mother answered. Trying to be courteous, he asked my Mother in Spanish how she was born instead of how she had awakened: *"Buenos días, Señora, ¿Cómo nació?"* instead of *"¿Cómo amaneció?"*

Some are not necessarily cognates but the mental mistranslations sometimes result in funny situations. My friend Rana has forever confused his Spanish with his English. As a high schooler, he was dazzled by a beautiful young woman and greeted her with "How are you going?" from *"¿Cómo te va?"* Even in English he had trouble. Lone Star Beer became Long Star, humble became noble, and misconstrew became misconstrue. In the context of a serious conversation the result is laughter.

Jokes abound about Latinos who come to this country and read English signs in Spanish. Back when Cokes were only a dime, a Mexicano put a ten cent coin in the machine but did not receive a bottle of Coke. He waited, hit it and nothing. Finally he read just above the coin slot where it said "Dime" (which translates to 'tell me' in Spanish). So he bent down to the slot and whispered into it, *"Dame una Coca Cola."*

We have all seen real estate signs that say "For Sale, No Lease." A newly arrived immigrant looking for housing, read the sign and kicked the door open. If you read that in Spanish and run the first two words together it reads, "force it, it's alright."

Introducing someone in Spanish is not the same as introducing someone in English. *Introducir* in Spanish means to put in, to infiltrate. The correct term is *presentar*. Yet *introducir* is used so often that people don't even catch it. Many bilingual cognates have returned to Mexico to become part of what is known as Mexican caló. *Chansa* comes from chance, for *oportunidades*. *Trakes* for tracks, *mechas* for matches, *chutear* for shooting, *raides* from rides. Mexican film actor Tin Tan and singer Juan Gabriel have been very influential in "introducing" Chicano terms to Mexico.

Most of the Spanish terminology for baseball comes from the English. *Ni ketcha, ni pitcha, ni deja batear* is a well-known proverb for someone who won't do anything and won't let anyone else do anything—He/she won't catch, doesn't pitch and won't let anyone bat.

One of my favorite anecdotes is the one about my good friend and ex-roommate Darío Prieto. Though it has little to do with cognates, it shows how our bilingual minds sometimes work. In a Washington, D.C., reception, he was once asked by our other roommate Ed Gutiérrez, "Hey Darío, where does the Lone Ranger take his trash?" Darío didn't know so Ed sang him the answer to the tune of the television show's theme, "to the dump, to the dump, to the dump! dump! dump! . . ."

Darío laughed heartily and then went to ask a couple the same question. But Darío always had to polish his English. He cleared his throat, something he always did, and asked, "Where does the Lone Ranger dispose of his debris?" The couple didn't know, so Darío sang the answer, "Ta-da-da, ta-da-da, ta-da-da, da, da . . ." The couple just stared at him.

~

Learning to Trust the Language
I Thought I'd Left Behind

Michael Awkward

In March, a few weeks after I'd received an acceptance letter from Penn, I went to Philadelphia with a group of black students, ostensibly to attend a party that the parents of one of my friends were throwing at her house in nearby Camden in honor of her twenty-first birthday. I tagged along in part because I wanted to experience the sense of community promised by such an exodus, and because this trip provided me a relatively inexpensive opportunity to see my mother and to see whether returning home seemed possible.

I was dropped off outside my apartment building at seven o'clock in the evening, and just a few minutes after I'd hugged my mother and set my bag on the bed of my room, the telephone rang. Insisting in mock self-importance that my fans were clearly monitoring my every move, I beat my mother to the phone and said, in the most authoritative voice I could muster, "Michael Awkward speaking."

"Hello. This is Houston Baker, calling from the English department at the University of Pennsylvania. Do you have a few minutes?"

I could barely speak. How'd he know I was here? What did he want? I'd wanted to rest, to relax, to forget about the decision I knew I'd have to make about graduate school in the next week or two. On the other end of the line, speaking in a voice heavy with authority, self-confidence, and urgency, was the man whose name I hadn't recalled in an earlier conversation with my mother. The man whose praises my advisers had sung and whose short book on the life and career of Countee Cullen I'd read twice when I was supposed to be writing my thesis.

With the exception of a single question I asked about the numbers of black Ph.D.'s Penn had produced in the previous decade, my contribution to the ten-minute conversation consisted mostly of nodding my head in affirmation and whispering "uh-huh" like someone entranced by a rollicking, awe-inspiring sermon in an urban black church where parishioner participation was utterly essential.

My primary reaction—to his call, to the excitement in his voice when he spoke about the prospects of mentoring me, to his forceful self-certainty—was fear. This voice could dance circles around me. It was a voice that radiated not money, like Fitzgerald's Daisy Buchanan, but something I suspected was even more intimidating: hard-won power. It slipped effortlessly between King's English and hood dialect, between authoritative assertion and sizzling slang, overwhelming me on each register. Standing in front of the table in my mother's apartment where the telephone had been securely stationed for more than a decade, I felt a thrill like being on a roller-coaster ride so terrifying that not even the most uncalculated of screams could register the sensory shock of its lows and highs, its dips and turns.

I wondered whether, in addition to all of the other things I knew I'd be expected to learn to get a Ph.D., I'd have to demonstrate something close to his level of linguistic dexterity to project myself as culturally black. Prep school and college provided few sites of black cultural expression (pickup basketball games, dances, closed dormitory room doors, the Brotherhood table). In other settings—especially in classrooms—its unacceptability, signaled in all sorts of ways by all sorts of people, caused me to repress its funky rhythms, its energetic rejection of standard speech. Except when I was speaking excitedly with my siblings and trusted friends, or talking shit on the court, black speech filled me with a tremendous sense of self-consciousness.

Part of my education consisted of forcing myself to speak differently, of naturalizing tonal arrangements, syllabic structures, and sentence formations that seemed, if not altogether unfamiliar, then deracinating to a boy whose formative years had been spent trying to learn the hip talk of the cool cats and boss chicks in my neighborhood.

As this voice assumed, abandoned, and took up again a range of discursive styles, I questioned the efficacy of my having spent seven years unlearning modes of speech that virtually all the people with whom I grew up employed as a rule. The notion that one could speak both right and black, could move effortlessly from proper to street discourse, from their to our forms of verbal address, hadn't occurred to me. As I spoke with him, and for months and years afterward, I longed for the sort of dexterity he displayed.

The fear I'd felt at the beginning of the call made some room in my imagination for wonder, awe, and excitement. I was thrilled by the prospect of having a committed black male mentor, developing such verbal fluency, and gaining access to my elite hometown university's luscious greens and well-protected buildings, which had seemed both so unwelcoming and so full of promise when I was a child.

When I got off of the phone, I smiled at my mother and told her that I planned to accept Penn's offer.

"Who was that on the phone? One of your girlfriends? Seems like you didn't get a word in edgewise."

"Mommy! That was that professor I told you about who teaches at Penn. His first name is Houston."

"That's a different name. Where's his people from?"

"We certainly can't talk about 'different names,' can we? He called to tell me he really wants me to come to school there."

"That's what you want to do?"

"Uh-huh."

Racially, culturally and linguistically *somos huérfanos,* we speak an orphan tongue.

—Gloria Anzaldúa

PART FIVE

EXCELLENCE AND NEGLECT IN THE SCHOOLING OF MULTILINGUAL CHILDREN

Oppressed groups are frequently placed in the situation of being listened to only if we frame our ideas in the language that is familiar to and comfortable for a dominant group.

—Patricia Hill Collins[1]

Principles of Successful Schools for Multilingual Children

Abridged from an article by Daniel Solórzano and Ronald Solórzano

Daniel G. Solórzano and Ronald W. Solórzano provide a synopsis explaining why the current educational system is not effective for the Latinos and, by ready extension, for the other marginalized communities. Educators and policymakers must come to understand the cumulative effects of the inadequate preparation of these students in the elementary and high school levels and how this affects access to higher education. The Solórzano brothers review several theories to explain Latino student achievement and underachievement. In addition, they provide an informative overview of two very successful college outreach efforts.

Solórzano and Solórzano investigate the environmental conditions in which Latino students learn at the elementary, secondary, and postsecondary levels of education. The authors found that in the Chicano and other predominantly minority schools, the academic emphasis at the elementary level tends to be on remediation rather than on an enrichment and acceleration of the curriculum. At the elementary level, "textbooks often exclude the Chicano social and historical experience" and reinforce negative stereotypes (295). According to the authors, low Chicano student participation in quality academic programs is a result of low expectations and a diminished sense of teacher responsibility for educating Chicano students.

These conditions are further compounded by other negative factors affecting Chicano students. The situation for limited-English-speaking students is even more precarious. At the high school level, quality programs for these students are rare. At the secondary level the situation does not seem to progress in favor of achievement. "College preparatory programs are less likely to be found in predominantly minority schools" than in predominantly white schools (295).* Even when such college preparatory programs exist in schools with concentrations of minority students, Chicano students tend to be tracked into vocational programs, away from college preparation courses. Further-

---

Editor: In 1999, academically motivated nonwhite high school students from Inglewood, California, were forced to file a class action lawsuit, *Williams v. State of California*, claiming they were denied equal access to higher education because their schools did not have the Advanced Placement classes that are now required to be a competitive candidate to attend the highest-ranked state universities, Berkeley and UCLA. See Louis Sahagun and Kenneth Weiss, "Bias Suit Targets Schools without Advanced Classes," *Los Angeles Times*, July 28, 1999, 1-A.

more, Latino high school teachers too often fail to function as role models for students at this level. Mentoring relationships, which often spark the aspiration to become future professionals, are too often ignored in poorly performing schools.

The postsecondary level brings new challenges to Chicana/o students. Once Chicanos reach the college level, the consequences of poor school preparation places them at a distinct disadvantage. The researchers found that even though there has been a modest increase in Chicano college enrollment, it is not proportional to the overall growth of the Chicano population; the increase is located mostly at the community college level, rather than four-year universities. To make things worse, a disproportionately larger number are part-time students in the community college. The majority of two-year college students do not transfer to four-year universities.

Compounding these troubling findings, once Chicano students are at four-year university, Chicano students are less likely to meet other Chicano students, less likely to have a class with a Chicano professor, and less likely able to find the Chicano experience integrated into the core curriculum (296).

Lastly, Chicano students and other racial minorities are "likely to find themselves on a racially hostile campus." Finally, "when bachelor, masters, and doctorates are awarded, Chicano students earn disproportionately fewer degrees than their white counterparts" (296).

To explain Chicano underachievement, as well as the public's viewpoint on this gross under-achievement, Solórzano and Solórzano distinguish four theories used to characterize the educational experience of Chicano students: the "genetic determinist, cultural determinist, school determinist, and societal determinist" theoretical models (297):

1. The **genetic determinist model** argues that the reason Chicano students underachieve collectively is attributed to their genetic makeup.
2. The **cultural determinist model** argues that Chicano cultural values prevent Chicanos from academic achievement. This model contrasts Chicano cultural values and Anglo cultural values. Such comparative values are: Chicano present time orientation versus White future time orientation; Chicano immediate gratification compared to White deferred gratification; Chicano emphasis on cooperation rather than on competition; and presumed Chicano lessened emphasis on education and upward mobility (297). Solórzano and Solórzano argue that the educational policy solutions that emerge from the cultural determinist model worked to the detriment of Chicano students because the educational policy emphasizes "acculturation of Chicano students to the values and behaviors of the culturally dominant group, while criticizing, downplaying, or ignoring the values and behaviors" of Chicano culture (298).

3. The **school/institutional determinist model** argues that "educational inequality exists because of the unequal conditions" found in predominantly Chicano schools. These inequalities are rooted in factors such as low teacher expectations, tracking, ability grouping, and the lack of academic resources (298).
4. The fourth model, the **societal determinist model**, "argues that Chicano educational inequality is rooted in the unequal class structure" of capitalist society (299).

Two New Approaches. The negative assumptions and pessimism of the four models lead Solórzano and Solórzano to support two new approaches to address the issue of low achievement among Chicano students. Their first model, fashioned on the work of Ronald Edmonds, is called the "Effective Schools Approach." This model rejects the genetic and cultural determinist models and is structured to counteract the effects of the other two models. Edmond's model focuses on the conditions of schools and how that impacts the students' achievement. This model cites five main characteristics of "Effective Schools":

- "high expectations and responsibility for student learning;
- strong instructional leadership;
- emphasis on basic skill acquisition;
- frequent monitoring of student progress;
- and an orderly and safe school environment" (303).

The Effective Schools Model is further elaborated in Henry M. Levin's Accelerated Schools Program. In this model, school officials and teachers worked to "accelerate rather than remediate the curriculum" and raise the achievement levels of so-called at-risk "minority students to grade level by the sixth grade" (303). By developing a common goal, enforcing accountability among educational leaders and teachers for educational decisions and results, requiring input from students and their families, and giving a crucial place to key cultural differences, the Accelerated Schools model attempts to increase students' achievement.

The first common characteristic of both models is that they create a successful schooling environment that has high expectations of these students. Teacher actions and attitudes directly affect the achievement of all students. Because a large number of teachers were raised in a society that maintains varieties of the deficit model,* they come to the Chicano classroom holding stereotypes that falsely characterize their Chicano students. Low expectations and lack of

---

*See Valencia and Solórzano, part III, for a discussion of deficit modeling in education.

teacher training with minority students in the classroom allows societal stereotypes to become a self-fulfilling prophecy.

A second characteristic is the need for a school to have strong instructional leadership. Even though traditionally this responsibility has fallen on principals, Solórzano and Solórzano emphasize the need for strong leadership among staff, students, and community members as well.

Thirdly, this strong administrative leadership must exist within a school environment to support successful programs for these students. Again, Solórzano and Solórzano emphasize the need to include not only administrators when defining the mission of the schools, but, more importantly, the entire community—not only administrators—must set the goals for their children.

Fourth, the traditional view of the acquisition of basic skills should be re-examined. Schools with a large low-income student body must look beyond the basic skills trap. "The primary focus of the Effective and Accelerated School models should be on the acquisition of higher order skills such as problem solving, critical thinking, logic, and creativity" (306). These skills have traditionally been part of the curricula in most suburban schools. Additionally, bilingual programs need to be integrated into the overall plan of the school and follow this same line of higher order skills, whenever possible, rather than remain remedial programs for students with deficits.

A fifth characteristic of the Effective and Accelerated Schools is the need to monitor the progress of students. Monitoring of students should be frequent and thorough in order to properly assess what measures should be taken to improve the achievement of the individual student, to spot weak educational practices, and to reward or hold educators accountable for their actions. Solórzano and Solórzano emphasize that the methods which are used to monitor students must "be linguistically and culturally sensitive" in order to attain sound results (307).

A sixth characteristic is that students have a safe and orderly school climate. When the students and staff do not have to be preoccupied with personal safety issues or worries, more time and energy is devoted to the learning and teaching processes. An orderly school climate also includes maintaining a low transience rate for teachers. The stability this provides is extremely important to maintaining a learning environment that truly nurtures academic as well as personal growth and is key to creating an effective school.

In order for these six characteristics to be successful, there must be parental involvement throughout this entire process. Solórzano and Solórzano criticize the genetic and cultural determinist models and shift "the primary responsibility for school failure from the students, their families, and their culture, to the school structure, resources, and processes" (308) in order to attack the root of educational deficit thinking and to create a successful educational model for Chicano and other socially marginalized students.

The Best Multilingual Schools

Abridged from an article by Tamara Lucas, Rosemary Henze,
and Rubén Donato

Perhaps it is human nature to crave effortless solutions to complex problems—to oversimplify what is in fact challenging. Today's multilinguistic school districts would indeed be a lot easier to run and judge if it were actually true that the students that "make it" (i.e., graduate, go on to college, etc.) are always the smartest and most deserving, while the kids who get left behind are simply not cut out for the academic life because they are lazy, have parents who do not support them, are simply slower . . . or don't speak English. It would make it all okay if it were the student's fault, but certain schools disprove this commonplace. Tamara Lucas, Rosemary Henze, and Rubén Donato show us that when schools make a concerted effort to promote the educational needs of the language minority students, their young people excel. In six exemplary schools, the language minority students not only achieve in academic and extracurricular activities, but they do so while being proud of their culture. Schools that excel make this a priority. The educators and administrators of the six incredibly successful schools have sought not to blame the students but to improve the practices of the schools. These six schools provide indispensable lessons regarding the most effective methods for dealing with not only language minority students but all of America's youth.

"In 'Effective Schools for the Urban Poor,' Ron Edmonds states: 'All children are eminently educable, and the behavior of the school is critical in determining the quality of the education'.[2] This way of thinking diverges from often-cited 'deficit' models of education, which account for student failure by reference to certain cultural, linguistic, and socioeconomic factors in students' backgrounds, thus making a liability out of difference. Language-minority students in particular have often been blamed for their underachievement in U.S. schools.[3] By considering them 'difficult' or culturally and linguistically 'deprived', schools have found it easy to absolve themselves of responsibility for the education of these students.* Edmonds, on the other hand, places the responsibility for quality education squarely in the hands of the schools" (315–316).

Lucas, Henze, and Donato state their position at the outset: "Because we believe that schools are responsible for the quality of education students receive, and that given a good education, all students can achieve, we are inter-

---

*See Valencia and Solórzano, part III, on the pervasive deficit ideology.

ested in what makes some schools more successful that others" (317). "In surveying the literature on effective schooling, we realized that little was known about successful schooling for language-minority students at the secondary level. To gather information, we . . . therefore conducted an exploratory study of schools promoting the achievement of language-minority students at the secondary level." We visited a total of six high schools in California and Arizona "that had large populations of Latino students and that had been recognized by local, state, and/or federal agencies for excellence" (319).

"Five of the six schools were relatively large, with 1,700 to 2,200 students. All had minority White populations, and in all but the smallest school, Latino students constituted the largest single group—more than one-third of the school population. The four schools with the larger proportions of non-White students . . . also had larger proportions of non-White staff. In none of the schools, however, was the ethnicity of the staff comparable to the student population; in all of them, a much larger proportion of staff than students was White. The percentage of students participating in a school lunch program—a rough measure of their socioeconomic status—varied considerably among the six schools." At two schools, "fewer than 25 percent of the students received such aid," at two others "about 33 percent did so," and at the last two "80 percent did so. Thus, socioeconomic status of students is not a feature shared by these schools overall, although . . . the Latino students whom we interviewed were largely working class."

"Through the exploratory case studies and the analysis across cases, eight features emerged which we believe to be the most important in promoting the success of language-minority students" (322). The following is a guide to understanding these key features, followed by specific examples of how these features benefit educators, administrators, and most importantly, students.

Eight Keys to Promote the Educational Success of Language-Minority Students

1. Place an especially high value on the students' languages and cultures.
2. Make high expectations for language-minority students' achievement concrete.
3. School leaders make the education of language-minority students a priority.
4. Staff development is designed to help teachers and other staff serve language-minority students more effectively.
5. Offer a variety of courses and programs for language-minority students.
6. Offer a counseling program to give special attention to language-minority students.

7. Encourage parents of language-minority students to become involved in their children's education.
8. School staff members share a strong commitment to empower language-minority students through education.

To succeed, these features cannot be mere lip service. Concrete daily actions based on these principles made the schools successful. In the six exemplary schools, these eight steps were implemented with the following specific elements:

1. *High value is placed on the students' languages and cultures.*
   a. Treat students as individuals, not as members of a group.
   b. Learn about students' cultures.
   c. Learn students' languages.
   d. Hire bilingual staff with similar cultural backgrounds to the students.
   e. Encourage students to develop their primary language skills.
   f. Allow students to speak their primary language, except when English development is the focus of instruction or interaction.
   g. Offer advanced as well as lower division content courses in the students' primary languages.
   h. Institute extracurricular activities that will attract language-minority students.

"Rather than ignoring barriers to equality and perpetuating the disenfranchisement of minority students, the principals, administrators, counselors, teachers, and other support staff at the schools we visited celebrated diversity. They gave language-minority students the message that their languages and cultures were valued and respected, thus promoting the self-esteem necessary for student achievement. They communicated this sense of value and respect in a number of concrete ways, translating the ideal into an everyday reality" (322). For example, the "ability to speak a language in addition to English was treated as an advantage rather than a liability. A number of White and Latino teachers and counselors who were not native speakers of Spanish had learned the language" in order to better understand and communicate with students (323).

"Besides showing respect for students' native language, staff in these schools also celebrated the students' cultures. Perhaps the most transparent and readily accessible aspects of culture are customs, holidays, and overtly stated values. While many schools give lip service to these aspects of culture, for example, by celebrating *Cinco de Mayo* and serving tacos on that day," the high-achieving "schools we visited affirmed the customs, values, and holidays of the language-minority students' countries in deeper and more consistent ways throughout the year" (323).

"Teachers, for example, made it their business to know about their students' past experiences. Some had visited public schools in Mexico to better understand their students' previous educational experiences. A group of teachers from one school had observed mathematics teaching in a Mexican school. One of them said that understanding how Mexican students were taught math in Mexico made teaching them easier. He could say to students, 'This is the way most of you were taught how to divide in Mexico. And that's OK. This is another way of doing it.' Without denigrating what they had learned in Mexico, he would ask which way was easiest for them" (323, 325).

Faculty and staff "recognized students' individual strengths, interests, problems, and concerns rather than characterizing them by reference to stereotypes. The assistant principal at one school said, "Basically, [Latino] kids are no different from other kids; they want to learn. Those who fall by the wayside are those whose needs aren't being met. Who wants to fail everyday?" (325).

The personnel who created the conditions for exemplary school recognized and acknowledged cultural differences. In these schools, there is no such thing as a generic Latino student. "Rather, people from Mexico, Nicaragua, El Salvador, Guatemala, Cuba, and other Spanish-speaking countries were known to have different histories and customs and to speak different varieties of Spanish. Mexican immigrants, Mexican Americans, and Chicanos were also recognized as different from one another, and variation among Mexican immigrants based upon socioeconomic background and educational attainment level was acknowledged" (326).

"A final and important way in which these high schools showed respect for the students' cultures and language was through their staffing" (326). As the head counselor at one successful high school stated: "Parents and students see Latinos in leadership positions, not just in the cafeteria or as janitors. People in the school understand problems in the community and have lived it themselves. . . . For example, I understand if a student has to stay home all week to take care of kids. . . . Parents come in because I speak Spanish and can understand their problems. I'm not from a middle-class, elite, intellectual background" (327).

2. *"High expectations of language-minority students are made concrete."*
   a. Hire minority staff in leadership positions to act as role models.
   b. Provide special programs to prepare language-minority students for college.
   c. Offer advanced and honors coursework in content areas in bilingual and sheltered classrooms.

    d.   Make it possible for students to exit ESL (English as a Second Language) programs quickly.

    e.   Challenge students in class and provide guidance to help them meet the challenge.

    f.   Provide counseling assistance (in the primary language if necessary) to help students apply to college and fill out scholarship and grant forms.

    g.   Bring in Latino representatives of colleges and graduates who are in college to talk to students.

    h.   Work with parents to gain their support for students going to college.

    i.   Formally recognize students who do well.

The schools visited demonstrate high expectations for Latino language-minority students. "One principal put it this way: 'I firmly believe that what you give to the best kids, you give to all,' while taking into account special needs and equity issues" (327).

"Recognizing that language-minority students do not have information that mainstream students possess, school counselors who understood students' languages and cultures helped them plan their high school programs, find information about different colleges, apply to college, fill out financial aid forms, and apply for scholarships. Counselors also communicated with parents to gain their support for their children to apply for college, understanding that if going to college is a new idea to the student, it is probably completely unfamiliar, perhaps even threatening, to the parents. As one female student noted, 'At first my parents weren't wanting me to go to college, but Mrs. C [the counselor] convinced them that it was okay.' College and university representatives were brought to the high school to talk with students. Former graduates of similar backgrounds who had gone to college were invited back to the high school to share their experiences and to encourage others to follow in their path" (327–328).

"In classes, teachers challenged students with difficult questions and problems. Complex ideas and materials were made more accessible to language-minority students through visuals, board work, group work, reading aloud, and clear and explicit class expectations. Teachers did not talk down to limited-English-proficient students in 'foreigner talk', but spoke clearly, with normal intonation, explaining difficult words and concepts as needed" (328).

The six excellent schools examined throughout the course of the study all utilized a variety of award programs such as: personal recognition by the principal, 'Student of the Month' luncheons, assemblies for students who had made the honor roll, where not only were the students awarded certificates—but the parents were also invited and honored. " 'It makes you want to try harder when you get an award,' noted one student. Latino language-minority students received these forms of recognition just as other students did" (328).

3. *"School leaders make the education of language-minority students a priority."*

   a. Hold very high academic expectations for language-minority students.

   b. Be knowledgeable about appropriate instructional and curricular approaches to teaching language-minority students and communicating this knowledge to staff.

   c. Take a strong leadership role in strengthening curriculum and instruction for all students, particularly language-minority students.

   d. Be bilingual minority-group member.

   e. Hire teachers who are bilingual and/or trained in methods for teaching language-minority students.

According to one high school principal, himself a Latino: "One of our major roles in this community is to develop a sense of confidence that we can compete in all areas, not just athletics, that we can go out there and be just as good as anybody else. I guess if I had a wish, I would like for the kids in the school to absolutely believe and know in their hearts that they are as good as anybody on this planet" (328).

"We found that good leadership can and does come from program directors, department chairpersons, and teachers in high schools as well as from principals. In some schools, these individuals had taken on strong leadership roles vis-à-vis the education of language-minority students." At another high school, "for example, a separate ESL department had been formed, and it was the chair of this department who advocated most strongly for the education of limited-English-proficient students.* The principal at this school played a less active role in this area, though the previous principal, it should be noted, had been very active in making changes for the language-minority population. This example of a leader who is not a principal serves as a reminder that the strength for change does not necessarily have to come from the top. Though a strong principal who is deeply committed to the needs of language-minority students is certainly desirable, the principal is not the only person who can make a difference. Teachers, program coordinators, and department chairs can also take it upon themselves to be leaders in the education of language-minority students" (329).

4. *"Staff development is explicitly designed to help teachers and other staff serve language-minority students more effectively."*

---

*Compare Guadalupe Valdés's comments, part III.

    a. Offer incentives and compensation so that school staff will take advantage of available staff development programs.

    b. Provide staff development for teachers and other school staff in:

       i. effective instructional approaches to teaching language-minority students, for example, cooperative learning methods, sheltered English, and reading and writing in the content areas;

      ii. principles of second-language acquisition;

     iii. the cultural backgrounds and experiences of the students;

     iv. the languages of the students;

      v. cross-cultural communication;

     vi. cross-cultural counseling, etc.

Teachers, administrators, and other professional staff of the exemplary schools "we visited received professional development through in-service workshops and conferences." Teachers were trained "in the principles of second language acquisition and effective instructional approaches for teaching language-minority students, such as sheltered content,[4] cooperative learning, and reading and writing in the content areas. Teachers and other staff learned about students' cultural backgrounds and experiences. Counselors became informed about cross-cultural counseling strategies. Professional staff worked to develop their ability in the native languages of their students, enabling them to communicate more effectively with language-minority students and their parents" (330). While some states have recently enacted legislation that restricts the use of native languages in classrooms, acquiring Spanish (or any other native language prevalent among such students) will indeed inspire and enhance communication with parents of limited-English-proficient students.

Of utmost importance: "*All* teachers and other professional staff were encouraged to participate in professional development of the sort described here, not just those who taught specific classes for this special student population. It appeared that all school staff took responsibility for teaching these students. No one expressed the attitude that one group of teachers would 'take care' of language-minority students and that the others therefore did not need to 'worry' about them. In fact, one principal had set a policy prohibiting bilingual teachers from teaching bilingual classes the entire day. He believed that bilingual teachers should teach mainstream as well as bilingual classes so they would not forget what they were preparing language-minority students to do" (330, emphasis in the original).

    5. *"A variety of courses and programs for language-minority students is offered."*

       a. Include courses in ESL and primary language instruction (both literacy and advanced placement) and bilingual and sheltered courses in content areas.

b. Insure that the course offerings for language-minority students do not limit their choices or trap them in low-level classes by offering advanced as well as basic courses taught through bilingual and sheltered methods.

c. Keep class size small (20–25 students) in order to maximize interaction.

d. Establish academic support programs that help language-minority students make the transition from ESL and bilingual classes to mainstream classes and prepare them to go to college.

In addition to implementing content courses appropriate to academic proficiency instead of English-fluency, the high schools visited also created special programs "to promote language-minority students' academic and social growth. These programs have the net effect of extending learning time through before- and after-school activities, a feature which many educational researchers, such as Wilson and Corcoran believe may be the 'critical difference between a mediocre school and an excellent one' "[5] (331).

In an advocacy program, "teachers were paired with students as tutors and advocates." One program called "BECA (Bilingual Excellence in Cognitive Achievement) provided tutoring, career planning, and multicultural awareness for both limited and fluent English-speaking Latino students at one high school.* UCO (University and College Opportunity) encouraged and prepared underrepresented minority students in another high school to go to college. The Tanner Bill Program . . . had a similar goal, though it targeted Latino students in particular. AVID (Advance Via Individual Determination) was a college-prep program for disadvantaged students in one high school that included one class specifically geared to limited-English-proficient students. These are only a few of the special programs that either targeted or included language-minority students" (331).

Other support programs examined during the study are: MESA (Math, Engineering, Science Achievement) at one school and PLATO (Programmed Logic for Automatic Teaching Operations) at another school. This second program is a "computer-training dropout program allowing students to attend school part of the day and work part-time" (332). Through PLATO, students are able to use computers for individualized instruction, obtain career and college counseling, and ultimately can receive a regular diploma.

One school instituted a program for students who have failed a class or two and/or have attendance problems. Students in this program are assigned to work with specially trained mentor teachers who volunteer their time.

---

*Beca in Spanish means 'scholarship'.

Another school established the Chapter I Program for "students in low socio-economic brackets who have scored below the 36th percentile" on state-required exams or their equivalent, focusing "on basic math and language arts and the use of computers" (332). Classes are limited to no more than twenty students.

Some extracurricular activities seen at the high schools were: "a group of students who learn and perform dances from different regions of Mexico; La Prensa Latina—a student journalism group that produces a Spanish-language newspaper called *El Mitotero*;* an International Club—a student group that sponsors events to increase intercultural awareness . . . MEChA (*Movimiento Estudiantil Chicano de Aztlán*)—a group that represents the interest of Chicano, Mexican and Latino students on college and high school campuses; Sports"—with "soccer and baseball emphasized over football," as well as the celebration of cultural events and holidays by the entire school (332).

6. *"A counseling program gives special attention to language-minority students."*
    a. Speak the students' languages and are of the same or similar cultural backgrounds.
    b. Be informed about post-secondary educational opportunities for language-minority students.
    c. Believe in, emphasize, and monitor the academic success of language-minority students.

"In our interviews with students, one question asked them to identify the teacher or other staff member who had helped them the most. Many students referred to counselors as being key to their adjustment to the new environment and to the clarification of future goals. 'At the beginning of the year,' said one student, 'I wasn't into school. Then I talked to Mrs. B [a counselor] and got into it. My mom said she was proud of me.' In the schools that exhibited excellence, there was at least one bilingual Latino counselor who was able to communicate effectively with newcomers, as well as with longer-term residents, and who understood the sociocultural backgrounds of the students. This person was also well informed about post-secondary educational opportunities for language-minority students—scholarships, fellowships, grants—and could guide the students in getting and filling out the appropriate forms. He or she could also communicate with parents about students' successes and problems in school and the value of a college or university education" (331, 333).

"One case we heard of involved a twelfth-grade student who lived with her aunt and uncle because her parents were in Mexico. The parents were reluctant to let their daughter, who had been accepted at a reputable college, move away

---

Mitotero 'gossip monger'.

from the family. The counselor took it upon herself to call the parents and talk it over with them, eventually convincing them of the wisdom of letting their daughter seize this opportunity. In a school with no bilingual counselor who cared as much as this one did, this student—and presumably others like her—would have become another statistic of the low college attendance of minority students. Simply having one or more bilingual counselors on the staff who are sensitive to students' cultures does not necessarily mean that language-minority students have access to that counselor, however. In talking with counselors and students, we learned about the importance of having an effective method of assigning students to counselors. Schools used a variety of methods, including assignment by class level, alphabetical order, special needs, and various combinations of these. Those that were most effective made sure that language-minority students were assigned to a counselor who could communicate with them, who was knowledgeable of post-secondary opportunities for language-minority students, and was sincerely committed to helping all students succeed in school and beyond. In the better counseling programs, case loads were relatively low, and bilingual Latino counselors were specifically designated for Latino language-minority students" (333).

7. *"Parents of language-minority students are encouraged to become involved in their children's education."*
    a. Staff who speak the parents' languages.
    b. On-campus ESL classes for parents.
    c. Monthly parents' nights.
    d. Parent involvement with counselors in planning their children's course schedules.
    e. Neighborhood meetings with school staff.
    f. Early morning meetings with parents.
    g. Telephone contacts to check on absent students.

Parent participation was the least developed component of these high schools. "The principals, counselors, and teachers at all of the schools commented that," in spite of their success, "more needed to be done to increase the school's interaction with the parents of language-minority students." This is not to say that nothing had been implemented. These exemplary schools had already "taken steps to encourage parents to take an active part in their children's education. Several schools had Parent Advisory Committees that met monthly and included parents of language-minority students. These committees typically reached out to other parents for assistance with parent-sponsored multicultural activities. Some schools regularly sent newsletters to parents in their native languages" (334).

The above-mentioned "Tanner Bill program for Latino students . . .

required that the teachers and parents of participating students meet twice a month. In addition, the program coordinator held evening meetings several times a year in the neighborhoods of the students in the program. Representatives of colleges and universities in the area attended these meetings to inform parents of the college programs offered by their institutions, the entry requirements, and the scholarships and other support services available to language-minority students. Generally, the college and university representatives who attended spoke the parents' native languages" (335).

Two schools "held early morning pancake breakfasts and invited parents to attend before they went to work; 800 people attended" such a breakfast of one school. The other school also held monthly Student-of-the-Month-Breakfasts for parents in which a high-achieving student in each department was formally applauded. This was in addition to a quarterly Honors Assembly "in which parents were asked to stand up and be recognized with their children. More than 750 people attended the most recent Honors Assembly." A third high school had "a full-time community liaison who spoke Spanish and offered ESL classes for parents on the school campus." Parents of students of this school had "come out on weekends to paint the school. Several schools contacted parents by telephone to check on students who were absent or to inform parents when a student had become ill and was returning home. The person making the contact spoke the parents' native language" (335).

"Although we did not interview parents, comments from students indicated that many Latino parents were very supportive of their children's education. The language barrier, lack of familiarity with the U.S. educational system, and their own lack of educational experience made it difficult for some parents to help directly with homework; however, they encouraged their children in other ways to pursue the education they had not had the opportunity to receive. One student reported, 'For my mom, the only thing is school. She said I could do anything. "All I want is for you to finish school." She pushes that I get educated. She herself dropped out and got married and regrets it. I dropped out too for awhile; it tore my mom and me apart.' The theme of 'becoming somebody' is a strong thread in the students' talk about parents and their own goals for the future. 'My dad is always telling me to work and study, to be somebody,' said one. 'Quiero seguir estudiando para llegar a ser alguien en la vida,'* said another. These comments by students attest to the strong desire among these Latino parents to do whatever they are able to do to gain a good education for their children. The schools we visited were working hard to find ways of making the schools accessible to parents" (335).

8. *"School staff members share a strong commitment to empower language-minority students through education."*

---

*'I want to keep studying so that I can become somebody in my life.'

a. Give extra time to work with language-minority students.
b. Take part in a political process that challenges the status quo.
c. Request training of various sorts to help language-minority students become more effective.
d. Reach out to students in ways that go beyond their job requirements, for example, by sponsoring extra-curricular activities.
e. Participate in community activities in which they act as advocates for Latinos and other minorities" (335–336)

"The most fundamental feature of all, and the most difficult to describe in concrete terms, is the commitment we heard about from most if not all of the school staff and students we interviewed. This commitment goes beyond the value the staff places on students' languages and cultures and beyond the high expectations staff members hold for language-minority students. One can value the language and culture of a student and expect that student to be successful, yet still remain passive when it comes to promoting that student in the world. Commitment and empowerment of students involve staff members reaching out, giving extra time to further the goals of a few students, and taking part in a political process that challenges the status quo" (335–336).

"Such commitment manifested itself in various ways at the schools we visited. Teachers and other staff at the schools were described as having students' best interests at heart and giving extra time and energy after school and during lunch or preparation time to counsel as well as teach them. For example, the Coordinator of Special Projects" at one high school "said that he had found the teachers there to be very eager to learn how to work effectively with language-minority students. He said that they considered it 'a very serious endeavor' to be sensitive to the needs of such students, and that they frequently requested training of various sorts to help them become more effective. At all of the schools, students mentioned teachers who had given them special help and attention, often crediting them with providing personal counseling as well as academic support. Typical student comments included the following: 'The teachers here don't just teach; they care about you' and 'Teachers stay after school to explain what we didn't understand'" (336). Of course sparing extra time is not always easy (in fact sometimes it is pretty near impossible), but the above examples certainly illustrate the impact a little extra time on the part of the teacher can have on his or her students.

"Besides their work in the school setting to promote the achievement and success of Latino and other language-minority students, staff at these schools also participated in various community activities, attended meetings, and held positions in their communities through which they acted as advocates for Latinos and other minorities. An assistant principal at Nogales High School, a

Latino from the community, had been" the city's mayor. "A teacher and MEChA advisor at [another] high school, also a Latino, was elected to the City Council." At a third high school the principal "described her work to develop an advocacy base in the community through her ongoing participation in a variety of community events and activities." She had received support from the school's alumni in the community, "some business people, and many parents—both Latino and Anglo—by participating in community activities herself. Some of these people had spoken out at school board meetings advocating programs and services that were crucial to the success of the district's language-minority students. Sensitive to the fact that the way certain issues are discussed can trigger negative reactions and therefore interfere with the achievement of desired goals, she worked to communicate effectively with different audiences. Above all, she said, 'I have not been naïve in thinking I can do it all by myself; I spent the first year getting a sense of who supported the equity issues that I'm concerned with'" (336–337).

"It was evident at these schools that teachers, counselors, administrators, and other staff were highly committed to promoting the success of language-minority students in school and beyond. Besides promoting the achievement of such students, they acknowledged the educational and social structures that surround the students and challenged these structures in productive ways through concrete actions, such as those described above. By taking their advocacy into the community, those who held elective offices and participated in community groups challenged negative attitudes and policies that may have been creating obstacles to the improvement of education for minority groups. Those who initiated and sponsored activities to expand language-minority students' knowledge and understanding helped them develop a sense of identity and community that knowledge of their own backgrounds could provide. Those who were putting their extra energy into helping students with their academic work were fighting to raise the low achievement records of language-minority students. This commitment and accompanying action provided the framework within which the attributes and processes we have described above were developed and carried out" (337).

Lucas, Henze, and Donato's review provides a rich array of programs for educational success, and real-life examples of how commitment, discussion, and compassion can lead to high accomplishment among language-minority and limited-English-proficient students. Most importantly, in order to effectively and positively educate these children, we must look within the school for what can be improved. To try addressing the so-called flaws of language-minority students themselves is deficit thinking, and only results in educational stigma and failure. Instead, building schools that work for these students leads to the successes exemplified here.

The Four Spokes of the Second Language Learning Wheel

Abridged from an article by Catherine Snow

Harvard professor of education Catherine Snow "provides a guide to basic research in second-language acquisition" by characterizing the distinct perspectives of foreign language teaching, first-language acquisition, psycholinguistics, and sociocultural factors. The research in these areas provides some answers to common questions about second-language acquisition, including those of optimum age, factors that facilitate learning, the consequences of bilingualism, individual differences, and assessment techniques" (16). Snow argues that the crucial insights of the sociocultural perspective must be kept in mind for adequate assessments of bilingual individuals and for meaningful evaluation of bilingual programs.

There are two aims of successful second-language acquisition programs for children: to learn the second language, and to learn educational content through that second language. This second objective cannot be achieved with simplistic assumptions—contrary to the views of the majority of the American public—since both of these language learning "processes are complex, and both raise many questions about process, conditions of learning, influences on learning, and prediction of success." In this article Snow offers cohesive responses to many of the inquiries posed by teachers of language-minority students by providing "an overview of the field of second-language-acquisition research" (16). The questions she addresses include:

- "Is there a best age to start second-language acquisition?
- How long does it take to learn a second language?
- How can second-language acquisition be facilitated?
- Can learners function as effectively in communicating, learning, reading, and talking in a second language as in a first?
- Does acquisition of a second language have any positive or negative consequences for the learner?
- Why do some people have so much trouble with second-language acquisition, when it is relatively fast and easy for others?
- How should we test the language proficiencies of second-language learners?
- How should we evaluate the outcomes of educational programs for language-minority children?" (16).

These are key questions for teachers, but they are not the questions that have "typically thrilled or motivated" second-language researchers. Snow emphasized that "second-language researchers come in different flavors, and each of the various camps of second-language researchers would approach these questions in slightly different ways" (16). Snow provides a thumbnail sketch of four schools of thought on language acquisition: foreign language learning researchers, developmentalists, psycholinguists and socioculturalists. Each school contributes a spoke to the wheel of the processes of language acquisition. With this four school understanding of second language acquisition, Snow then answers the questions listed above.

Foreign language learning research. According to Snow, second language acquisition research originated with foreign language teachers thinking about their teaching methods, curricula, and the performance of their students.

"The assumption made by foreign-language-oriented second-language researchers is that careful, sequenced presentation of information about the second language is crucial to successful learning; this perspective does not have much relevance to the case of children too young to benefit from formal second language study." On the other hand, these researchers "have been thoughtful about questions of testing proficiency. They have put considerable effort into assessing the reliability and predictive validity of standardized testing instruments like the Test of English for Speakers of Foreign Languages (TOEFL), of general proficiency indicators like the cloze,* and of instruments designed to reflect functioning in real-world settings, like the Foreign Service Institute interview and its recent adaptation for lower level learners. The shortcomings of foreign-language-oriented second-language research derive from its exclusive focus on learning as what happens in classrooms." In this line of research "a second language is defined as a curricular outcome, rather than as an abstract system of knowledge" (16).

In brief, this school of research makes several simplifying assumptions to achieve its focused objective. It disregards several key aspects of language and language use. "Any language system is extremely complex." "Many aspects of the grammar have never been described and thus cannot be taught." "The knowledge acquired by a competent speaker goes far beyond the information

---

Editor: A cloze test is a written passage in which gaps replace carefully selected words. The test taker is asked to replace the deleted words. Both linguistic competence and literacy skills are required to succeed, as in the following:

"There was a young _____ named Bright / Whose speed was much faster than _____.
She set out one _____ / In a _____ way, / And returned on the previous _____." Example from www.hf.uio.no/east/bulg/mat/cloze/bright.html.

given" during classroom instruction. "The active, creative role of the learner is more important than the role of the teacher in any successful language-learning process" (16).

Moreover, "foreign-language-based models tend to emphasize intellectual factors such as aptitude as the distinguishing features of good second language learners, underemphasizing such factors as access to social contact with native speakers, motivation, and the sociocultural meaning of the second language in the life of the learner" (16–17).

Developmentalists. Developmentalists have elaborated a theory that takes the orientation that second language acquisition has many of the characteristics of first language acquisition. It is the "result of a natural, creative, active process of analysis of language data made available through social interaction with native speakers" (17). This line of research focuses on the consequences of second language learning for the learner—the cognitive advantages young bilingual children and second language learners have in certain types of tasks. Developmentalists also "emphasize the interdependence between performance on first-language and second-language tasks" (17). Two of their views may be summarized in the following statements:

1. "Certain levels of achievement in a first language constitute a threshold for the easy addition of a second."
2. "Patterns of second language skill directly reflect conditions of acquisition, for example, a learner might have quite different skills in the language learned at home and the one acquired at school" (17).

Developmentalists define language proficiency differently than foreign-language-oriented researchers. For them, language proficiency is "the ability to be communicatively effective in the tasks one must carry out, not in terms of grammatical correctness or good pronunciation as the foreign-language-based researchers tend to do" (17).

According to Snow, while the first language-oriented line of research has helped us acknowledge the developmental and cognitive issues involved in second language acquisition, developmentalists "tend to ignore both the social and cultural situatedness of language learning and use" (17).

Psycholinguists. The third group of language researchers provide another important and different perspective on language acquisition. Psycholinguists think of second language acquisition "more as learning than as development. They treat language acquisition as a special sort of information processing. . . . According to this view, learning a language and understanding a language are not so very different" (17).

Psycholinguistic-based research holds the position that the major difference between the skilled speaker and the learner is that the person who is a skilled speaker/hearer "will more readily question or reject a string" of language information, that is to say a stretch of spoken or written speech, "if interpretation proves difficult, whereas the learner is under pressure to try to incorporate all newly encountered" language information" (17).

Psycholinguists have rejected two standard assumptions of the preceding two schools of thought. They question and tend to reject the distinction between comprehension and learning. They also find the distinction between first and second languages to be problematic. According to this third school of thought, first language acquisition and second language acquisition are more similar than different, "except for the amount of information one starts with. They also put into considerable jeopardy notions like the *native speaker*, since acquisition is conceived as continuing throughout one's lifetime" (17).

Socioculturalists. "When psychologists and linguists think about language acquisition, they emphasize cognition—the problems faced by the learner acquiring a complex system that has more or less overlap with complex systems already acquired. Anthropologists, social psychologists, and sociolinguists, on the other hand, concentrate on the social context of bilingualism." The facts that they emphasize include:

- "Multilingualism is very common across the world."
- "More children grow up learning two languages than one."
- "Language use is tied closely to personal identity, to cultural identification, to national or ethnic pride, to specific communicative tasks or situations, and to a set of attitudes and beliefs that may have an impact on the course of second language acquisition."
- "Becoming too good a second language speaker can threaten the personal identity of the learner."
- A "second language with negative associations for the learner is unlikely to be easy to learn."
- "Perfect control over accent or grammar may not relate to effectiveness in achieving communicative aims" (17).

The three other schools of thought "identify a linguistic norm, typically defined by the competence of the native speaker, toward which the learner is clearly moving" (17). In contrast, sociocultural schools of thought radically reconsider this notion of the linguistic norm by focusing on the social nature of language use. They emphasize that it is impossible to establish, in purely linguistic terms, better or worse varieties of any language. In other words, all verdicts about the quality or superiority of one variety over another are arbitrary, conventional social judgments. When we hear a nonstandard form and conclude that it is bad, inferior, or the result of laziness or poor grammar, we have imposed a social norm. No language variety is linguistically inferior. As a consequence, "many issues that seem intractable within [the previously mentioned] cognitively oriented approaches are easily dealt with from the sociocultural perspective" (17).

"Within sociocultural approaches, notions like *language proficiency* are replaced by notions like *communicative effectiveness* and *social appropriateness*" (17, editor's emphasis). Developmentalists and psycholinguists "struggle with the question of whether adult learners can become so-called 'perfect bilinguals'." On the other hand, the sociocultural school of thought emphasizes "the effective functioning of bilinguals in a variety of cultures." They want all of us to consider the educational utility of presuming that there is such a thing as "a single so-called 'standard' language" or dialect (17). This school of thought opens avenues of understanding "the social and cultural pressures affecting learners in situations where different social value is attached to their two languages" (18). There is much to say about this point of view. In brief, "understanding the patterns of language choice and language proficiency for an individual or a community requires understanding that language is a sociocultural phenomenon as well as a cognitive achievement" (18).

Some answers. Since none of the four schools of thought, by itself, "gives a fully satisfactory picture of second language acquisition," Snow is not surprised that teachers "are tempted to judge research findings as irrelevant to real-world problems. In fact though, the research efforts summarized here have successfully answered questions posed within their own paradigms" (18):

1. *Is there a best age to start second-language acquisition?*
   It may surprise you, but younger is not better. "Foreign-language-oriented researchers are clear that their methods work best with older learners." Younger learners are not as good as older children at the formal study of second languages. It is true that younger children do well "in untutored settings where real communication is at stake. They can succeed in the relatively simple communicative tasks they face with rudimentary second language skills, and thus be encouraged to go on and learn more. They also benefit from relative free-

dom from both personal-identity issues and cultural stereotypes that block easy second language acquisition." But as children get older, their capacity to benefit from formal second language teaching gradually increases. It is important to note that "even adults need consequential communicative interactions in second language to achieve real proficiency" (18).

2. How long does it take to learn a second language?

"One can learn enough of a second language in a few hours to perform some tasks in it. Other tasks (including some challenging academic and literacy-related tasks) may take years to conquer, even for native speakers. Both the psycholinguistic and the sociocultural approaches have shown us how fragile are concepts like *the native speaker* or *the perfect bilingual*. Both first language and second language speakers continue to acquire vocabulary, rhetorical skills, and new communicative abilities as long as they encounter new communicative settings" (18).

3. How can second-language acquisition be facilitated?

"Successful communicative exchanges with native speakers lead to opportunities for learning about the language. Positive regard for the culture associated with the language also helps, as do well-designed curricula and good teachers" (18). In other words, children learn a second language when they have good and fun reasons to speak it, when they have educational materials and programs that are designed for their needs, and when they have teachers who are patient, flexible, and hold a positive attitude towards helping students in this long-term task.

4. Can learners function as effectively in communicating, learning, reading, and talking in a second language as in a first?

"Learners can come to function better in their second language than their first language, especially on tasks rarely encountered and not practiced in the first language. Optimal functioning in both languages requires exposure to a full range of language experiences in both languages" (18).

5. Does acquisition of a second language have any positive or negative consequences for the learner?

"Acquiring a second language can give young learners some advantage" in certain cognitive "tasks but can also increase processing times slightly for both languages. Both these effects are quite small, and the costs in processing speed certainly do not outweigh the advantage of knowing two languages" (18).

6. Why do some people have so much trouble with second-language acquisition, when it is relatively fast and easy for others?

Foreign-language-based researchers have noted two things. One, there are sizeable differences in individual aptitude that make a difference. Two, teaching techniques have a great deal to do with the effectiveness of second language learning. But this is not the whole story. The sociocultural school adds other factors to the cognitive accounts. To understand success versus failure, one must incorporate the student's personal regard—positive or negative—for the second language speakers, for the second language, and for its associated culture. Also, one must factor how authentic are the learner's opportunities to communicate effectively and pleasantly in the second language. "Second language acquisition is a very complex process; its success or failure will not be explained by a single factor or theory" (18).

7. How should we test the language proficiencies of second language learners?

"Proficiency assessment techniques make no sense unless they relate to the goals of the assessment. Second language learners' skills can vary widely across domains (reading vs. listening) and across tasks (telling jokes vs. telling stories)." It is crucial to note that "proficiency on conversational assessments does not predict academic performance. Especially for second language speakers, assessment of the ability to learn in [the] second language offers much better prediction than assessment of what they already know. Social appropriateness and communicative effectiveness are aspects of second language proficiency as important as formal correctness" (18).

8. How should we evaluate the outcomes of educational programs for language-minority children?

"Speed and success of second language acquisition is dependent on the quality of the linguistic environment within which it occurs; thus, assessing the quality of a bilingual education program is crucial in evaluating it. [No] one would argue that poor bilingual programs are better than excellent English-as-a-second-language or submersion settings. Even in excellent environments, however, normal children can take several years to acquire a full range of skills in a second language, and they can only demonstrate language skills that they have had a chance to acquire and practice" (18).

"In order to effectively evaluate bilingual programs, or to promote individual and societal bilingualism, we must understand both the individual, cognitive achievements of the second language learner and the cultural, social meaning of second language acquisition. Educational researchers cannot permit themselves the luxury of prematurely aligning themselves with particular theoretical positions or respecting disciplinary boundaries. . . . . Research on evaluation of bilingual programs has been carried out largely from a foreign-language perspective, with some recent influence of the developmental model. The crucial insights of the sociocultural perspective have been missing and must be introduced if we are to have adequate assessments of bilingual individuals or evaluation of bilingual programs" (18–19).

◠

Teaching Multilingual Children

Abridged from chapters by Virginia Collier

Professor Collier believes that teaching continues to be one of today's most fulfilling professions. She presents an assortment of options for today's teachers who are facing numerous multilingual students—whether bilingual, ESL, or mainstream. The guidelines can orient teachers to approach these classes with confidence as well as offer parents an idea of what to expect for their children. It is time not only to reconsider what students trying to acquire English need but also to recognize how many talented teachers can greatly improve their personal and professional reward as well as their students' advancements.

"Once upon a time there was a grown-up who loved children. One child who came to know this person was eager to find out about many things. Together they discovered the intimate secrets of time and space and nature and the way things work. They played with language. They both grew in wisdom and they learned how infinite and mysterious knowledge is . . ."

Some questions come to mind right away: Don't we as teachers wish that somehow we could capture this romanticized vision of what learning is all about? Don't we parents want our child's relationship to the teacher to resemble this vision? Why does twenty-first century technological society have to be so complicated, educational politics so confused, education so bureaucratized and standardized? How do we prepare students to face this complicated world we have created and yet allow them to retain their love of learning? (87)

These questions present many challenges for teachers at today's schools. Things become even more complicated when we enter increasingly multilingual classrooms. Being a bilingual teacher seems to multiply the complications of teaching. "One must teach in two languages, affirm the cultural values of both home and school, teach standardized forms of the two languages but respect and affirm the multiple varieties and dialects represented among students in class, be a creative and flexible teacher, serve as a catalyst for discovery as students learn to operate effectively in their multiple worlds, be able to mediate and resolve intercultural conflicts, keep students on task and on and on. An ESL teacher is expected to teach English at breakneck speed, provide meaningful content-area instruction in all subject areas, solve all problems of limited-English-proficient students, and serve as a mediating link between home and school. In other words, bilingual and ESL staff are to be super-people!" (57, 1st edition)

More questions: How can you teach enough English in less than one year?* How do you teach (standard) English in a way that respects and affirms the multiple home languages and dialects represented among students in class? How do you affirm the cultural values of both home and school? If English has to be taught in a speedy fashion and students have to acquire the language rapidly enough to survive academically, how can teachers do this?

Beginning answers: Teachers must be creative and flexible, serve as a catalyst for discovery as students learn to operate effectively in their multiple worlds, be able to mediate and resolve intercultural conflicts, keep students on task, and serve as a support base. "Teaching is complicated, but it is also rewarding in ways that many other jobs can never be. You have the chance to interact daily with live, growing, thinking, maturing human beings, and that time is special, despite the complications of managing a bureaucratized, overcrowded classroom of overtested, underchallenged students" (58, 1st edition).

However idyllic the original vision of teaching may be, the reality is that in the complicated school world of proposals and governmental superplans, there are things that can still be done! Everything depends on one key concept, a crucial point of view. The key is the true appreciation of the different linguistic and cultural values that students bring into the classroom. Seven guidelines are offered to better understand how teaching English to second-language learners can become an enriching experience when appreciating students' different languages and life situations. Guideline #1 draws on the research findings of psycholinguists and child development researchers:†

1. Be aware that children use first language acquisition strategies for learning or acquiring a second language (127).

The picture, which has emerged thus far from first language acquisition research, is that children actively engage in a gradual, subconscious, and creative proof-discovery procedure through which they acquire the rule system of the language. There are predictable stages and strategies in this process, which all first language acquirers go through. The strategies of the young second language acquirer are similar. They tacitly identify patterns; they attempt

---

*Editor: Only 180 days of bilingual education—one school year—is permitted under the restrictions imposed by Proposition 227, the antibilingual education referendum, which was passed in California in 1998. In recent years, other states have implemented equally misguided legislation.

†Refer to Snow, in part V, for further discussion of these findings.

to simplify and use words and phrases (even if the meanings and structures are only partial approximations); they find ways of figuring out socially embedded language (not only as a means of gaining confirmation of meaning but also as a way of learning culturally appropriate patterns); and they take risks to try to use analogies of the first language, knowing that these analogies may be only partially correct in meaning and structure. There are differences between first language and second language acquisition in children. These include variables such as the child's age, place and time of second language acquisition, individual learning style, the broader society's social perceptions of the status of the child's identity group, and the child's desire or need to understand and/or identify with speakers of the new language (127). For younger children, it is recommended that the teacher's focus be on the message—which is the child's focus—rather than on the form of the message. Children acquiring second language will self-correct their own utterances over time as they progress through the various stages of second language development, which are similar to those experienced by a child learning her or his first language (128).

Two concepts, and an important distinction are associated with Guideline #1. One, teachers should be aware of the special kind of speech that mothers and fathers use automatically with their children, and try to emulate this. "Caregiver speech" has six features:

a. Caregivers talk about what is going on here and now. The child is actively involved in the immediate context, rather than dealing with abstractions.

b. Caregivers speak in short and simple sentences. As the child moves from one stage of acquisition to the next, sentences become longer and more complex. Caregiver sentences are on the level that the child controls or the next higher level.

c. Caregivers repeat themselves using the same syntactic patterns, not through exact repetition, but through rephrasing.

d. When they find they must slow down, caregivers insert pauses; they do not distort words and intonation.

e. Caregivers provide models to children by saying for them what the children seem to want to say.

f. When caregivers do any kind of correcting, speakers focus attention not on the error, but on trying to communicate well with the child. The focus of the whole conversation is on communication, not on grammatical form or pronunciation.

Two, it is critical to be aware of the social and emotional factors which affect the second language learner. Students do not learn or acquire everything in second language to which they are exposed. Some input may be incomprehensible. The student, because of conscious or unconscious emotional or social factors that keep him or her from taking in maximum input at that time, may miss other input. Many attitude studies in second language acquisition have shown a positive influence on second language acquisition of low anxiety, self-esteem and self-confidence, an outgoing personality, and high motivation for instrumental (practical use) or integrative (identity with another group) purposes (140–145).

The critical distinction to maintain is between how children acquire the capacity to converse casually in a second language, and how they learn to become proficient students using second language. These are two entirely different processes.

On the one hand, children automatically acquire, as a part of their human endowment, proficiency for context-embedded face-to-face communication. This level of English proficiency in the U.S. context includes the ability to handle complex conversation (one might call it the ability to get along in the outside world) using contextual cues such as gestures and intonation from the other speakers, and situational cues to meaning. Native-like conversational proficiency generally takes students two to three years to master. It is not intellectually as demanding as school or academic language (128–129).

On the other hand, teachers are responsible for facilitating academic language development. Academic language does not come to kids automatically, just because they are in a dominant English-speaking locale. Academic language is context-reduced and intellectually much more demanding. Context-reduced communication relies heavily on linguistic cues alone. It involves abstract thinking. It is what we think of when we speak about traditional academic instruction at secondary and adult levels. When language-minority students work academically only in the second language, it seems to take them from five to seven years to master commonly accepted age-grade norms in context-reduced aspects of English proficiency. Furthermore, academic skills developed in the first language tend to automatically transfer to the second language (129).

Schools sometimes use linguistic proficiency tests that assume that a student's full proficiency in English can be ascertained on the basis of conversational skills. People untrained in linguistics, particularly politicians, tend to believe that if limited English proficient students can converse with their monolingual English-speaking peers, then these English-language learners can compete with them on an equal footing. If it were only so easy! English-language learners who can chat comfortably in English do not automatically develop the academic language skills needed to compete. They often have significant educational difficulties upon transition. It is worse for many students who are placed in English-only classrooms with teachers who have no training in second language acquisition and who use an English-only curriculum. So, the choice of language in which the student works academically is less important than success in mastering school skills, or academic language proficiency.

A bilingual teacher, it often seems, needs to be all things to all people. Regarding the teaching of language alone, a bilingual teacher in a two-way Spanish/English classroom, for example, must know something about English language arts to native speakers, teaching standard English as a second dialect, and teaching English as a second language. The same teacher, or team teacher or aide, must understand the teaching of Spanish language arts, standard Spanish as a second dialect, and Spanish as a second language. One teacher may indeed be given all these responsibilities—a tough assignment indeed!

Guideline #2 is a decisive challenge for all teachers who are themselves products of public or private schools. They must reflect on their tacit beliefs and overt actions in the classroom, and consciously reexamine the commonplace beliefs of U.S. society:

2. Do not think of yourself as a remedial teacher expected to correct so-called "deficiencies" of your students.

Instead, whether in English, Korean, Spanish, Greek, or Portuguese, you are working to develop the child's language as an effective instrument of intellectual growth. The difficulty with teaching languages to native speakers is that many teachers have been trained to teach them as foreign languages. Or they automatically revert to the orientation of foreign-language teachers. Second-language or foreign-language methods are inappropriate for native speakers. Also a foreign-language teacher, upon first assessing his or her students, may see the particular dialect represented in class as needing remediation.

Thinking about a student's home dialect gets even more complicated when one considers that some home dialects are socially stigmatized. Educators have tended to blame the language variety and/or home environment for a child's lack of success in school. The solution proposed in the past has been eradication of the stigmatized variety.

"Eradication, which may be said to be the traditional view of the language-teaching profession as a whole, looks upon dialects other than standard as deficient in themselves, as deserving of the stigma they have attracted, and as the causes of severe problems in the total learning process including the acquisition of reading and writing skills." Guadalupe Valdés continues: "Educators who hold this view look upon the educational process as a means by which one is made to distinguish 'right' from 'wrong'. They see themselves as the tools by which a particular student can rid himself of stigmatized dialect features and become a speaker of the 'right' type of the standard language—the passport to achievement, success, and acceptance. As educators, they insist that they have a solemn duty to their students, which includes the total eradication of non-standard dialects."[6] Moreover, eradication has been tried and proven to be effective only to turn off students from schooling. It has never served to encourage school achievement of minority students. Guideline #3 follows, stated as a prohibition.

3. Don't teach a second language in any way that challenges or seeks to eliminate the first language.

Instead of eradication, the most popular view among linguists and bilingual educators requires the teacher's conscious recognition of "bi-dialectism." This position affirms the importance of home dialect and its appropriate use within the community in which it is spoken while at the same time students are taught the standard variety. Students will produce utterances in the classroom in their native dialect. To affirm the home language means that they will not be told that they are wrong, or that what they say is vulgar or bad. Instead, the teacher analyzes with the students the differences between their dialect and the standard variety: grammatical patterns, pronunciation differences, vocabulary items, varying social contexts, and so on. Most importantly, your goal is to help your students master the language used in formal schooling (academic language proficiency) and at the same time give your students language tools for use in all contexts in the outside world (169). This bi-dialectal or multilingual approach builds can be expressed in the affirmative as Guideline #4.

4. Teach the standard form of English and students' home language together with an appreciation of dialect differences to create an environment of language recognition in the classroom.

One of the most difficult things for teachers to do when teaching a second language to native speakers of other languages is to fully accept and give complete credence to the different languages and dialects they bring to the classroom. It is the social bias that language-minority students experience most often in school. When the children are very young, it is experienced as personal inadequacy. When the child is older, it is taken as an indictment, a personal and familial affront. To rectify this bias, the first step is to recognize that English and all other "spoken languages are constantly in a process of change," and that they "change when they come in contact with other languages" (167). So, when children come to class with their non-standard varieties of English and home language, teachers must look at the benefits of having multiple ways of talking in the classroom.

Thus the reorganized task of the teacher is to model his or her own variety of English, as well as the second language of the bilingual classroom, noting that there are many varieties and many standard Englishes and standard varieties of Spanish and other languages, making it clear to the students where he or she is from and helping them to become aware of language differences between countries and regions. Teachers can affirm the varieties represented by students in class, and as students become older and more cognitively aware, they can benefit from understanding the contrasts and affirming them as language differences not to be looked down on (167). Only in this way the classroom becomes the ideal setting to affirm the importance of home dialect and its appropriate use within the community in which it is spoken while at the same time students are taught the standard variety (169).

Teaching in a Bilingual Classroom. On first hearing about bilingual education, everyone immediately wants to know the method of teaching. In most ways, a bilingual classroom is just like any other classroom. A bilingual teacher learns how to become a teacher first of all. Methods of teaching language arts, reading, second language, math, science, and social studies are the same as for any other teacher. Differences, however, are created by the two major variables of language and culture. How the two languages are used in the classroom is one aspect of methodology. A second aspect, which we will not cover in this summary, concerns culture. There are as many bilingual methods as there are bilingual teachers. To oversimplify, there are three major models in actual practice in the United States today: transitional, maintenance, two-way enrichment. As in all education, politics and ideology are expressed by the selection of a given model. By far the most common form is the transitional model. On the other end of the scale is the two-way enrichment model, which carries the ideological claim that no one language has precedence, and education in two languages is better than in just one.

Each community should be able to determine its language and education ideology on the basis of informed discussion. Once the overall philosophical-political goals of a bilingual program are determined, the model(s) of bilingual instruction for a school district can be chosen. Ideally, the models are based on detailed examination of community needs—which in turn are based on factors such as the sociological, economic, political, religious, cultural, geographical, demographic, historical, and linguistic makeup of the community. Each school would then operate its program based on the needs of the total population attending that school. Some school districts bus students to a special school for a portion of a day or a full day for their bilingual or ESL classes. Others have a sufficiently large population of multilingual students to offer a special program at each school.

The main distinction from monolingual classes for any bilingual class (whether transitional, maintenance, or two-way) is the balance in use of the two languages. A second variable that affects the process of classroom organization is who teaches: a team, a teacher and an aide, or one teacher alone. The third variable comes from the structure of the school model. In transitional bilingual and pullout ESL classes, the students are probably not with the bilingual teacher for a full day. Maintenance and two-way bilingual instruction involve a comprehensive, full-day program.

When two languages are used in the school curriculum, the teacher should plan the precise times to use each language. Bilingual pedagogy research indicates that the teacher should clearly separate the two languages of instruction. For example, the teacher should speak Spanish when the instructional language is Spanish, and speak English when instructional language is English. On the other hand, young children should be permitted to speak the language they know best. This includes code-switching. Only after a few years in the bilingual classroom (for example after having attended such a school from preschool or kindergarten to second grade) can students be expected to be proficient enough in each language to sustain the instructional language. Since children code-switch spontaneously, teachers must understand the functions of code-switching in a bilingual setting to determine how best to respond to it in the classroom.

A corollary of Guideline #4 follows. Code-switching, the alternate use of two languages, may strike the monolingual teacher as "broken speech," but it is a normal occurrence in bilingual communities. It can occur at the word, phrase, clause, or sentence level. Code-switching is considered by linguists to be a creative use of language by bilinguals who know both codes (languages) well. In code-switching the items inserted in the second language represent a "clean break" between the two phonemic and morphologic systems. Guideline #5 defends the child's use of code-switching:

5. *Do not forbid young students from code-switching in the classroom. Understand the functions that code-switching serves.*

When bilingual people use both languages in speech, alternating between the two, they code-switch. Code-switching occurs at the word, phrase, clause, or sentence level. Linguists consider code-switching to be a creative use of language by bilinguals who know both languages well.

This is not so-called first language "interference," which is now referred to by the less pejorative term first language influence. For example, first-language influence might affect a student's pronunciation or word order in the second language. In code-switching the items inserted in the second language represent a "clean break" between the two phonemic and morphologic systems.

Code-switching also should not to be confused with borrowing, in which words from one language are "borrowed."* Most borrowed words are incorporated into the sound and grammatical systems of the second language. Consider the English/Spanish sentence: *Los muchachos están puchando la troca* 'The boys are pushing the truck'. Here the verb *puchar,* and the noun *la troca* have been borrowed from English.[7] The monolingual Spanish words for the same concepts are *empujar* 'to push' and *camioneta* 'truck'.

Whenever speakers of two languages come in contact with each other, these three natural processes occur: code-switching, language influence, and word borrowing. Code-switching, the most creative and dynamic process of the three, is highly structured. It is governed by the grammars of both the first and second languages. It is not a linguistic weakness. In reality, code-switching is a display of the integrated and sophisticated use of both languages. As adults, bilinguals code-switch only with speakers who know both languages. Guadalupe Valdés has stated, "Bilingual speakers are aware that each of their languages has certain strengths and that two languages can be used simultaneously to convey the most precise meaning."[8]

Research on code-switching has shown a wide variety of reasons for the switches from one language to the other. An excellent summary is found in the table below, drawn from the work of Valdés.[9] The examples given are in Spanish/English, but code-switching occurs naturally in all bilingual community settings.

Code-switching by students should be accepted, and not penalized. The insights of Valdés have been advanced and refined, not superseded. Many subsequent researchers have confirmed that it is preferable that children code-switch at the ends of sentences. Even when they code-switch within a sentence, it should be accepted, if not used by the teacher. "The natural phenomenon of code-switching should not be forbidden." One kind of code-switch is conversational, which can be a signal "that the students feel a common bond among themselves and a teacher." To allow the child to express him/herself can motivate the student, which encourages learning. The teacher should recognize the natural aspects of language contact settings, and the normal developmental processes of second language acquisition. Accepting code-switching "might produce better academic results than a constant preoccupation with maintaining a single language."

The decision of the teacher to switch or not to switch will vary according to the goals of the community, the type of bilingual program design, the specific classroom structure, the bilingual competence of the teacher, and the formality

---

Editor: Since a "borrowed" word is never "given back," perhaps a better way to think about this language contact process is that a word is "cloned" in one language from a word of another language.

Principal Code-Switching Patterns

Patterns	Definitions	Examples
SOCIAL FACTORS ASSOCIATED WITH CODE-SWITCHING		
Situational switches	Related to the social role of speakers	Mother uses English to chat with daughters, but switches to Spanish to reprimand son.
Contextual switches	Situation, topic, setting, etc., linked to the other language	Students speaking Spanish switch to English to discuss details of a math exam.
Identity markers	In-group membership stressed	*Ese bato* 'That guy' *Órale* 'Alright' *Ándale pues* 'Let's do it'. (Such markers are used in English conversations, regardless of actual Spanish fluency.)
Quotations and paraphrases	Contextual: related to language used by the original speaker	*Y luego me dijo el Mr. Johnson que I have to study.* 'And then Mr. Johnson said I have to study'. (Teacher's remark was originally made in English.)
LINGUISTIC FACTORS ASSOCIATED WITH CODE-SWITCHING		
Random switches of high-frequency items	Unpredictable; do not relate to topic, situation, setting, or language dominance; occur only on word level	*Fuimos al party ayer y estuvo tan suave la fiesta.* 'We went to the party yesterday and the party was really great'.
Switches that reflect lexical needs	Related to language dominance, memory, and spontaneous versus automatic speech	Include the "tip of the tongue" phenomenon; item may be momentarily forgotten.
Triggered switches	Due to the preceding or following items	*Yo lo ví, you know, but I didn't speak to him.* 'I saw him, you know, but I didn't speak to him'. (Switch is triggered by the formulaic expression, 'you know'.)

Principal Code-Switching Patterns (continued)

Patterns	Definitions	Examples
Fixed expressions	Include linguistic routines and automatic speech	*You know . . .* *Glad to meet you . . .* *Thanks for calling . . .* *No te molestes . . .* *¿Qué hay de nuevo?, etc.*
Discourse markers	Similar to *but, and, of course*, etc.	*Este . . . este . . . yo si quería ir.* 'Well . . . well . . . I did want to go'.
Quotations and paraphrases	Noncontextual: not related to language used by original speaker	*He insistió que no me fuera. But I did anyway.* 'He insisted that I not go . . .'. (Remark was originally made in English.)
Stylistic switches	Obvious stylistic devices used for emphasis or contrast	*Me tombé toda la cafetera, the whole coffee pot.* 'I dropped the whole coffee pot'.
Sequential switches	Involve using the last language used by the preceding speaker	Certain speakers will always follow the language switches of other speakers; others will not.

Source: Valdés-Fallis, 1978, p. 16.

or informality of the specific classroom tasks. Code-switching is appropriate in creative, informal, casual, and intimate speech among bilingual speakers.*

Literacy and the English-Language Learner. This final section covers just a few key points regarding literacy teaching in bilingual and ESL classrooms. Many transitional or ESL programs do not emphasize the backbone of school success: academic literacy. On the false premise that English oral competence is all that an immigrant child needs to compete with native English speaking peers, too many ESL or other English-language learner programs fail to provide a literacy curriculum for their unique needs. This curricular failure cheats immigrant stu-

---

*Editor: Code-switching can be found in many of the creative works in *Tongue-Tied.* Code-switching is the literary analogy to a visual artist's using two media. It is a rich linguistic resource that is displayed in bilingual poetry and other expressive culture. See examples in Burciaga, part IV; and Gina Valdés, part VI. Code-switching can also be regarded as happening within a single language, as between dialects or between speech registers (that is to say, socially distinct linguistic varieties), as discussed by Awkward, part IV.

dents, since literacy is indispensable for lifelong success. Indeed, literacy is the ultimate aspiration of all schooling. As Sarah Hudelson states, the goal of reading and writing is to enable students "to learn about and interpret the world and reflect upon themselves in relation to people and events around them . . . to explain, analyze, argue about, and act upon the world."[10] Hence Guideline #6:

6. Provide a literacy development curriculum that is specifically designed for English-language learners.

Guideline #6 immediately generates a question. Which language is best for English-language learner literacy development: the home language, English (the second language), or both? Happily, the research is clear about the best choice. The "most successful long-term academic achievement occurs where the students' primary language is the initial language of literacy" (174). First, at the early stages of instruction, using the home language for literacy builds the self-worth of language minority students. Further, literacy research states that first language literacy favorably influences subsequent second language literacy (175). Once a child becomes literate in the home language, literacy skills swiftly transfer to second language settings. The skills that transfer include general literacy strategies and reading-ready skills, habits and attitudes toward text interpretation, knowledge about text structure and rhetorical devices, sensori-motor skills, visual/perceptual training, and literacy related cognitive functions. Any academic home language development that benefits a child's cognitive development, whether oral or written, will transfer to the second language. It turns out that first language transfer is swift, even when the writing systems are not the same!

The second option, developing literacy in both languages simultaneously, is far better than the third option, literacy development in the second language before the home language. Children may experience a bit of confusion with simultaneous literacy development, but the research literature indicates few long-term academic problems result.

Sadly, the worst option is too often the only one offered to immigrant students. This occurs in spite of the research literature, which speaks with one voice: To dismiss the home language in literacy development instantly places immigrant children at risk. This risk does not recede over time, but accumulates. Collier's own research indicates that the English reading skills of fourth graders who were not literate in their home language, were three years behind fourth graders who had received three years of schooling in their home language before arriving in the U.S. It is a distressing state of affairs that teachers must encourage immigrant parents to promote home language literacy, not because it is a best practice for English-language learner literacy development, but because some states forbid schools to offer these tools directly to the children.

In our information century, reading and writing have become profoundly social phenomena, natural processes that students readily "acquire" when classroom environments make full use of the natural reading activities that surround them (176, 179).

In spite of the world's wealth of textual information, learning to read and write is often trying for average students. Nonetheless, it is essential, since reading and writing enables students to learn about and act upon the world. It is evermore important for immigrant students. Many of these students are refugees or older preliterate students. For them the challenge is greater. The teacher's challenge is to find ways to integrate immigrant students with other students their age, while presenting meaningful lessons both at their level of maturity and their level of cognitive development (176). The best way for all students is for teachers to use all the available language resources at hand. Sadly, classroom materials on the teaching of listening, speaking, reading, and writing tend to separate the skills. In reality, all the skills are intimately integrated, and should be offered in this way. Hence Guideline #7:

7. *Provide a balanced and integrated approach to the four language skills: listening, speaking, reading and writing.*

In the literate world, children become aware very early of the importance of written language through books, the media, signs, printed containers, logos, instructions, and endless forms of environmental print. They might first learn to read stories that they themselves dictated to their teacher, as well as through games, recipes, and maps. Dialogue journals are used extensively in bilingual and ESL classrooms to develop writing and communication skills, using a notebook in which two-way written dialogue is carried on between the student and the teacher (177). The teacher corrects no errors, but instead endeavors to be supportive and responsive. Formal writing involves several stages, again interweaving the four language skills, with a lengthy prewriting stage, followed by the getting-ideas-on-paper stage where fluency (not accuracy) is the operative word. Next, a sharing stage begins, to be followed by the revising-in response-to-feedback stage. Only then is editing for usage and spelling undertaken. And the publishing stage follows. In print-rich settings, writing stimulates reading, which in turn incites more reading. "And talking about one's own writing and other authors' writing, as well as connected life experiences, leads to continuing cognitive and academic growth through language acquisition: a full circle" (178). Literacy emerges among student partners in classrooms where sharing oral and written personal narratives, journal writing, and conversational writing occurs regularly. It blossoms when fluent readers (including the teacher) recite newly composed or predictable and familiar (especially multicultural) literature, and when the whole class of students participate in read-alongs and sing-alongs, story mappings, and shared oral narratives from home (such as storytelling, commenting, questioning, teasing, jokes and song).*

In sum, "language is enchanting, powerful, magical, useful, personal, natural, all-important" (181). The reasons to use this whole range of activities in the classroom is to eliminate boredom, raise awareness, and make language teaching as well as learning as culturally relevant as possible for students. In this manner, it is hoped that the learning process will not only enrich the life of the student, but also that of his or her teacher.

Editor: Collier points out that a rich but underutilized resource for literacy development is the "funds of knowledge" from language minority home and community that students can share. See Moll and González, part III.

~

Suite for Ebony and Phonics: Reflections on African American English

Abridged from an article by John Rickford

Stanford University linguistics professor John Rickford offers a straightforward analysis of Ebonics, the English dialect of many African Americans. Rickford demonstrates that it is a highly structured, grammatically consistent dialect that is quite distinct from regional Anglo-American English dialects. He holds that Ebonics is not a distinct language, in contrast to many authorities who maintain an Afrocentric viewpoint. His clear discussion demonstrates why linguistic science is very useful to shed light on social and educational issues involving the way people talk.

To James Baldwin, writing in 1979, it was "this passion, this skill . . . this incredible music." Toni Morrison, two years later, was impressed by its "five present tenses" and felt that "the worst of all possible things that could happen would be to lose that language." What these novelists were talking about was Ebonics, the informal speech of many African Americans, which rocketed to public attention after the Oakland School Board approved a resolution in December 1996, recognizing it as the primary language of African American students.

The reaction of most people across the country—in the media, at holiday gatherings, and on electronic bulletin boards—was overwhelmingly negative. In the flash flood of e-mail on America Online, Ebonics was described as "lazy English," "bastardized English," "poor grammar," and "fractured slang." Oakland's decision to recognize Ebonics and use it to facilitate mastery of Standard English also elicited superlatives of negativity: "ridiculous, ludicrous," "VERY, VERY STUPID," "a terrible mistake."

However, linguists—who study the sounds, words, and grammars of languages and dialects—though less rhapsodic about Ebonics than the novelists, were much more positive than the general public. In January 1997, at the annual meeting of the Linguistic Society of America, my colleagues and I unanimously approved a resolution describing Ebonics as "systematic and rule-governed like all natural speech varieties." Moreover, we agreed that the Oakland resolution was "linguistically and pedagogically sound."

Why do we linguists see the issue so differently from most other people? A founding principle of our science is that we describe *how* people talk; we don't judge how language should or should not be used. A second principle is that all languages, if they have enough speakers, have dialects—regional or social

236

varieties that develop when people are separated by geographic or social barriers. And a third principle, vital for understanding linguists' reactions to the Ebonics controversy, is that all languages and dialects are systematic and rule-governed. Every human language and dialect that we have studied to date—and we have studied thousands—obeys distinct rules of grammar and pronunciation.

What this means, first of all, is that Ebonics is not slang. Slang refers just to a small set of new and usually short-lived words in the vocabulary of a dialect or language. Although Ebonics certainly has slang words—such as *chillin*, 'relaxing', or *homey*, 'close friend', to pick two that have found wide dissemination by the media—its linguistic identity is described by distinctive patterns of pronunciation and grammar.

But is Ebonics a different language from English or a different dialect of English? Linguists tend to sidestep such questions, noting that the answers can depend on historical and political considerations. For instance, spoken Cantonese and Mandarin are mutually unintelligible, but they are usually regarded as 'dialects' of Chinese because their speakers use the same writing system and see themselves as part of a common Chinese tradition. By contrast, although Norwegian and Swedish are so similar that their speakers can generally understand each other, they are usually regarded as different languages because their speakers are citizens of different countries. As for Ebonics, most linguists agree that Ebonics is more of a dialect of English than a separate language, because it shares many words and other features with other informal varieties of American English. And its speakers can easily communicate with speakers of other American English dialects.

Yet Ebonics is one of the most distinctive varieties of American English, differing from Standard English—the educated standard—in several ways. Consider, for instance, its verb tenses and aspects. (*Tense* refers to when an event occurs; *aspect* to how it occurs, whether habitual or ongoing.) When Toni Morrison referred to the "five present tenses" of Ebonics, she probably had usages like these—each one different from Standard English—in mind:

1. *He runnin.*	'He is running.'
2. *He be runnin.*	'He is usually running.'
3. *He be steady runnin.*	'He is usually running in an intensive, sustained manner.'
4. *He bin runnin.*	'He has been running.'
5. *He BIN runnin.*	'He has been running for a long time and still is.'

In Standard English, the distinction between habitual or non-habitual events can be expressed only with adverbs like *usually*. Of course, there are also simple present tense forms, such as *he runs*, for habitual events, but they do not carry the meaning of an ongoing action, because they lack the *-ing* suffix. Note too that *bin* in example (4) is unstressed, while *BIN* in example (5) is stressed. The former can usually be understood by non-Ebonics speakers as equivalent to *has been* with the *has* deleted, but the stressed BIN form can be badly misunderstood. Years ago, I presented the Ebonics sentence *She BIN married* to 25 whites and 25 African Americans from various parts of the United States and asked them if they understood the speaker to be still married or not. While 23 of the African Americans said yes, only 8 of the whites gave the correct answer.

Word pronunciation is another distinctive aspect of dialects, and the regularity of these differences can be very subtle. Most of the so-called rules we follow when speaking Standard English are obeyed unconsciously. Take for instance English plurals. Although grammar books tell us that we add *-s* to a word to form a regular English plural, as in *cats* and *dogs*, that's true only for writing. In speech, what we actually add in the case of *cat* is an *s* sound; in the case of *dog* we add *z*. The difference is that *s* is voiceless, with the vocal cords spread apart, while *z* is voiced, with the vocal cords held closely together and noisily vibrating. Because we spell both plural endings with *-s*, we're not aware that English speakers make this systematic difference every day, and I'll bet your English teacher never told you about voiced and voiceless plurals. But you follow the 'rules' for using them anyway, and anyone who doesn't—for instance, someone who says "bookz"—strikes an English speaker as sounding funny.

One reason people might regard Ebonics as 'lazy English' is its tendency to omit consonants at the ends of words—especially if they come after another consonant, as in *tes(t)* and *han(d)*. But if one were just being lazy or cussed or both, why not also leave out the final consonant in a word like *pant*? This is not permitted in Ebonics; the 'rules' of the dialect do not allow the deletion of the second consonant at the end of a word unless both consonants are either voiceless, as with *-st*, or voiced, as with *-nd*. In the case of *pant*, the final *-t* is voiceless, but the preceding *-n* is voiced, so the consonants are both spoken. In short, the manner in which Ebonics differs from Standard English is highly ordered; it is no more lazy English than Italian is lazy Latin. Only by carefully analyzing each dialect can we appreciate the complex rules that native speakers follow effortlessly and unconsciously in their daily lives.

Who speaks Ebonics? If we made a list of all the ways in which the pronunciation and grammar of Ebonics differ from Standard English, we probably couldn't find anyone who always uses all of them. While its features are found most commonly among African Americans (*Ebonics* is itself derived from *ebony* and *phonics*, meaning 'black sounds'), not all African Americans speak it. The features of Ebonics, especially the distinctive tenses, are more common among working-class than among middle-class speakers, among adolescents than among the middle-aged, and in informal contexts (a conversation on the street) rather than formal ones (a sermon at church) or writing.

The genesis of Ebonics lies in the distinctive cultural background and relative isolation of African Americans, which originated in the slaveholding South. But contemporary social networks, too, influence who uses Ebonics. For example, lawyers and doctors and their families are more likely to have more contact with Standard English speakers—in schools, work, and neighborhoods—than do blue-collar workers and the unemployed. Language can also be used to reinforce a sense of community. Working-class speakers, and adolescents in particular, often embrace Ebonics features as markers of African American identity, while middle-class speakers (in public at least) tend to eschew them.

How did Ebonics arise? What we do know is that the ancestors of most African Americans came to this country as slaves. They first arrived in Jamestown in 1619, and a steady stream continued to arrive until at least 1808, when the slave trade ended, at least officially. Like the forebears of many other Americans, these waves of African 'immigrants' spoke languages other than English. Their languages were from the Niger-Congo language family, especially the West Atlantic, Mande, and Kwa subgroups spoken from Senegal and Gambia to the Cameroons, and the Bantu subgroup spoken farther south. Arriving in an American milieu in which English was dominant, the slaves learned English. But how quickly and completely they did so and with how much influence from their African languages are matters of dispute among linguists.

The Afrocentric view is that most of the distinctive features of Ebonics represent imports from Africa. As West African slaves acquired English, they restructured it according to the patterns of Niger-Congo languages. Most Afrocentrists, however, do not cite a particular West African language source. Although many linguists acknowledge continuing African influences in some Ebonics and American English words, they want more proof of its influence on Ebonics pronunciation and grammar.

A second view, the Eurocentric—or dialectologist—view, is that African slaves learned English from white settlers, and that they did so relatively quickly and successfully, retaining little trace of their African linguistic heritage. Vernacular or nonstandard features of Ebonics, including omitting final consonants and habitual *be*, are seen as imports from dialects spoken by colonial English, Irish, or Scotch-Irish settlers, many of whom were indentured servants. Or they may be features that emerged in the twentieth century, after African Americans became more isolated in urban ghettos. However, as with Afrocentric arguments, we still do not have enough historical details to settle the question.

A third view, the creolist view, is that many African slaves, in acquiring English, developed a pidgin language—a simplified fusion of English and African languages—from which Ebonics evolved. Native to none of its speakers, a pidgin is a mixed language, incorporating elements of its users' native languages but with less complex grammar and fewer words than either parent language. A pidgin language emerges to facilitate communication between speakers who do not share a language; it becomes a creole language when it takes root and becomes the primary tongue among its users.

Creole speech might have been introduced to the American colonies through the large numbers of slaves imported from the colonies of Jamaica and Barbados, where creoles were common. In these regions the percentage of Africans ran from 65 to 90 percent. And some slaves who came directly from Africa may have brought with them pidgins or creoles that developed around West African trading forts.

My own view is that the creolist hypothesis incorporates the strengths of the other hypotheses and avoids their weaknesses. But we linguists may never be able to settle that particular issue one way or another. What we can settle on is the unique identity of Ebonics as an English dialect.

So what does all this scholarship have to do with the Oakland School Board's proposal? Some readers might be fuming that it is one thing to identify Ebonics as a dialect and quite another to promote its usage. Don't linguists realize that nonstandard dialects are stigmatized in the larger society, and that Ebonics speakers who cannot shift to Standard English are less likely to do well in school and on the job front? Well, yes. The resolution that we put forward . . . in fact stated that "there are benefits in acquiring Standard English." But there is experimental evidence both from the United States and Europe that mastering the standard language might be easier if the differences in the student vernacular and Standard English were made explicit rather than entirely ignored.

To give only one example: At Aurora University, outside Chicago, inner-city African American students were taught by an approach that contrasted Standard English and Ebonics features through explicit instruction and drills. After eleven weeks, this group showed a 59 percent reduction in their use of

Ebonics features in their Standard English writing. But a control group taught by conventional methods showed an 8.5 percent increase in such features.

This is the technique the Oakland School Board was promoting. The approach is not new; it is part of the sixteen-year-old Standard English Proficiency Program, which is being used in some three hundred California schools. Since the media uproar over its original proposal, the Oakland School Board clarified its intent: the point is not to teach Ebonics as a distinct language but to use it as a tool to increase mastery of Standard English among Ebonics speakers. The support of linguists for this approach may strike nonlinguists as unorthodox, but that is where our principles—and the evidence—lead us.

What Should Teachers Do about Ebonics?

Lisa Delpit

The educational outlook for many African-American children is achingly bleak. Not only are schools failing to meet the educational needs of these students, but the national controversy surrounding the legitimacy of Ebonics (a.k.a. Black English) serves two dangerous purposes. One is to question the validity of a group's native language. The other is to detract attention from taking appropriate steps to remedy those problems that have historically afflicted these students. Lisa Delpit moves beyond this struggle. She states that whether one is in favor of Ebonics or not, its reality must be recognized: "It is the language spoken by many of our African-American children. It is the language they heard as their mothers nursed them and changed their diapers and played peek-a-boo with them. It is the language through which they first encountered love, nurturance, and joy." Delpit situates Ebonics at the center of the African-American community and articulates its role in African-American students' successful education. However, the power of this revelation can only be employed when teachers themselves understand how to correctly incorporate this language into their class work.

The national debate about Ebonics created much more heat than light. For teachers who must ask what classroom lessons should be drawn, almost no enlightenment can be found. "I have been asked often enough recently 'What do you think about Ebonics? Are you for it or against it?' My answer must be neither. I can be neither for Ebonics or against Ebonics any more than I can be for or against air. It exists. It is the language spoken by many of our African-American children. It is the language they heard as their mothers nursed them and changed their diapers and played peek-a-boo with them. It is the language through which they first encountered love, nurturance, and joy" (17).

"On the other hand, most teachers of those African-American children who have been least well-served by educational systems believe that their students' life chances will be further hampered if they do not learn Standard English. In the stratified society in which we live, they are absolutely correct. While having access to the politically mandated language form will not, by any means, guarantee economic success, not having access will almost certainly guarantee failure" (17).

"So what must teachers do? Should they spend their time relentlessly 'correcting' their Ebonics-speaking children's language so that it might conform to what we have learned to refer to as Standard English? Despite good intentions, constant correction seldom has the desired effect. Such correction increases cognitive monitoring of speech [on the part of the student], thereby making talking difficult. To illustrate, I have frequently taught a relatively simple new 'dialect' to classes of preservice teachers. In this dialect, the phonetic element 'iz' is added after the first consonant or consonant cluster in each syllable of a word. (*Maybe* becomes miz-ay-biz-ee and *apple*, iz-ap-piz-le.) After a bit of drill and practice, the students are asked to" explain, in Izlanguage, why they decided to become teachers. "Most only haltingly attempt a few words before lapsing into either silence or into Standard English. During a follow-up discussion, all students invariably speak of the impossibility of attempting to apply rules while trying to formulate and express a thought." As this demonstration clearly shows, "forcing speakers to monitor their language typically produces silence" (17–18).

Group Identity. "Issues of group identity may also affect students' oral production of a different dialect. In a study of phonologic aspects of Pima Indian language, Sharon Nelson-Barber found that, in grades 1–3, the children's English most approximated the standard dialect of their teachers. But surprisingly, by fourth grade, when one might assume growing competence in standard forms, their language moved significantly toward the local dialect. These fourth graders had the *competence* to express themselves in a more standard form but chose, consciously or unconsciously, to use the language of those in their local environments. The researcher believes that, by ages eight to nine, these children became aware of their group membership and its importance to their well-being, and this realization was reflected in their language.[11] They may also have become increasingly aware of the school's negative attitude toward their community and found it necessary—through choice of linguistic form—to decide with which camp to identify" (18–19).

Techniques. "What should teachers do about helping students acquire an additional oral form? First, they should recognize that the linguistic form a student brings to school is intimately connected to loved ones, community, and personal identity. To suggest that this form is 'wrong' or, even worse, ignorant, is to suggest that something is wrong with the student and his or her family. To denigrate your language is, then, in African-American terms, to 'talk about your mama.' Anyone who knows anything about African-American culture knows the consequences of that speech act!" (19).

"On the other hand, it is equally important to understand that students who do not have access to the politically popular dialect form in this country are less likely to succeed economically than their peers who do. How can both realities be embraced in classroom instruction?" (19).

"It is possible and desirable to make the actual study of language diversity a part of the curriculum for all students. For younger children, discussions about the differences in the ways TV characters from different cultural groups speak can provide a starting point. A collection of the many children's books written in the dialects of various cultural groups can also provide a wonderful basis for learning about linguistic diversity,* as can audiotaped stories narrated by individuals from different cultures, including taped books read by members of the children's home communities." Students can become 'language detectives' who interview "a variety of individuals and listen to the radio and TV to discover the differences and similarities in the ways people talked.[12] Children can learn that there are many ways of saying the same thing, and that certain contexts suggest particular kinds of linguistic performances" (19).

"Some teachers have groups of students create bilingual dictionaries of their own language form and Standard English. Both the students and the teacher become engaged in identifying terms and deciding upon the best translations. This can be done as generational dictionaries, too, given the proliferation of 'youth culture' terms growing out of the Ebonics-influenced tendency for the continual regeneration of vocabulary. Contrastive grammatical structures can be studied similarly," but teachers must be aware of the grammatical structure of Ebonics and the other nonstandard and ethnic dialects represented in their classrooms "before they can launch into this complex study" (19–20).

"Other teachers have had students become involved with standard forms through various kinds of role-play. For example, memorizing parts for drama productions allows students to practice and 'get the feel' of speaking Standard English while not under the threat of correction. A master teacher of African-American children in Oakland, Carrie Secret, uses this technique and extends it so that students videotape their practice performances and self-critique them as to the appropriate use of Standard English" (20).

"Young students can create puppet shows or role-play cartoon characters—many 'superheroes' speak almost hypercorrect standard English! Playing a role eliminates the possibility of implying that the child's language is inadequate and suggests, instead, that different language forms are appropriate in different

---

Author's Note: Some of these books include Lucille Clifton, *All us come 'cross the water* (New York: Holt, Rinehart, and Winston, 1973); Paul Green (aided by Abbe Abbott), *I am Eskimo—Aknik my name* (Juneau: Alaska Northwest Publishing, 1959); Howard Jacobs and Jim Rice, *Once upon a bayou* (New Orleans: Phideaux Publications, 1983); Tim Elder, *Santa's Cajun Christmas Adventure* (Baton Rouge: Little Cajun Books, 1981) and a series of biographies produced by Yukon-Koyukkuk School District of Alaska and published by Hancock House Publishers in North Vancouver, B.C., Canada.

contexts. Some other teachers in New York City have had their students produce a news show every day for the rest of the school. The students take on the personae of famous newscasters, keeping in character as they develop and read their news reports. Discussions ensue about whether Tom Brokaw would have said it that way, again taking the focus off the child's speech" (20–21).

Discourse Styles. "Although most educators think of Black Language as primarily differing in grammar and syntax, there are other differences in oral language of which teachers should be aware in a multicultural context, particularly in discourse style and language use. Harvard University researcher Sarah Michaels and other researchers identified differences in children's narratives at 'sharing time.'[13] They found that there was a tendency among young White children to tell 'topic-centered' narratives—stories focused on one event—and a tendency among Black youngsters, especially girls, to tell 'episodic' narratives—stories that include shifting scenes and are typically longer. While these differences are interesting in themselves, what is of greater significance is adults' responses to the differences" (21).

Reactions to Children Speaking Ebonics. "In responding to the retelling of a Black child's story, the White adults were uniformly negative, making such comments as "terrible story, incoherent." When asked to judge this child's academic competence, all of the White adults rated her below the children who told 'topic-centered' stories. Most of these adults also predicted difficulties for this child's future school career, such as "This child might have trouble reading," that she exhibited "language problems that affect school achievement," and that "family problems" or "emotional problems" might hamper her academic progress" (21).

"The Black adults had very different reactions. They found this child's story "well formed, easy to understand, and interesting, with lots of detail and description." Even though all five of these adults mentioned the 'shifts' and 'associations' or 'nonlinear' quality of the story, they did not find these features distracting. Three of the Black adults selected the story as the best of the five they had heard, and all but one judged the child as exceptionally bright, highly verbal, and successful in school" (21–22).

"This is not a story about racism, but one about cultural familiarity. However, when differences in narrative style produce differences in interpretation of competence, the pedagogical implications are evident. If children who produce stories based on differing discourse styles are expected to have trouble reading and viewed as having language, family, or emotional problems, as was the case with the informants" quoted by the researchers, "they are unlikely to be viewed as ready for the same challenging instruction awarded students whose language patterns more closely parallel the teacher's" (22).

∿

Reading. "Most teachers are particularly concerned about how speaking Ebonics might affect learning to read. There is little evidence that speaking another mutually intelligible language form, per se, negatively affects one's ability to learn to read. For commonsensical proof, one need only reflect on nonstandard English-speaking Africans who, though enslaved, not only taught themselves to read English, but did so under threat of severe punishment and death. But children who speak Ebonics do have a more difficult time becoming proficient readers. Why?"

"In part, appropriate instructional methodologies are frequently not adopted. There is ample evidence that children who do not come to school with knowledge about letters, sounds, and symbols need to experience some explicit instruction in these areas in order to become independent readers" (22).

"Another explanation is that, where teachers' assessments of competence are influenced by the language children speak, teachers may develop low expectations for certain students and subsequently teach them less."[14,*]

"A third explanation rests in teachers' confusing the teaching of reading with the teaching of a new language form. Reading researcher Patricia Cunningham found that teachers across the United States were more likely to correct reading miscues that were 'dialect'-related (*Here go a table* for *Here is a table*) than those that were 'non-dialect'-related (*Here is a dog* for *There is a dog*). Seventy-eight percent of the former types of miscues were corrected, compared with only twenty-seven percent of the latter" leading her to conclude that "teachers were acting out of ignorance, not realizing that *here go* and *here is* represent the same meaning in some Black children's language" (22–23).

"In my observations of many classrooms, however, even when teachers recognize the similarity of meaning, they are likely to correct Ebonics-related miscues. Consider a typical example:

Text: Yesterday I washed my brother's clothes.
Student's spoken rendition: Yesterday I wash my bruvver close.

The subsequent exchange between student and teacher sounds something like this:

---

*See Valencia and Solórzano's article on self-fulfilling prophecies, in part III.

Teacher: Wait, let's go back. What's that word again? (*Points at washed.*)

Student: Wash.

Teacher: No. Look at it again. What letters do you see at the end? You see *–ed*. Do you remember what we say when we see those letters on the end of the word?

Student: *–ed*.

Teacher: OK, but in this case we say washed. Can you say that?

Student: Wash*ed*.

Teacher: Good. Now read it again.

Student: Yesterday I wash*ed* my bruvver . . .

Teacher: Wait a minute, what's that word again? (*Points at brother.*)

Student: Bruvver.

Teacher: No. Look at these letters in the middle. (*Points at brother.*) Remember to read what you see. Do you remember how we say that sound? Put your tongue between your teeth and say /th/.

"The lesson continues in such a fashion, the teacher proceeding to correct the student's Ebonics-influenced pronunciations and grammar while ignoring that fact that the student had to have comprehended the sentence in order to translate it into her own language. Such instruction occurs daily and blocks reading development in a number of ways" (23).

"First, because children become better readers by having the opportunity to read, the overcorrection exhibited in this lesson means that this child will be less likely to become a fluent reader than other children that are not interrupted so consistently" (23–24).

"Second, a complete focus on code and pronunciation blocks children's understanding that reading is essentially a meaning-making process. This child, who understands the text, is led to believe that she is doing something wrong. She is encouraged to think of reading not as something you do to get a message, but something you pronounce" (24).

"Third, constant corrections by the teacher are likely to cause this student and others like her to resist reading and to resent the teacher" (24).

"The moral of this story is not to confuse learning a new language form with reading comprehension. To do so will only confuse the child, leading her away from those intuitive understandings about language that will promote reading development and toward a school career of resistance and a lifetime of avoiding reading" (25).

"The teacher's job is to provide access to the national 'standard' as well as to understand the language the children speak sufficiently to celebrate its beauty. The verbal adroitness, the cogent and quick wit, the brilliant use of metaphor, the facility in rhythm and rhyme, evident in the language of Jesse

Jackson, Whoopi Goldberg, Toni Morrison, Henry Louis Gates, Jr., Tupac Shakur, and Maya Angelou, as well as in that of many inner-city Black students, may all be drawn upon to facilitate school learning. The teacher must know how to effectively teach reading and writing to students whose culture and language differ from that of the school, and must understand how and why students decide to add another language form to their repertoire. All we can do is provide students with access to additional language forms. Inevitably, each speaker will make his or her own decision about what to say in any context" (25–26).

Notes

1. Patricia Hill Collins, *Black Feminist Thought* (New York: Routledge), xiii, cited in Pat Mora's *Nepantla: Essays for the Land in the Middle* (Albuquerque: University of New Mexico Press, 1993), 15.

2. Ron Edmonds, "Effective schools for the urban poor," *Educational Leadership*, volume 37, number 1 (1979, May 5), 15–27.

3. *Authors' note:* We will use the phrase 'language-minority students' to refer to those who come from families where a language other than English is spoken. Such students may or may not speak English fluently. [The editor of *Tongue-Tied* expands the term to include students whose native English dialect is nonstandard, such as Chicano English, African American English, and various types of American Indian English.]

4. *Authors' note:* The term *sheltered content* refers to an approach to teaching content classes for [students who are learning the English language] in which the development of English language skills is emphasized along with content area development. Teachers use whatever means they can to make the content comprehensible and meaningful to the students: for example, simplified speech, vocabulary work, visuals, hands-on activities, and highly structured lessons (see L. Northcutt and D. Watson. *SET: Sheltered English Teaching Handbook.* [San Marcos, CA: AM Graphics and Printing, 1986]).

5. Bruce L. Wilson and Thomas B. Corcoran. *Successful secondary schools: Visions of excellence in American public education* (New York: Falmer Press, 1988), page 58.

6. Guadalupe Valdés, "Pedagogical Implications of Teaching Spanish to the Spanish-Speaking in the United States," in *Teaching Spanish to the Hispanic Bilingual: Issues, Aims, and Methods,* ed. Guadalupe Valdés, Anthony G. Lozano, Rodolfo García-Moya (New York: Teachers College, Columbia University, 1981), 3–20.

7. Spanish/English examples of borrowing and code-switching are drawn from Guadalupe Valdés-Fallis's book, *Code Switching and the Classroom Teacher* (Arlington, VA: Center for Applied Linguistics, 1978).

8. Valdés-Fallis, 1978, p. 7.

9. Valdés-Fallis, 1978, p. 16.

10. Sarah J. Hudelson. "Literacy development of second language children," in *Educating Second Language Children: The Whole Child, the Whole Curriculum, the Whole Community,* ed. Fred Genesee. (New York: Cambridge University Press, 1994), 130.

11. Sharon Nelson-Barber, "Phonological variations of Pima English." In *Language Renewal among American Indian Tribes: Issues, Problems and Prospects,* ed. Robert St. Clair and William Leap. (Rosslyn, VA: National Clearinghouse for Bilingual Education, 1982).

12. Cited in Shirley Brice Heath, *Ways with Words: Language, Life, and Work in Communities and Classrooms* (Cambridge and New York: Cambridge University Press, 1983).

13. S. Michaels and Courney B. Cazden, "Teacher-Child Collaboration on Oral Preparation for Literacy." In *The Acquisition of Literacy: Ethnographic Perspectives,* ed. Bambi B. Schieffelin and Perry Gilmore. (Norwood, NJ: Ablex, 1986).

14. R. Sims, "Dialect and Reading: Toward Redefining the Issues." In *Reader Meets Author / Bridging the Gap,* ed. Judith A. Langer and M. Trika Smith-Burke. (Newark, DE: International Reading Association, 1982).

15. Njabulo Ndebele, *South African Literature and Culture: Rediscovery of the Ordinary* (Manchester, England, and New York: Manchester University Press [distributed by St. Martin's Press]), 114.

The problem of society will also be the problem of the predominant language of that society. It is the carrier of its perception, its attitudes, and its goals, for through it, speakers absorb entrenched attitudes. The guilt of English then must be recognized and appreciated before its continued use can be advocated.

—Njabulo Ndebele[15]

PART SIX

RAGE, REGRET, AND RESISTANCE

Shifting how we think about language and how we use it necessarily alters how we know what we know. . . . I suggest that we do not necessarily need to hear and know what is stated in its entirety, that we do not need to 'master' or conquer the narrative as a whole, that we may know in fragments. I suggest that we may learn from spaces of silence as well as spaces of speech, that in the patient act of listening to another tongue . . . we may disrupt that cultural imperialism that suggests one is worthy of being heard only if one speaks in standard English.

—bell hooks

I Want to Write an American Poem II

Excerpt from an essay by Benjamin Alire Sáenz

There is no "degree zero" of culture, just as there is no "degree zero" of history.

—Eduardo Galeano

Several years ago, the Russian poet Joseph Brodsky came to visit our writing workshop at Stanford. When it came time to discuss the poem I had written, he remarked that my poem was the "most regrettable of the lot." One of the pieces of advice he gave me was to keep foreign languages out my poems, since I was working in an "English tradition." (I had used a childhood poem rendered in Spanish, since Spanish was the predominant language of my childhood.) He later went on to recite a poem with a Latin phrase in it. What Mr. Brodsky was objecting to was not my use of a foreign language per se, but my use of Spanish—a language that has not traditionally held an esteemed place in American letters—unlike Latin, Greek, and French. Clearly, in the "English tradition," some languages are more foreign than others. Mr. Brodsky also warned me about expressing my politics via my poetry. As it turns out, I came to the same conclusion as Brodsky regarding my poem—I eventually threw it out. But I have since spent a great deal of time pondering Brodsky's attitudes toward American 'poetics' (if that is what they are). Brodsky assumes that an American poet is *necessarily and by definition* working in the Anglo-American tradition. It never occurred to Brodsky that there are many literary and cultural traditions that coexist in America, and not every poet who writes "in English" is necessarily enamored of the Anglo-American tradition. Brodsky's attitude suggests that I set aside my culture, my working-class roots, and my bilingual heritage if I wish to be an American poet.

Brodsky asks the impossible. I cling to my culture because it is my memory—and what is a poet without memory? I cling to my culture because it is my skin, because it is my heart, because it is my voice, because it breathes my mother's mother's mother into me. My culture is the genesis and the center of my writing—the most authentic space I have to write from. I am blind without the lenses of my culture. Robert Frost's New England is not even a remote possibility for me, nor is Pablo Neruda's Isla Negra. Paterson, New Jersey, was no Paris, but it was a big enough place to give William Carlos Williams his wonderful and particular vision of the world—but Paterson is not my city. What I have is a desert—and it is all I have—and it is a big enough place to write from for a lifetime. Like every poet, I would like to be read and appreciated—and not just by other Chicanos. By refusing to write out of any other space, I run the risk of being labeled nothing more than an 'ethnic writer'—applauded by some for no other reason than my 'ethnicity' and held in contempt by others for the same reason.

This is the truth of the matter: I have no choice. I cannot write out of a white space, and this for the obvious reason that I am not white. It is true that my writing wears a sign: THIS POEM WAS WRITTEN BY A CHICANO, but it is also true that almost everything I read also wears a sign that ANNOUNCES ITS AUTHOR'S CULTURE, GENDER, AND CLASS. Robert Lowell's poetry is filled with his very male obsessions, his Yankee history, his Catholic/Puritan angst, his academic, formal training—none of these qualities validates or invalidates his poetry. Every writer has his obsessions, and there are very real personal, psychological, historical, and political backgrounds for those obsessions. My particular obsession is my culture—a culture less familiar to most audiences in the United States than Robert Lowell's, but no less 'American'.

Often, people do not read Chicano, Native American, or African-American poets because they are not interested in 'ethnic' subject matters. But, as a Chicano, I do not read non-Chicano poets merely because I am necessarily enamored of the cultures from which they come and which they represent, but because I am interested in learning about the different poetic traditions that form and inform the broader culture around me. If Wallace Stevens's formal verse is complex and formidable, is it honest to dismiss the poetry of Langston Hughes because it fails to meet Stevens's poetics? Hughes himself once said, "I believe that poetry should be direct, comprehensible, and the epitome of simplicity"—a far different goal from Stevens's—a goal I find completely genuine and admirable. Hughes attempted to develop a poetics that was based on the music and life of black culture—a poetry that included his own people as part of the audience for his work. He could not afford to ignore the racism confronting the circumstances of his people. This very knowledge became a part of his aesthetic. Hughes's position in society (a position defined by his 'blackness') became central to his poetics, just as Stevens's position in *his* culture was central to his formation as a poet. Like Stevens and Hughes, I too have a particular position vis-à-vis American culture, and it would be impossible to escape this position, even if I wanted to. I've learned to embrace the space out of which I write. It is a curse. But it is also a blessing.

Teaching New Worlds/New Words

bell hooks

Like desire, language disrupts, refuses to be contained within boundaries. It speaks itself against our will, in words and thoughts that intrude, even violate the most private spaces of mind and body. It was in my first year of college that I read Adrienne Rich's poem, "The Burning of Paper Instead of Children." That poem, speaking against domination, against racism and class oppression, attempts to illustrate graphically that stopping the political persecution and torture of living beings is a more vital issue than censorship, than burning books. One line of this poem that moved and disturbed something within me: "This is the oppressor's language yet I need it to talk to you." I've never forgotten it. Perhaps I could not have forgotten it even if I tried to erase it from memory. Words impose themselves, take root in our memory against our will. The words of this poem begat a life in my memory that I could not abort or change.

When I find myself thinking about language now, these words are there, as if they were always waiting to challenge and assist me. I find myself silently speaking them over and over again with the intensity of a chant. They startle me, shaking me into an awareness of the link between languages and domination. Initially, I resist the idea of the "oppressor's language," certain that this construct has the potential to disempower those of is who are just learning to speak, who are just learning to claim language as a place where we make ourselves subject. *"This is the oppressor's language yet I need it to talk to you."* Adrienne Rich's words. Then, when I first read these words, and now, they make me think of standard English, of learning to speak against black vernacular, against the ruptured and broken speech of a dispossessed and displaced people. Standard English is not the speech of exile. It is the language of conquest and domination; in the United States, it is the mask which hides the loss of so many tongues, all those sounds of diverse, native communities we will never hear, the speech of the Gullah, Yiddish, and so many other unremembered tongues.

Reflecting on Adrienne Rich's words, I know that it is not the English language that hurts me, but what the oppressors do with it, how they shape it to become a territory that limits and defines, how they make it a weapon that can shame, humiliate, colonize. Gloria Anzaldúa reminds us of this pain in *Borderlands/La Frontera* when she asserts, "So, if you want to really hurt me, talk badly about my language."* We have so little knowledge of how displaced, enslaved,

---

*See Gloria Anzaldúa's essay in part VI.

or free Africans who came or were brought against their will to the United States felt about the loss of language, about learning English. Only as a woman did I begin to think about these black people in relation to language, to think about their trauma as they were compelled to witness their language rendered meaningless with a colonizing European culture, where voices deemed foreign could not be spoken, were outlawed tongues, renegade speech. When I realize how long it has taken for white Americans to acknowledge the diverse languages of Native Americans, to accept that the speech their ancestral colonizers declared as merely grunts or gibberish was indeed *language*, it is difficult not to hear in Standard English always the sound of slaughter and conquest. I think now of the grief of displaced "homeless" Africans, forced to inhabit a world where they saw folks like themselves, inhabiting the same skin, the same condition, but who had no shared language to talk with one another, who needed "the oppressor's language." *"This is the oppressor's language yet I need it to talk to you."* When I imagine the terror of Africans on board slave ships, on auction blocks, inhabiting the unfamiliar architecture of plantations, I consider that this terror extended beyond fear of punishment, that it resided also in the anguish of hearing a language they could not comprehend. The very sound of English had to terrify. I think of black people meeting one another in a space away from the diverse cultures and languages that distinguished them from one another, compelled by circumstance to find ways to speak with one another in a "new world" where blackness or the darkness of one's skin and not language would become the space of bonding. How to remember, to reinvoke this terror. How to describe what it must have been like for Africans whose deepest bonds were historically forged in the place of shared speech to be transported abruptly to a world where the very sound of one's mother tongue had no meaning.

I imagine them hearing spoken English as the oppressor's language, yet I imagine them also realizing that this language would need to be possessed, taken, claimed as a space of resistance. I imagine that the moment they realized the oppressor's language, seized and spoken by tongues of the colonized, could be a space of bonding was joyous. For in that recognition was the understanding that intimacy could be restored, that a culture of resistance could be formed that would make recovery from the trauma of enslavement possible. I imagine, then, Africans first hearing English as "the oppressor's language" and then rehearing it as a potential site of resistance. Learning English, learning to speak the alien tongue, was one way enslaved Africans began to reclaim their personal power within a context of domination. Possessing a shared language, black folks could find again a way to make community, and a means to create the political solidarity necessary to resist.

Needing the oppressor's language to speak with one another they nevertheless also reinvented, remade that language so that it would speak beyond the boundaries of conquest and domination. In the mouths of black Africans in the so-called "New World," English was altered, transformed, and became a different speech. Enslaved black people took broken bits of English and made of them a counter-language. They put together their words in such a way that the colonizer had to rethink the meaning of English language. Though it has become common in contemporary culture to talk about the messages of resistance that emerged in the music created by slaves, particularly spirituals, less is said about the grammatical construction of sentences in these songs. Often, the English used in the song reflected the broken, ruptured world of the slave. When the slaves sang "nobody knows de trouble I see—" their usage of the word "nobody" adds a richer meaning than if they had used the phrase "no one," for it was the slaves *body* that was the concrete site of suffering. And even as emancipated black people sang spirituals, they did not change the language, the sentence structure, of our ancestors. For in the incorrect usage of words, in the incorrect placement of words, was a spirit of rebellion that claimed language as a site of resistance. Using English in a way that ruptured standard usage and meaning, so that white folks could often not understand black speech, made English into more than the oppressor's language.

An unbroken connection exists between the broken English of the displaced, enslaved African and the diverse black vernacular speech black folks use today. In both cases, the rupture of standard English enabled and enables rebellion and resistance. By transforming the oppressor's language, making a culture of resistance, black people created an intimate speech that could say far more than was permissible within the boundaries of standard English. The power of this speech is not simply that it enables resistance to white supremacy, but that it also forges a space for alternative cultural production and alternative epistemologies—different ways of thinking and knowing that were crucial to creating a counter-hegemonic worldview. It is absolutely essential that the revolutionary power of black vernacular speech not be lost in contemporary culture. That power resides in the capacity of black vernacular to intervene on the boundaries and limitations of standard English.

In contemporary black popular culture, rap music has become one of the spaces where black vernacular speech is used in a manner that invites dominant mainstream cultures to listen—to hear—and, to some extent, be transformed. However, one of the risks of this attempt at cultural translation is that it will trivialize black vernacular speech. When young white kids imitate this speech in ways that suggest it is the speech of those who are stupid or who are only interested in entertaining or being funny, then the subversive power of this speech is undermined. In academic circles, both in the sphere of teaching and that of writing, there has been little effort made to utilize black vernacular—or, for that matter, any language other than standard English. When I asked an ethnically diverse group of students in a course I was teaching on black women writers why we only hear standard English spoken in the classroom, they were momentarily rendered speechless. Though many of them were individuals for whom standard English was a second or third language, it had simply never occurred to them that it was possible to say something in another language, in another way. No wonder, then, that we continue to think, "This is the oppressor's language yet I need it to talk to you."

I have realized that I was in danger of losing my relationship to black vernacular speech because I too rarely use it in the predominantly white settings that I am most often in, both professionally and socially. And so I have begun to work at integrating into a variety of settings the particular Southern black vernacular speech I grew up hearing and speaking. It has been hardest to integrate black vernacular in writing, particularly for academic journals. When I first began to incorporate black vernacular in critical essays, editors would send the work back to me in standard English. Using the vernacular means that translation into standard English may be needed if one wishes to reach a more inclusive audience. In the classroom setting, I encourage students to use their first language and translate it so they do not feel that seeking higher education will necessarily estrange them from that language and culture they know most intimately. Not surprisingly, when students in my Black Women Writers class began to speak using diverse language and speech, white students often complained. This seemed particularly the case with black vernacular. It was particularly disturbing to the white students because they could hear the words that were said but could not comprehend their meaning. Pedagogically, I encouraged them to think of the moment of not understanding what someone says as a space to learn. Such a space provides not only the opportunity to listen without "mastery," without owning or possessing speech through interpretation, but also the experience of hearing non-English words. These lessons seem particularly crucial in a multicultural society that remains white supremacist, that uses standard English as a weapon to silence and censor. June Jordan reminds us of this in *On Call* when she declares:

> I am talking about majority problems of language in a democratic state, problems of a currency that someone has stolen and hidden away then homogenized into an official "English" language that can only express nonevents involving nobody responsible, or lies. If we lived in a democratic state our language would have to hurtle, fly, curse, and sing, in all the common American names, all the undeniable and representative participating voices of everybody here. We would not tolerate the language of the powerful and, thereby, lose all respect for words, per se. We would make our language conform to the truth of our many selves and we would make our language lead us into the equality of power that a democratic state must represent.

That the students in the course on black women writers were repressing all longing to speak in tongues other than standard English without seeing this repression as political was an indication of the way we act unconsciously, in complicity with a culture of domination.

Recent discussions of diversity and multiculturalism tend to downplay or ignore the question of language. Critical feminist writings focused on issues of difference and voice have made important theoretical interventions, calling for a recognition of the primacy of voices that are often silenced, censored, or marginalized. This call for the acknowledgment and celebration of diverse voices, and consequently diverse language and speech, necessarily disrupts the primacy of standard English. When advocates of feminism first spoke about the desire for diverse participation in women's movement, there was no discussion of language. It was simply assumed that standard English would remain the primary vehicle for the transmission of feminist thought. Now that the audience for feminist writing and speaking has become more diverse, it is evident that we must change conventional ways of thinking about language, creating spaces where diverse voices can speak in words other than English or in broken, vernacular speech. This means that at a lecture or even in a written work there will be fragments of speech that may or may not be accessible to every individual. Shifting how we think about language and how we use it necessarily alters how we know what we know. At a lecture where I might use Southern black vernacular, the particular patois of my region, or where I might use very abstract thought in conjunction with plain speech, responding to a diverse audience, I suggest that we do not necessarily need to hear and know what is stated in its entirety, that we do not need to "master" or conquer the narrative as a whole, that we may know in fragments. I suggest that we may learn from spaces of silence as well as spaces of speech, that in the patient act of listening to another tongue we may subvert that culture of capitalist frenzy and consumption that demands all desire must be satisfied immediately, or we may disrupt that cultural imperialism that suggests one is worthy of being heard only if one speaks in standard English.

Adrienne Rich concludes her poem with this statement:

I am composing on the typewriter late at night, thinking of today. How well we all spoke. A language is a map of our failures. Frederick Douglass wrote an English purer than Milton's. People suffer highly in poverty. There are methods but we do not use them. Joan, who could not read, spoke some peasant form of French. Some of the suffering are: it is hard to tell the truth; this is America; I cannot touch you now. In America we have only the present tense. I am in danger. You are in danger. The burning of a book arouses no sensation in me. I know it hurts to burn. There are flames of napalm in Catonsville, Maryland. I know it hurts to burn. The typewriter is overheated, my mouth is burning, I cannot touch you and this is the oppressor's language.

To recognize that we touch one another in language seems particularly difficult in a society that would have us believe that there is no dignity in the experience of passion, that to feel deeply is to be inferior, for within the dualism of Western metaphysical thought, ideas are always more important than language. To heal the splitting of mind and body, we marginalized and oppressed people attempt to recover ourselves and our experiences in language. We seek to make a place for intimacy. Unable to find such a place in standard English, we create the ruptured, broken, unruly speech of vernacular. When I need to say words that do more than simply mirror or address the dominant reality, I speak black vernacular. There, in that location, we make English do what we want it to do. We take the oppressor's language and turn it against itself. We make our words a counter-hegemonic speech, liberating ourselves in language.

Desmet, Idaho, March 1969

Janet Campbell Hale

At my father's wake,
The old people
     Knew me,
   Though I
     Knew them not,
And spoke to me
In our tribe's
Ancient tongue,
Ignoring
The fact
That I
Don't speak
The language,
And so
I listened
As if I understood
What it was all about,
And,
Oh,
How it
Stirred me
To hear again
That strange,
   Softly
   Flowing
Native tongue,
So
Familiar to
My childhood ear.

~

Speaking in Tongues: A Letter to 3rd World Women Writers

Excerpted from an essay by Gloria Anzaldúa

My dear *hermanas*, the dangers we face as women writers of color are not the same as those of white women though we have many in common. We don't have as much to lose—we never had any privileges. I wanted to call the dangers "obstacles" but that would be a kind of lying. We can't *transcend* the dangers, can't rise above them. We must go through them and hope we won't have to repeat the performance.

Unlikely to be friends of people in high literary places, the beginning woman of color is invisible both in the white male mainstream world and in the white women's feminist world, though in the latter this is gradually changing. The *lesbian* of color is not only invisible, she doesn't even exist. Our speech, too, is inaudible. We speak in tongues like the outcast and the insane.

Because white eyes do not want to know us, they do not bother to learn our language, the language which reflects us, our culture, our spirit. The schools we attended or didn't attend did not give us the skills for writing nor the confidence that we were correct in using our class and ethnic languages. I, for one, became adept at, and majored in English to spite, to show up, the arrogant racist teachers who thought all Chicano children were dumb and dirty. And Spanish was not taught in grade school. And Spanish was not required in High School. And though now I write my poems in Spanish as well as English I feel the rip-off of my native tongue.

> I *lack imagination* you say
> *No.* I lack language.
>
> The language to clarify
> my resistance to the literate.
> Words are a war to me.
> They threaten my family.
>
> To gain the word
> to describe the loss
> I risk losing everything.
> I may create a monster
> the word's length and body

swelling up colorful and thrilling
looming over my *mother*, characterized.
Her voice in the distance
unintelligible illiterate.

These are the monster's words.

—Cherríe Moraga*

Who gave us permission to perform the act of writing? Why does writing seem so unnatural for me? I'll do anything to postpone it—empty the trash, answer the telephone. The voice recurs in me: *Who am I, a poor Chicanita from the sticks, to think I could write?* How dare I even considered becoming a writer as I stooped over the tomato fields bending, bending under the hot sun, hands broadened and calloused, not fit to hold the quill, numbed into an animal stupor by the heat.

How hard it is for us to *think* we can choose to become writers, much less *feel* and *believe* that we can. What have we to contribute, to give? Our own expectations condition us. Does not our class, our culture as well as the white man tell us writing is not for women such as us?

The white man speaks: *Perhaps if you scrape the dark off of your face. Maybe if you bleach your bones. Stop speaking in tongues, stop writing left-handed. Don't cultivate your colored skins nor tongues of fire if you want to make it in a right-handed world.*

---

*Cherríe Moraga, excerpt from "It's the Poverty," *Loving in the War Years: lo que nunca pasó por sus labios* (Cambridge, MA: South End Press, 2000), 54–55.

Two Languages in Mind, but Just One in the Heart

Louise Erdrich

For years now I have been in love with a language other than the English in
which I write, and it is a rough affair. Every day I try to learn a little more
Ojibwe. I have taken to carrying verb conjugation charts in my purse, along
with the tiny notebook I've always kept for jotting down book ideas, overheard conversations, language detritus, phrases that pop into my head. Now
that little notebook includes an increasing volume of Ojibwe words. My
English is jealous, my Ojibwe elusive. Like a besieged unfaithful lover, I'm
trying to appease them both.

Ojibwemowin, or Anishinabemowin, the Chippewa language, was last spoken in our family by Patrick Gourneau, my maternal grandfather, a Turtle
Mountain Ojibwe who used it mainly in his prayers. Growing up off reservation, I thought Ojibwemowin mainly was a language for prayers, like Latin in
the Catholic liturgy. I was unaware for many years that Ojibwemowin was
spoken in Canada, Minnesota and Wisconsin, though by a dwindling number
of people. By the time I began to study the language, I was living in New
Hampshire, so for the first few years I used language tapes.

I never learned more than a few polite phrases that way, but the sound of
the language in the author Basil Johnson's calm and dignified Anishinabe voice
sustained me through bouts of homesickness. I spoke basic Ojibwe in the isolation of my car traveling here and there on twisting New England roads. Back
then, as now, I carried my tapes everywhere.

The language bit deep into my heart, but it was an unfulfilled longing. I had
nobody to speak it with, nobody who remembered my grandfather's standing
with his sacred pipe in the woods next to a box elder tree, talking to the spirits.
Not until I moved back to the Midwest and settled in Minneapolis did I find
a fellow Ojibweg to learn with, and a teacher.

Mille Lac's Ojibwe elder Jim Clark—Naawi-giizis, or Center of the
Day—is a magnetically pleasant, sunny, crew-cut World War II veteran with a
mysterious kindliness that shows in his slightest gesture. When he laughs,
everything about him laughs; and when he is serious, his eyes round like a
boy's.

Naawi-giizis introduced me to the deep intelligence of the language and
forever set me on a quest to speak it for one reason: I want to get the jokes. I
also want to understand the prayers and the adisookaanug, the sacred stories,
but the irresistible part of language for me is the explosion of hilarity that

attends every other minute of an Ojibwe visit. As most speakers are now bilingual, the language is spiked with puns on both English and Ojibwe, most playing on the oddness of gichi-mookomaan, that is, big knife or American, habits and behavior.

This desire to deepen my alternate language puts me in an odd relationship to my first love, English. It is, after all, the language stuffed into my mother's ancestors' mouths. English is the reason she didn't speak her native language and the reason I can barely limp along in mine. English is an all-devouring language that has moved across North America like the fabulous plagues of locusts that darkened the sky and devoured even the handles of rakes and hoes. Yet the omnivorous nature of a colonial language is a writer's gift. Raised in the English language, I partake of a mongrel feast.

A hundred years ago most Ojibwe people spoke Ojibwemowin, but the Bureau of Indian Affairs and religious boarding schools punished and humiliated children who spoke native languages. The program worked, and there are now almost no fluent speakers of Ojibwe in the United States under the age of 30. Speakers like Naawi-giizis value the language partly because it has been physically beaten out of so many people. Fluent speakers have had to fight for the language with their own flesh, have endured ridicule, have resisted shame and stubbornly pledged themselves to keep on talking the talk.

My relationship is of course very different. How do you go back to a language you never had? Why should a writer who loves her first language find it necessary and essential to complicate her life with another? Simple reasons, personal and impersonal. In the past few years I've found that I can talk to God only in this language, that somehow my grandfather's use of the language penetrated. The sound comforts me.

What the Ojibwe call the Gizhe Manidoo, the great and kind spirit residing in all that lives, what the Lakota call the Great Mystery, is associated for me with the flow of Ojibwemowin. My Catholic training touched me intellectually and symbolically but apparently never engaged my heart.

There is also this: Ojibwemowin is one of the few surviving languages that evolved to the present here in North America. The intelligence of this language is adapted as no other to the philosophy bound up in northern land, lakes, rivers, forests, arid plains; to the animals and their particular habits; to the shades of meaning in the very placement of stones. As a North American writer it is essential to me that I try to understand our human relationship to place in the deepest way possible, using my favorite tool, language.

There are place names in Ojibwe and Dakota for every physical feature of Minnesota, including recent additions like city parks and dredged lakes. Ojibwemowin is not static, not confined to describing the world of some out-of-reach and sacred past. There are words for e-mail, computers, Internet, fax.

For exotic animals in zoos. Anaamibiig gookoosh, the underwater pig, is a hippopotamus. Nandookomeshiinh, the lice hunter, is the monkey.

There are words for the serenity prayer used in 12-step programs and translations of nursery rhymes. The varieties of people other than Ojibwe or Anishinabe are also named: Aiibiishaabookewininiwag, the tea people, are Asians. Agongosininiwag, the chipmunk people, are Scandinavians. I'm still trying to find out why.

For years I saw only the surface of Ojibwemowin. With any study at all one looks deep into a stunning complex of verbs. Ojibwemowin is a language of verbs. All action. Two-thirds of the words are verbs, and for each verb there are as many as 6,000 forms. The storm of verb forms makes it a wildly adaptive and powerfully precise language. Changite-ige describes the way a duck tips itself up in the water butt first. There is a word for what would happen if a man fell off a motorcycle with a pipe in his mouth and the stem of it went through the back of his head. There can be a verb for anything.

When it comes to nouns, there is some relief. There aren't many objects. With a modest if inadvertent political correctness, there are no designations of gender in Ojibwemowin. There are no feminine or masculine possessives or articles.

Nouns are mainly designated as alive or dead, animate or inanimate. The word for stone, asin, is animate. Stones are called grandfathers and grandmothers and are extremely important in Ojibwe philosophy. Once I began to think of stones as animate, I started to wonder whether I was picking up a stone or it was putting itself into my hand. Stones are not the same as they were to me in English. I can't write about a stone without considering it in Ojibwe and acknowledging that the Anishinabe universe began with a conversation between stones.

Ojibwemowin is also a language of emotions; shades of feeling can be mixed like paints. There is a word for what occurs when your heart is silently shedding tears. Ojibwe is especially good at describing intellectual states and the fine points of moral responsibility.

Ozozamenimaa pertains to a misuse of one's talents getting out of control. Ozozamichige implies you can still set things right. There are many more kinds of love than there are in English. There are myriad shades of emotional meaning to designate various family and clan members. It is a language that also recognizes the humanity of a creaturely God, and the absurd and wondrous sexuality of even the most deeply religious beings.

Slowly the language has crept into my writing, replacing a word here, a concept there, beginning to carry weight. I've thought of course of writing stories in Ojibwe, like a reverse Nabokov. With my Ojibwe at the level of a dreamy 4-year-old child's, I probably won't.

Though it was not originally a written language, people simply adapted the English alphabet and wrote phonetically. During the Second World War, Naawi-giizis wrote Ojibwe letters to his uncle from Europe. He spoke freely about his movements, as no censor could understand his writing. Ojibwe orthography has recently been standardized. Even so, it is an all-day task for me to write even one paragraph using verbs in their correct arcane forms. And even then, there are so many dialects of Ojibwe that, for many speakers, I'll still have gotten it wrong.

As awful as my own Ojibwe must sound to a fluent speaker, I have never, ever, been greeted with a moment of impatience or laughter. Perhaps people wait until I've left the room. But more likely, I think, there is an urgency about attempting to speak the language. To Ojibwe speakers the language is a deeply loved entity. There is a spirit or an originating genius belonging to each word.

Before attempting to speak this language, a learner must acknowledge these spirits with gifts of tobacco and food. Anyone who attempts Ojibwemowin is engaged in something more than learning tongue twisters. However awkward my nouns, unstable my verbs, however stumbling my delivery, to engage in the language is to engage the spirit. Perhaps that is what my teachers know, and what my English will forgive.

Mi Problema

Michele M. Serros

My sincerity isn't good enough.
Eyebrows raise
when I request: *"Hable más despacio, por favor."**
My skin is brown
just like theirs,
but now I'm unworthy of the color
'cause I don't speak Spanish
the way I should.
Then they laugh and talk about
mi problema
in the language I stumble over.

A white person gets encouragement,
praise,
for weak attempts at a second language.
"Maybe he wants to be brown
like us."
and that is good.

My earnest attempts
make me look bad,
dumb.
"Perhaps she wanted to be white
like THEM."
and that is bad.

I keep my flash cards hidden
a practice cassette tape
not labeled
'cause I am ashamed.
I "should know better"
they tell me
"Spanish is in your blood."

---

*Hable más despacio, por favor 'Speak slower to me, please'.

I search for S.S.L. classes,
(Spanish as a second language)
in college catalogs
and practice
with my grandma.
who gives me patience,
permission to learn.

And then one day,
I'll be a perfected "r" rolling
tilde using Spanish speaker.
A true Mexican at last!

∽

Linguistic Terrorism

Excerpt from an essay by Gloria Anzaldúa

Deslenguadas. Somos los del español deficiente. We are your linguistic nightmare, your linguistic aberration, your linguistic *mestizaje*, the subject of your *burla*. Because we speak with tongues of fire we are culturally crucified. Racially, culturally and linguistically *somos huérfanos*—we speak an orphan tongue.*

Chicanas who grew up speaking Chicano Spanish have internalized the belief that we speak poor Spanish. It is illegitimate, a bastard language. And because we internalize how our language has been used against us by the dominant culture, we use our language differences against each other.

Chicana feminists often skirt around each other with suspicion and hesitation. For the longest time I couldn't figure it out. Then it dawned on me. To be close to another Chicana is like looking into the mirror. We are afraid of what we'll see there. *Pena.* Shame. Low estimation of self. In childhood we are told that our language is wrong. Repeated attacks on our native tongue diminish our sense of self. The attacks continue throughout our lives.†

Chicanas feel uncomfortable talking in Spanish to Latinas, afraid of their censure. Their language was not outlawed in their countries. They had a whole lifetime of being immersed in their native tongue; generations, centuries in which Spanish was a first language, taught in school, heard on radio and TV, and read in the newspaper.

If a person, Chicana or Latina, has a low estimation of my native tongue, she also has a low estimation of me. Often with *mexicanas y latinas* we'll speak English as a neutral language. Even among Chicanas we tend to speak English at parties or conferences. Yet, at the same time, we're afraid the other will think we're *agringadas* because we don't speak Chicano Spanish.‡ We oppress each other trying to out-Chicano each other, vying to be the "real" Chicanas, to speak like Chicanos. There is no one Chicano language just as there is no one Chicano experience. A monolingual Chicana whose first language is English or Spanish is just as much a Chicana as one who speaks several variants of Spanish. A Chicana from Michigan or Chicago or Detroit is just as much a Chicana

---

*Editor's translations: *Deslenguadas. Somos los del español deficiente.* 'Those with tongues cut out. We are the ones with deficient Spanish.' *mestizaje* 'mixing of European and American races', *burla* 'ridicule', *Somos huérfanos* 'We are orphans'.

†*Pena* 'shame'.

‡*Agringada*, derogatory term for 'Anglicized, acculturated'.

as one from the Southwest. Chicano Spanish is as diverse linguistically as it is regionally.

By the end of this century, Spanish speakers will comprise the biggest minority group in the U.S., a country where students in high schools and colleges are encouraged to take French classes because French is considered more "cultured." But for a language to remain alive it must be used. By the end of this century English, and not Spanish, will be the mother tongue of most Chicanos and Latinos.

So, if you want to really hurt me, talk badly about my language. Ethnic identity is twin skin to linguistic identity—I am my language. Until I can take pride in my language, I cannot take pride in myself. Until I can accept as legitimate Chicano Texas Spanish, Tex-Mex and all other languages I speak, I cannot accept the legitimacy of myself. Until I am free to write bilingually and to switch codes without having always to translate, while I still have to speak English or Spanish when I would rather speak Spanglish, and as long as I have to accommodate the English speakers rather then having them accommodate me, my tongue will be illegitimate.

I will no longer be made to feel ashamed of existing. I will have my voice: Indian, Spanish, white. I will have my serpent's tongue—my woman's voice, my sexual voice, my poet's voice. I will overcome the tradition of silence.

I Recognize You

Rosario Morales

I recognize you. Spitting out four, five, six-syllable English words, your tongue turning a tight grammatical sentence, flipping adjectives and adverbs into line faster than you can say *Oxford Unabridged Dictionary* and pinning all of it in place with commas, colons, semicolons, and parentheses.

You were the one I couldn't beat at spelling bees, the other girl who got *A* in grammar two semesters in a row. You're the one who went on to college, or maybe didn't, but took classes after work, who reads and reads and worries whether you're reading enough or the right thing.

I know without meeting you that you're working class, or a woman of color, or an immigrant, or child of immigrants. That you keep your mama language for the kitchen, hardly ever pronounce it in public, never on the written page.

You're proud. You've done this by yourself, or with your family behind you. And I'm impressed. You can make the English language roll over, bark on command, sit up and beg, you—who were raised on spuds, grits, rice, or tortillas.

But I'm sad, too. For the English language robbed of the beat your home talk could give it, the words you could lend, the accent, the music, the word-order reordering, the grammatical twist. I'm sad for you, too, for the shame with which you store away—hide—a whole treasure box of other, mother, language. It's too rough-mannered you say, too strange, too exotic, too untutored, too low class.

You're robbing us, robbing the young one saying her first sentence, reading her first book, writing her first poem. You're confirming her scorn of her cradle tongue. You're robbing her of a fine brew of language, a stew of words and ways that could inspire her to self-loving invention.

And you're robbing yourself . . . no, we're robbing ourselves, of selfness, of wholeness, of the joys of writing with *all* our words, of the sound of your Mama's voice, my Papa's voice, of the smell of the kitchen on the page.

The New World

Eva Hoffman

If all neurosis is a form of repression, then surely, the denial of suffering, and of helplessness, is also a form of neurosis. Surely, all our attempts to escape sorrow twist themselves into the specific, acrid pain of self-suppression. And if that is so, then a culture that insists on cheerfulness and staying in control is a culture that—in one of those ironies that prevails in the unruly realm of the inner life—propagates its own kind of pain.

Perhaps perversely, I sometimes wish for that older kind of suffering—the capacity and the time for a patient listening to the winds of love and hate that can blow you like a reed, for that long descent into yourself in which you touch bottom and recognize the poor, two-forked creature that we all are.

For me, therapy is partly translation therapy, the talking cure a second-language cure. My going to a shrink is, among other things, a rite of initiation: initiation into the language of the subculture within which I happen to live, into a way of explaining myself to myself. But gradually, it becomes a project of translating backward. The way to jump over my Great Divide is to crawl backward over it in English. It's only when I retell my whole story, back to the beginning, and from the beginning onward, in one language, that I can reconcile the voices within me with each other; it is only then that the person who judges the voices and tells the stories begins to emerge.

The tiny gap that opened when my sister and I were given new names can never be fully closed up; I can't have one name again. My sister has returned to her Polish name—Alina. It takes a while for me to switch back to it; Alina, in English, is a different word than it is in Polish: it has the stamp of the unusual, its syllables don't fall as easily on an English speaker's tongue. In order to transport a single word without distortion, one would have to transport the entire language around it. My sister no longer has one, authentic name, the name that is inseparable from her single essence.

When I talk to myself now, I talk in English. English is the language in which I've become an adult, in which I've seen my favorite movies and read my favorite novels, and sung along with Janis Joplin records. In Polish, whole provinces of adult experience are missing. I don't know Polish words for "microchips," or "pathetic fallacy," or *The Importance of Being Earnest*. If I tried talking to myself in my native tongue, it would be a stumbling conversation indeed, interlaced with English expressions.

So at those moments when I am alone, walking, or letting my thoughts meander before falling asleep, the internal dialogue proceeds in English. I no longer triangulate to Polish as to an authentic criterion, no longer refer back to it as to a point of origin. Still, underneath the relatively distinct monologue, there's an even more interior buzz, as of countless words compressed into an electric blur moving along a telephone wire. Occasionally, Polish words emerge unbidden from the buzz. They are usually words from the primary palette of feeling: "I'm so happy," a voice says with bell-like clarity, or "Why does he want to harm her?" The Polish phrases have roundness and a surprising certainty, as if they were announcing the simple truth.

Occasionally, the hum makes minute oscillations. "I'm learning a lot about intimacy in this relationship," I tell myself sternly, and a barely discernible presence whispers, pianissimo, I love him, that's all. . . . "The reason he's so territorial is because he's insecure," I think of a difficult colleague, and an imp of the perverse says, "Well, simply, he's a bastard. . . ." But I'm less likely to say the latter to my American friends, and therefore the phrase has a weaker life. In order to translate a language, or a text, without changing its meaning, one would have to transport its audience as well.

No, there's no returning to the point of origin, no regaining of childhood unity. Experience creates style, and style, in turn, creates a new woman. Polish is no longer the one, true language against which others live their secondary life. Polish insights cannot be regained in their purity; there's something I know in English too. The wholeness of childhood truths is intermingled with the divisiveness of adult doubt. When I speak Polish now, it is infiltrated, permeated, and inflected by the English in my head. Each language modifies the other, crossbreeds with it, fertilizes it. Each language makes the other relative. Like everybody, I am the sum of my languages—the language of my family and childhood, and education and friendship, and love, and the larger, changing world—though perhaps I tend to be more aware than most of the fractures between them, and of the building blocks. The fissures sometimes cause me pain, but in a way, they're how I know that I'm alive. Suffering and conflict are the best proof that there's something like a psyche, a soul; or else, what is it that suffers? Why would we need to suffer when fed and warm and out of the rain, were it not for that other entity within us making its odd, unreasonable, never fulfillable demands?

But in my translation therapy, I keep going back and forth over the rifts, not to heal them but to see that I—one person, first-person singular—have been on both sides. Patiently, I use English as a conduit to go back and down; all the way down to childhood, almost to the beginning. When I learn to say those smallest, first things in the language that has served for detachment and irony and abstraction, I begin to see where the languages I've spoken have their correspondences—how I can move between them without being split by the difference.

The gap cannot be fully closed, but I begin to trust English to speak my childhood self as well, to say what has so long been hidden, to touch the tenderest spots. Perhaps any language, if pursued far enough, leads to exactly the same place. And so, while therapy offers me instruments and the vocabulary of self-control, it also becomes, in the long run, a route back to that loss which for me is the model of all loss, and to that proper sadness of which children are never really afraid; in English, I wind my way back to my old, Polish melancholy. When I meet it, I reenter myself, fold myself again in my own skin. I'm cured of the space sickness of transcendence. It is possible that when we travel deep enough, we always encounter an element of sadness, for full awareness of ourselves always includes the knowledge of our own ephemerality and the passage of time. But it is only in that knowledge—not its denial—that things gain their true dimensions, and we begin to feel the simplicity of being alive. It is only that knowledge that is large enough to cradle a tenderness for everything that is always to be lost—a tenderness for each of our moments, for others and for the world.

The gap has also become a chink, a window through which I can observe the diversity of the world. The apertures of perception have widened because they were once pried apart. Just as the number "2" implies all other numbers, so a bivalent consciousness is necessarily a multivalent consciousness.

Multivalence is no more than the condition of a contemporary awareness, and no more than the contemporary world demands. The weight of the world used to be vertical: it used to come from the past, or from the hierarchy of heaven and earth and hell; now it's horizontal, made up of the endless multiplicity of events going on at once and pressing at each moment on our minds and our living rooms. Dislocation is the norm rather than the aberration in our time, but even in the unlikely event that we spend an entire lifetime in one place, the fabulous diverseness with which we live reminds us constantly that we are no longer the norm or the center, that there is no one geographic center pulling the world together and glowing with the allure of the real thing; there are, instead, scattered nodules competing for our attention. New York, Warsaw, Tehran, Tokyo, Kabul—they all make claims on our imaginations, all remind us that in a decentered world we are always simultaneously in the center and on the periphery, that every competing center makes us marginal.

It may be only in my daily consciousness of this that the residue of my sudden expulsion remains. All immigrants and exiles know the peculiar restlessness of an imagination that can never again have faith in its own absoluteness. "Only exiles are truly irreligious," a contemporary philosopher has said. Because I have learned the relativity of cultural meanings on my skin, I can never take any one set of meanings as final. I doubt that I'll ever become an ideologue of any stripe; I doubt that I'll become an avid acolyte of any school of thought. I know that I've been written in a variety of languages; I know to what extent I'm a script. In my public, group life, I'll probably always find myself in the chinks between cultures and subcultures, between the scenarios of political beliefs and aesthetic credos. It's not the worst place to live; it gives you an Archimedean leverage from which to see the world.

I'm writing a story in my journal, and I'm searching for a true voice. I make my way through layers of acquired voices, silly voices, sententious voices, voices that are too cool and too overheated. Then they all quiet down, and I reach what I'm searching for: silence. I hold still to steady myself in it. This is the white blank center, the level ground that was there before Babel was built, that is always there before the Babel of our multiple selves is constructed. From this white plenitude, a voice begins to emerge: it's an even voice, and it's capable of saying things straight, without exaggeration or triviality. As the story progresses, the voice grows and diverges into different tonalities and timbres; sometimes, spontaneously, the force of feeling or of thought compresses language into metaphor, or an image, in which words and consciousness are magically fused. But the voice always returns to its point of departure, to ground zero.

This is the point to which I have tried to triangulate, this private place, this unassimilable part of myself. We all need to find this place in order to know that we exist not only within culture but also outside it. We need to triangulate to something—the past, the future, our own untamed perceptions, another place—if we're not to be subsumed by the temporal and temporary ideas of our time, if we're not to become creatures of ephemeral fashion. Perhaps finding such a point of calibration is particularly difficult now, when our collective air is oversaturated with trivial and important and contradictory and mutually canceling messages. And yet, I could not have found this true axis, could not have made my way through the maze, if I had not assimilated and mastered the voices of my time and place—the only language through which we can learn to think and speak. The silence that comes out of inarticulateness is the inchoate and desperate silence of chaos. The silence that comes after words is the fullness from which the truth of our perceptions can crystallize. It's only after I've taken in disparate bits of cultural matter, after I've accepted its seductions and its snares, that I can make my way through the medium of language to distill my own meanings; and it's only coming from the ground up that I can hit the tenor of my own sensibility, hit home.

"Hello, silly little Polish person," Miriam says, greeting me at the Boston airport.

"Good grief, it's good to see you," I say.

"Is the article done so we can play tomorrow?"

"Almost, almost," I say. "How's the mood?"

"Oh, the mood," she says. "The mood has its moods."

"How has Tom been this week?" I ask, as we get into her car.

"Quite well behaved," she says briskly, and we smile. "Except for an unfortunately regressive episode yesterday. . . . Well, I'll tell you tomorrow. I've scheduled two hours of uninterrupted conversation after breakfast."

"Great," I say, and walk into her house, and into "my" room, where I've stayed over the years.

"You wouldn't guess who called me this week," I say as I hang up my clothes. "Ricky."

"No," Miriam says. "Where was he calling from?"

"Well, you wouldn't guess that either. London. Can you see Ricky in London? Except he seems to be doing very well. He's in some high-tech optics business, and he's managed to be married and divorced twice since we last saw him, and now he's married again and terribly in love. I guess that means he's doing well, right?"

"Good God, who knows what it means?" Miriam says. "It's certainly getting harder to keep up with one's friends. I wonder if we're going to meet this new individual he's married to."

We meander like this for a while; we know that tomorrow we'll go into various items in greater depth, that we'll register the most minute developments in our lives and circle around them until they yield some insight, or at least a few satisfactory remarks. We've carried on this conversation for a long time now, through our respective affairs, marriages, divorces, work crises, the composition of short stories, political disagreements, and indecisions about our fall wardrobes.

We've known each other for nearly twenty years, as occasionally we're wont to remind each other. This simple fact continues to astonish us partly because we're of a generation that was supposed to stay forever young, and a friendship that long demonstrates indisputably that we too are subject to the passage of time; it continues to amaze us because, after all, Miriam is from St. Louis, and I from Cracow, and our friendship sometimes seems as fortuitous and unlikely as that comical and incongruous distance suggests. For me, there is an additional jolt: so I've been here this long.

Well, yes. I've been here this long. I have a whole American past, extended enough to produce its own repetitions and recurrences: on the radio, songs that I'd first heard as wild, grunting sounds now have the mellow quaintness of something that summons one's youth; boyfriends resurface to replay former relationships at speeded-up tempo; I go back to Houston, where I hadn't been in years, and where I walk around the Rice campus with a double sense of surprise and recognition. These repetitions give my American life heft and substance, the weight of reality. Those who don't understand the past may be condemned to repeat it, but those who never repeat it are condemned not to understand it. The one-night stand, or the motel in which we stop on the periphery of a town we don't know, the job at which we once spent five months, and which doesn't fit on our curriculum vitae—such passing, isolated events can give us the brief excitement of stepping outside the fabric of ordinary meaning; but they also leave behind the gloominess of evanescence, the flat aftertaste of meaninglessness.

As long as the world around me has been new each time, it has not become my world; I lived with my teeth clenched against the next assault of the unfamiliar. But now, the year has assumed an understandable sequence within which I play the variations of a professional New York life. The social world in which I move has comprehensible elements and dimensions. I am no longer mystified by the rules and rituals of friendship and of love. It is only within such frames and patterns that any one moment is intelligible, that stimulus transforms itself into experience and movement into purpose. And it is only within an intelligible human context that a face can become dear, a person known. Pattern is the soil of significance; and it is surely one of the hazards of emigration, and exile, and extreme mobility, that one is uprooted from that soil.

Over the years, I have learned to read the play of wit and feeling and intelligence on Miriam's face, which at first seemed to me flat and impassive. I've learned to trust the subtlety of her judgments, and I can distinguish the quarter tones of happiness and unhappiness within the intonations of her urbane, civilized talk. I know when she's dissimulating, for her own or my benefit, and through this knowledge I can also detect her truths. I can triangulate from her concealments and confessions to what she feels. To some extent, I've assimilated the tenor of her mind and the accents of her speech, and sometimes, I recognize the phrases I've used in her conversation. It's difficult to tell the truth to another person. The self is a complicated mechanism, and to speak it forth honestly requires not only sincerity but the agility to catch insight on the wing and the artistry to give it accurate words. It also requires a listener who can catch our nuances as they fly by. Spoken truth shrivels when it falls on a tin ear. But Miriam and I have been each other's highly attentive listeners. We've woven intricate designs for each other, and have subjected them to close mutual investigation. To a large extent, we're the keepers of each other's stories, and the shape of these stories has unfolded in part from our interwoven accounts. Human beings don't only search for meanings, they are themselves units of meaning; but we can mean something only within the fabric of larger significations. Miriam is one of the people through whom I've gained a meaning here. Starting so far apart, we have, through painstaking back and forth, forged a language in common. We keep describing the flow of experience to each other with the impetus to truth, and thus we keep creating new maps and tapestries of a shared reality.

The sense of the future returns like a benediction, to balance the earlier annunciation of loss. It returns in the simplest of ways: in an image of a crooked Paris street, where I'll go on my vacation, or in a peaceful picture of myself, at my desk, writing. Quiet, modest images light up the forward trajectory, and these flickers that suppose a pleasurable extension in time feel very much like hope.

Psychological pleasure or unpleasure is, I think, channeled in time, as physical pain or satisfaction runs along the conduits of our nerves. When time compresses and shortens, it strangles pleasure; when it diffuses itself into aimlessness, the self thins out into affectless torpor. Pleasure exists in middle time, in time that is neither too accelerated or too slowed down.

For quite a while I've woken up tensed, coiled against the next disaster, right up against the wall of a possible end. But now, a succession of tomorrows begins to exfoliate like a faith.

It seems a tremendous, Pascalian gamble, this leap into the future, into the moving stream. It means, after all, that I give up on trying to stop time, trying to keep that ship from moving away from the Baltic shore, and that I begin to greet whatever awaits me willingly. When I image, imagine, those shimmers of nonexistent possibility suspended on a thread of purely mental light, time expands and creates a breathing space in which sensations can be savored, as I once savored the churning butter or the minor triad. If images, as some philosophers theorize, congeal out of the matrix of language, then perhaps I've had to wait to have enough linguistic concentrate for hope to arise. Or perhaps I've had to gather enough knowledge of my new world to trust it, and enough affection for it to breathe life into it, to image it forth. But once time uncoils and regains its forward dimension, the present moment becomes a fulcrum on which I can stand more lightly, balanced between the past and the future, balanced in time.

⌒

"Azalea, hyacinth, forsythia, delphinium," Miriam says, pointing at the flowers with a mock-didactic gesture. "I'm going to make you feel at home in the New World." I look at the flowers; some of them I've never seen before; some names I've read but haven't put together with the flowers themselves. This is the kind of thing that comes latest in my strange building of the language from the roof down. "Azalea," I repeat. "Forsythia, delphinium." The names are beautiful, and they fit the flowers perfectly. They are the flowers, these particular flowers in this Cambridge garden. For now, there are no Platonic azaleas, no Polish hyacinths against which these are compared. I breathe in the fresh spring air. Right now, this is the place where I'm alive. How could there be any other place? Be here now, I think to myself in the faintly ironic tones in which the phrase is uttered by the likes of me. Then the phrase dissolves. The brilliant colors are refracted by the sun. The small space of the garden expands into the dimensions of peace. Time pulses through my blood like a river. The language of this is sufficient. I am here now.

I Want to Write an American Poem III

Excerpt from an essay by Benjamin Alire Sáenz

When my mother was in the ninth grade, she was awarded a medal for out-standing academic achievement. A few years ago, she handed me her medal. It reads, "For God and Country." That same year she dropped out of school to help support her large family because her mother was sick. At fifteen she became a maid and part-time mother to her brothers and sisters. My father experienced such racism in West Texas that he still says bitterly, "I wouldn't shit in the best part of Texas." In the early 1960s what passed for plumbing in the "house" I lived in was one pipe that brought in cold water. My mother would rise in the morning and heat water to scrub us before we went to school. I sometimes still feel her washcloth rubbing my skin raw. She wanted us to be clean; she would not have her children be called "dirty." I am not likely to privilege what I have learned in educational institutions over the experiences of my family. For too many years I have seen the cycle of poverty of our peo-ple. All of my life I have seen more wasted minds and lives than Allen Ginsberg ever dreamed of seeing. I could launch into full and graphic descriptions—to do so would be to utter an endless litany of despair. I write to fight despair.

Though I work in language, language is not my primary concern (which is not to say that I am disconnected from and unconcerned about the language I work in—the words I choose). According to Alexander Pope, "Language is the dress of thought." I have always struggled to "dress" my thoughts appro-priately. When I say that language is not my main concern, I am not implying that I do not pay attention to sound, rhythms, line breaks, imagery, metaphors, similes, and the rest of the poetic and literary devices available to me as a poet—this goes without saying. No poet is exempt from learning his craft. No artist is exempt from immersing himself in his discipline. But it should be remembered that a poet ought to be judged according to his own particular tradition. It is disingenuous, inappropriate, and chauvinistic to judge the poetry of the indigenous peoples of the Americas by the poetic standards of English culture. (In the United States, the English literary tradition has been con-structed as the central poetic tradition—but it is not central to many poets who find that particular tradition culturally and artistically foreign.) I am primarily concerned—perhaps even obsessed—with the desire to write the unwritten into history—into time. We have bled. We have died unnecessarily. We have lived. *We live now.* We are worthy of being represented in history, in art, in poetry (and not merely assigned to be studied by cultural anthropologists and social scientists).

In Joyce's *A Portrait of the Artist as a Young Man*, Stephen Dedalus is speaking to an *English* Jesuit. As he does so, he reflects about this relationship to the English language because of his Irishness. He writes:

> The language in which we are speaking is his before it is mine. How different are the words *home*, *Christ*, *ale*, *master*, on his lips and on mine! I cannot speak or write these words without unrest of spirit. His language, so familiar and so foreign, will always be for me an acquired speech. I have not made or accepted its words. My voice holds them at bay. My soul frets in the shadow of his language.

My soul, too, frets in the shadow of those who take for granted their ownership of the English language. Because the language of my family was Spanish and not English, I have always had an ambivalent relationship to the language of my country. The language I am writing in will always be someone else's before it is mine. English was the language of my education; it was the language of power—of empowerment—of intelligence. To speak Spanish, when I entered grade school in 1960, was to be dumb in every sense of that word. If "in the beginning was the word," then the word belonged to the gods who spoke English. The word was not mine—the word was the possession of the gringo. It was my task as a student to receive the word and, having received it, to forget the language of the home. But to erase a language is to erase a culture. We were treated as inferior and we knew it, though we did not know the word "inferior." We learned shame early, and despite my mother's efforts we *were* looked upon as dirty.

But a child knows more than he can say in language. James Baldwin spoke for many when he wrote:

> All this enters the child's consciousness much sooner than we as adults would like to think it does. As adults, we are easily fooled because we are anxious to be fooled. But children are very different. . . . They don't have the vocabulary to express what they see, and we, their elders, know how to intimidate them very easily and very soon. But a black child, looking out at the world around him, though he cannot quite know what to make of it, is aware there is a reason why his mother works so hard, why his father is always on the edge. . . . He is aware that there is some terrible weight on his parents' shoulders which menaces him. And it isn't long—in fact it begins when he is in school—before he discovers the shape of oppression.

A child senses all the splits of his universe though he cannot give them names. Often, he does not even learn the names of the many oppressions and inequalities from the adults around him because the adults are all trying very hard to deny that they exist. Silence is a difficult habit to break. I did not have a word for racism and cultural domination until I was much older—and even then, I first thought it applied only to what whites felt for blacks. It was only much later that I understood that in southern New Mexico, it was we who were the blacks.

$\sim$

Speaking Spanglish

Abby Figueroa

Hace un año tuve una discusión con un amigo que insistía que si yo no podía hablar el español absolutamente correcta, mejor que me quedara expresándome en inglés. Él siempre había hablado español en su casa. Por contrario yo estaba acostumbrada a oír y hablar dos idiomas todo el tiempo. Él hablaba perfectamente los dos idiomas sin olvidar las reglas de gramática o el vocabulario.* I'd usually butcher the grammar in both languages and grapple for that exact word I wanted.

Mi profesora de castellano insiste que aprendamos hablar el idioma de acuerdo a la manera "correcta." Eso es, la manera de la academia de España. Los otros estudiantes no lo disputan. Ellos también creen que la línea entre el español e inglés es inmovible.†

Everytime I find myself thinking, speaking, writing and breathing in two languages though, I disagree with everyone who thinks that speaking both simultaneously is a disgrace. Well, make that almost two languages. I'm the first to admit that my Spanish isn't perfect. Far from it. But not for a second do I believe that my deliberate Spanglish, my twisting and turning through dos idiomas, is wrong. At the very least it helps me express myself more precisely. A larger vocabulary, dozens more idioms, más chistes, all this and more makes my world more colorful. Le da más sabor a mis pensamientos.‡

I've been thinking in two languages ever since my parents spoke to me in Spanish and I answered back in English. I've been thinking in two languages ever since they spoke to me in English, and I corrected their grammar. And I've been thinking, quite clearly, in two languages ever since they spoke to me in English y yo les contesté en español. I start in one y termino en otra.§

---

*'A year ago I had an argument with a friend who insisted that if I was unable to speak Spanish absolutely correctly, it was better to express myself in English. He had always spoken Spanish at home. On the contrary, I was used to listening to and speaking two languages all the time. He spoke both languages perfectly without forgetting grammatical rules or vocabulary.'

†'My professor of Peninsular Spanish insists that we learn to speak "correctly." That is to say, in the manner of the Spanish Royal Academy. The other students don't dispute this. They, too, believe that the line between Spanish and English is fixed.'

‡*dos idiomas* 'two languages'; *más chistes* 'more jokes'; *Le da más sabor a mis pensamientos* 'It gives more flavor to my thought'.

§. . . *yo les contesté en español* '. . . I answered in Spanish'; *y termino en otra* 'and I finish in another'.

Speak it right, or don't speak it at all. That's what many people think. I'm insulting the Spanish language, corrupting it even, they say.* But the language I speak is simply a reflection of the culture I embrace. Es una cultura tan complicada pero también tan rica, that it takes two languages to describe and live through it everyday.†

Si los países de Latinoamérica creerían que the utmost authority over the language rests with los españoles, then, well, that would be a mess. So instead cada país tiene su academia que se encarga del idioma nacional.‡ Language evolves. Someone has to keep track of the ever-changing lexicon and definitions that mark the passing of time and distinctiveness of the region.

Language is a tool. Without a firm grasp of it you drown in your inability to express yourself well. Dining rooms, locker rooms and classrooms all have their specific language that must be spoken for entrance and acceptance. Conociendo el lenguaje partícular de un grupo,§ opens doors and allows you in to places that would exclude you otherwise.

Language most importantly is a weapon. It can be manipulated, contorted, and misrepresented. Whoever controls language—what we say and how we say it—controls every aspect of our lives. The heated debates over ebonics, bilingual education and illegalizing foreign languages in the workplace leave no doubt about this.

I swerve between two languages. I sometimes skirt the edges of proper grammar and social acceptance, and often crash into a linguistic wall. What's that word? ¿Cómo se dice? And then I remember que lo que yo quería decir es muy simplemente expresado en español, or maybe in English, or maybe necesito combinar palabras y frases from both languages to get right to the heart, el corazón de lo que deseo explicar. There's something exhilarating about being able to race through una conversación sin frenando cuando me encuentro trabada and I have the thoughts, the poem, the word at the tip of my

---

Editor: One such elitist statement: "Spanglish . . . poses a grave danger to Hispanic culture and to the advancement of Hispanics in . . . America. . . . Spanglish is primarily the language of poor Hispanics, many barely literate in either language. They . . . lack . . . vocabulary and education in Spanish. . . . Educated Hispanics who do likewise have a different motivation: Some are embarrassed by their background. . . . Politically, Spanglish is a capitulation; it indicates marginalization, not enfranchisement. . . ." —Roberto González Echevarría, Yale professor of comparative literature, in "Is Spanglish a Language?" *New York Times,* March 28, 1997.

†*Es una cultura tan complicada pero también tan rica* 'It is such a complicated culture, but also so very rich . . .'

‡*Si los países de Latinoamérica creerían que . . .* 'If Latin American countries believe that . . .'; *los españoles* 'the Spaniards'; *cada país tiene su academia que se encarga del idioma nacional* 'each country has its own academy in charge of its national language'

§*Conociendo el lenguaje partícular de un grupo . . .* 'Knowing the language specific to a group . . .'

tongue just itching to get out but I scramble por recordarme por la palabra exacta but then I just switch and boom I finished what I had to say and it quite incredibly makes perfect sense.*

Am I bilingual? Almost. The day I can speak and write Spanish with no embarrassing gaffes or awkward stumbling, when I can use it as effectively and creatively as I do English, then I'll be 100 percent bilingual. Mientras cuando esté en El Salvador, or wherever only Spanish is spoken, no usaré mi inglés at all. Pero aquí, donde los dos idiomas y culturas chocan, I defiantly use both and can express myself twice as well.†

Admittedly, my friends and I, when we talk, cuando platicamos, we're not really speaking true, perfect and proper Spanish or English. That is, Spanish according to los españoles o salvadoreños o mexicanos. But we're not corrupting the languages either. Language is a tool and a weapon, but most importantly it belongs to no one. It isn't static or unforgiving. It is constantly being reshaped.

With two ways to say everything I'm hardly at a disadvantage. How I speak Spanish and English is a reflection of the culture I live everyday. And unless there's something wrong about my almost bilingual and very bicultural life, then there's nothing wrong with combining the two languages I grew up with. Yo hablaré en dos idiomas‡ as long as I can think in two.

---

*¿Cómo se dice? 'How's it said?'; que lo que yo quería decir es muy simplemente expresado en español 'what I wanted to say can be expressed concisely in Spanish'; necesito combinar palabras y frases 'I need to combine words and phrases'; el corazón de lo que deseo explicar 'the heart of what I wish to explain'; una conversación sin frenando cuando me encuentro trabada 'a conversation without braking when I find myself tongue-tied'; por recordarme por la palabra exacta 'to remember the exact word'.

†Mientras cuando esté en El Salvador 'when I am in El Salvador'; no usaré mi inglés 'I will not use English'; Pero aquí, donde los dos idiomas y culturas chocan . . . 'But here, where the two languages and cultures collide . . .'.

‡Yo hablaré en dos idiomas . . . 'I will speak in two languages . . .'.

English con Salsa

Gina Valdés

Welcome to ESL 100, English Surely Latinized,
inglés con chile y cilantro, English as American
as Benito Juárez. Welcome, muchachos from Xochicalco,
learn the language of dólares and dolores, of kings
and queens, of Donald Duck and Batman. Holy Toluca!
In four months you'll be speaking like George Washington,
in four weeks you can ask, More coffee? In two months
you can say, May I take your order? In one year you
can ask for a raise, cool as the Tuxpan River.

Welcome, muchachas from Teocaltiche, in this class
we speak English refrito, English con sal y limón,
English thick as mango juice, English poured from
a clay jug, English tuned like a requinto from Uruapán,
English lighted by Oaxacan dawns, English spiked
with mezcal from Juchitán, English with a red cactus
flower blooming in its heart.

Welcome, welcome, amigos del sur, bring your Zapotec
tongues, your Nahuatl tones, your patience of pyramids,
your red suns and golden moons, your guardian angels,
your duendes, your patron saints, Santa Tristeza,
Santa Alegría, Santo Todolopuede. We will sprinkle
holy water on pronouns, make the sign of the cross
on past participles, jump like fish from Lake Pátzcuaro
on gerunds, pour tequila from Jalisco on future perfects,
say shoes and shit, grab a cool verb and a pollo loco
and dance on the walls like chapulines.

When a teacher from La Jolla or a cowboy from Santee
asks you, Do you speak English? You'll answer, Sí,
yes, simón, of course. I love English!
                                    And you'll hum
a Mixtec chant that touches la tierra and the heavens.

To heal the splitting of the mind and body, we marginalized and oppressed people attempt to recover ourselves and our experiences in language. We seek to make a place for intimacy. Unable to find such a place in standard English, we create the ruptured, broken, unruly speech of vernacular.

—bell hooks

The need to maintain control over English by its native speakers has given birth to a policy of manipulative open-mindedness in which it is held that English belongs to all who use it provided that it is used correctly. This is the art of giving away the bride while insisting that she still belongs to you.

—Njabulo Ndebele*

---

*Njabulo Ndebele, *South African Literature and Culture: Rediscovery of the Ordinary* (Manchester, England, and New York: Manchester University Press [distributed by St. Martin's Press], 1994), 100.

~

Sources and Permissions

Introduction

Dorene Day, "The People's Gift," in *Angwamas Minosewag Anishinabeg: Time of the Indian,* vol. 8, Saint Paul Community Programs in the Arts and Sciences (Saint Paul, MN: Indian Country Communications, 1977). Reproduced by permission of the author.

Part I

1. Carole Yazzie-Shaw, "Cut into Me," appears here for the first time, by permission of the author.

2. Kit Yuen Quan, "The Girl Who Wouldn't Sing." © 1990 by Kit Yuen Quan. From *Making Face, Making Soul (Haciendo Caras): Creative and Critical Perspectives by Women of Color,* ed. Gloria Anzaldúa (San Francisco: Aunt Lute Books, 1990), 212–20. © 1990 by Gloria Anzaldúa. Reprinted with permission from Aunt Lute Books.

3. Joe Nieto, "Prospectus," in *Arrow V: Creative Writing Project of the Bureau of Indian Affairs,* ed. T. D. Allan (Pacific Grove Press, 1973), 2. Reprinted with permission from the author.

4. Maria Mazziotti Gillan, "Learning Silence" in *Identity Lessons: Contemporary Writing about Learning to Be American,* ed. Maria Mazziotti Gillan and Jennifer Gillan (New York: Penguin Books, 1999), 140–41. Copyright © 1999 by Maria Mazziotti Gillan and Jennifer Gillan. Used by permission of Penguin, a division of Penguin Putnam.

5. Luis J. Rodríguez, *Always Running—La Vida Loca, Gang Days in L.A.* (New York: Simon & Schuster, 1993), 26–27. Copyright © 1993 by Luis J. Rodríguez. Reprinted with permission of Curbstone Press. Distributed by Consortium.

6. Eva Hoffman, *Lost in Translation: A Life in a New Language* (New York: E. P. Dutton, 1989), 104–8. Copyright © 1989 by Eva Hoffman. Used by permission of Dutton, a division of Penguin Putnam.

7. Phil George, "Name Giveaway," in *Voices of the Rainbow: Contemporary Poetry by American Indians,* ed. Kenneth Rosen (New York: Viking Press, 1975), 160. Copyright © 1975, 1993 by Kenneth Rosen.

8. Margaret E. Montoya, "Mascaras, Trenzas, y Greñas: Un/Masking of the Self while Un/Braiding Latina Stories and Legal Discourse," *Harvard Women's Law Journal* 17 (1994): 185–86, as well as in *Chicano-Latino Law Review* 15 (1994): 1. Adapted by permission. Copyright © 1994 by the President and Fellows of Harvard College.

9. Richard Rodriguez, *Hunger of Memory: The Education of Richard Rodriguez* (New York: Bantam Books, 1982), 19–26. Reprinted by permission of David R. Godine, Publisher. Copyright ©1982 by Richard Rodriguez.

10. Simon J. Ortiz, "Language and Consciousness," in *Woven Stone* (Tucson: University of Arizona Press, 1992), 5–12. Copyright © 1992 by Simon J. Ortiz. Reprinted by permission of the author.

11. Carole Yazzie-Shaw, "Back in Those Days," in *Returning the Gift: Poetry and Prose from the First North American Native Writers' Festival*, ed. Joseph Bruchac (Tucson: University of Arizona Press, 1994), 330–37. Copyright © by the University of Arizona Board of Regents. Reprinted by permission of the author.

12. Sherman Alexie, "Indian Boy Love Song (#2)," in *The Business of Fancydancing: Stories and Poems* (Brooklyn, NY: Hanging Loose Press, 1992), 55. Copyright © 1992 by Sherman Alexie, by permission of Hanging Loose Press.

13. Delphine Red Shirt, "Wašicuia ya he? Do you speak English?" in *Bead on an Anthill: A Lakota Childhood* (Lincoln: University of Nebraska Press, 1998), 96–106. Copyright © 1998 by the University of Nebraska Press. Reprinted by permission of the University of Nebraska Press.

14. Paula Gunn Allen, "Off Reservation Blues," in *Shadow Country,* Native American Series (Los Angeles: American Indian Studies Center, 1982), 24–26. Copyright © 1992 Regents of the University of California. Reproduced by permission of the American Indian Studies Center, University of California, Los Angeles.

15. Antonia Castañeda, "Language and Other Lethal Weapons: Cultural Politics and the Rites of Children as Translators of Culture," in *Mapping Multiculturalism*, ed. Avery F. Gordon and Christopher Newfield (Minneapolis: University of Minnesota Press, 1996), 201–14. Copyright © by the Regents of the University of Minnesota.

16. Armand Garnet Ruffo, "No Questions Asked," in *Returning the Gift: Poetry and Prose from the First North American Native Writers' Festival*, ed. Joseph Bruchac (Tucson: University of Arizona Press, 1994), 242. Copyright © by the University of Arizona Board of Regents. Reprinted by permission of the author. Originally published in Ruffo's *Opening in the Sky* (Theytus Books, 1994).

17. David Sedaris. "Me Talk Pretty One Day," in *Me Talk Pretty One Day* (Boston: Little, Brown, 2000), 166–73. Copyright © 2000 by David Sedaris. Reprinted by permission of Little, Brown and Company, Inc.

18. Julia Kristeva, "The Silence of Polyglots," in *Etrangers à Nous-mêmes,* trans. Leon S. Roudiez (New York: Columbia University Press, 1991), 15–16. Copyright ©1991 Columbia University Press. Reprinted with permission of the publisher.

19. Juanita M. Sánchez, "voz en una cárcel," in *Chicana Lesbians: The Girls Our Mothers Warned Us About*, ed. Carla Trujillo (Berkeley: Third Woman Press, 1991), 79. Copyright © 1991 by Third Woman Press. Reprinted by permission of Third Woman Press.

20. Maxine Hong Kingston, *The Woman Warrior: Memoirs of a Girlhood among Ghosts* (New York: Vintage Books, 1975), 163–69. Copyright © 1975, 1976 by Maxine Hong Kingston. Used by permission of Alfred A. Knopf, a division of Random House.

Part III

1. Guadalupe Valdés, "The World Outside and Inside Schools: Language and Immigrant Children," *Educational Researcher* 27, no. 6 (August/September 1998): 4–18. Copyright ©1998 by the American Educational Research Association. Adapted by permission of the author and the publisher.

2. Herbert Kohl, *36 Children* (New York: Plume, 1988), 33–38. Copyright ©1967 by Herbert Kohl. Used by permission of Dutton Signet, a division of Penguin Putnam.

3. Richard R. Valencia and Daniel G. Solórzano, "Contemporary Deficit Thinking," in *The Evolution of Deficit Thinking: Educational Thought and Practice*, ed. Richard R. Valencia (Washington D.C.: Falmer Press, 1997), 160–210. Copyright © by Falmer Press. Adapted by permission of the authors.

4. William Labov, "Academic Ignorance and Black Intelligence," *Atlantic* 229, no. 6 (June 1972): 59–67. Copyright © by William Labov. Reproduced by permission of the author.

5. Luis C. Moll and Norma González, "Teachers as Social Scientists: Learning about Culture from Household Research," in *Race, Ethnicity and Multiculturalism: Policy and Practice*, ed. Peter M. Hall. Missouri Symposium on Research and Educational Policy, vol. 1 (New York: Garland Publishing, 1997), 89–114. Copyright © 1997 from *Race, Ethnicity and Multiculturalism* by Peter M. Hall. Adapted by permission of the authors and Routledge/ Taylor & Francis Books, Inc.

6. Alberto Alvaro Ríos, "Translating Translation: Finding the Beginning," *Prairie Schooner* 68, no. 4 (Winter 1994): 5–8. Copyright © 1994 by the University of Nebraska Press. Reprinted by permission of the University of Nebraska Press.

Part IV

1. Pat Mora, "Elena," in *Chants* (Houston, TX: Arte Público Press, 1984), 50. Copyright © 1984 by Pat Mora. Reprinted with permission from the publisher of Mora's *Chants* (Houston: Arte Público Press—University of Houston, 1985).

2. Jimmy Santiago Baca, "Five," in *Healing Earthquakes: A Love Story in Poems* (New York: Grove Press, 2001), 12–14, 16–17. Copyright © 2001 by Jimmy Santiago Baca. Reproduced by permission of Grove/Atlantic, Inc.

3. Amy Tan, "Mother Tongue," *The Three Penny Review*, 1990, 197–202. Copyright 1990 © by Amy Tan. Reprinted by permission of the author and the Sandra Dijkstra Literary Agency.

4. Delphine Red Shirt, "Lakota Words," in *Bead on an Anthill: A Lakota Childhood* (Lincoln: University of Nebraska Press, 1998), 91–96. Copyright © 1998 by the University of Nebraska Press. Reprinted by permission of the University of Nebraska Press.

5. Pat Mora, "Immigrants," in *Borders* (Houston, TX: Arte Público Press, 1986), 15. Copyright © 1986 by Arte Público Press. Reprinted with permission of Arte Público Press—University of Houston.

6. Nana Veary, "My Hawai'i" from *Change We Must: My Spiritual Journey* (Honolulu, Hawaii: Institute of Zen Studies, 1989), 19–26. Copyright © 1989 by Institute of Zen Studies. Reprinted by permission of Gordon Greene, Director of Publications, Institute of Zen Studies.

7. José Antonio Burciaga, "Chief Wachuseh," in *Drink Cultura: Chicanismo* (Santa Barbara, CA: Joshua Odell Editions, 1993), 3–5. Copyright © by José Antonio Burciaga. Reproduced by permission of Cecilia Preciado Burciaga.

8. Rhina Espaillat, "Translation," in *Other Words: Literature by Latinas of the United States*, ed. Roberta Fernández (Houston, TX: Arte Público Press, 1994), 83. Copyright © by Arte Público Press. Reprinted by permission.

9. José Antonio Burciaga, "Bilingual Cognates," in *Spilling the Beans: Lotería Chicana* (Santa Barbara, CA: Joshua Odell Editions, 1995), 170–73. Copyright © by José Antonio Burciaga. Reproduced by permission of Cecilia Preciado Burciaga.

10. Michael Awkward, "Learning to Trust the Language I Thought I'd Left Behind," in *Scenes of Instruction: A Memoir* (Durham, NC: Duke University Press, 2002), 153–55. Copyright © 1999 by Duke University Press. All rights reserved. Reprinted with permission.

Part V

1. Daniel G. Solórzano and Ronald W. Solórzano, "The Chicano Educational Experience: A Framework for Effective Schools in Chicano Communities," *Educational Policy* 9, no. 3 (September, 1995): 293–314. Copyright © by Corwin Press, Inc. Adapted by permission of the authors and Corwin Press.

2. Tamara Lucas, Rosemary Henze, and Rubén Donato, "Promoting the Success of Latino LEP Students: An Exploratory Study of Six High Schools," *Harvard Educational Review* 60, no. 3 (1990): 315–40. Adapted with permission of the authors and the Harvard Educational Publishing Group.

3. Catherine E. Snow, "Perspectives on Second-Language Development: Implications for Bilingual Education," *Educational Researcher* 21, no. 2 (March 1992): 16–19. Copyright © 1992 by the American Educational Research Association. Adapted by permission of the author and the publisher.

4. Virginia Collier, "Teaching" (chapter 3) and "Language" (chapter 4), in *Bilingual and ESL Classrooms: Teaching in Multicultural Contexts*, 3d ed., authored by Carlos J. Ovando, Virginia P. Collier, and Mary Carol Combs (New York: McGraw-Hill, 2003), 86–185. As coauthors of the 3d ed., Carlos J. Ovando and Mary Carol Combs updated the teachings and language chapters of Collier. Copyright © by McGraw-Hill. Adapted by permission of the coauthors and McGraw-Hill.

5. John R. Rickford, "Suite for Ebony and Phonics: Reflections on the Richness and Utility of the African American English Dialect," *Discover* 18, no. 12 (December 1997): 84–87. Reprinted by permission of the author.

6. Lisa Delpit, "What Should Teachers Do? Ebonics and Culturally Responsive Instruction," *The Real Ebonics Debate: Power, Language, and the Education of African American Children*, ed. Theresa Perry and Lisa Delpit (Boston: Beacon Press, 1998), 17–26. Copyright ©1998 by Theresa Perry and Lisa Delpit. Reprinted by permission of Beacon Press, Boston.

Part VI

1. Benjamin Alire Sáenz, "I Want to Write an American Poem," in *Currents from the Dancing River: Contemporary Latinos Fiction, Non-Fiction, and Poetry*, ed. Ray González

(Orlando, FL: Harcourt Brace, 1994), 522–36. Copyright © 1992 by Benjamin Alire Sáenz. Used by permission of the author.

2. bell hooks, "Language: Teaching New Worlds/New Words," in *Teaching to Transgress: Education as the Practice of Freedom* (New York: Routledge, 1994), 167–76. Copyright ©1994 by bell hooks. Reproduced by permission of Routledge, part of the Taylor and Francis Group.

3. Janet Campbell Hale, "Desmet, Idaho, March 1969" in *Voices of the Rainbow: Contemporary Poetry by American Indians*, ed. Kenneth Rosen (New York: Viking Press, 1975), 49. Copyright © 1975, 1993 by Kenneth Rosen.

4. Gloria Anzaldúa, "Speaking in Tongues: A Letter to 3rd World Women Writers," in *This Bridge Called My Back: Writings by Radical Women of Color*, ed. Cherríe Moraga and Gloria Anzaldúa (Watertown, MS: Persephone Press, 1981), 165–66. Copyright © by Cherríe Moraga and Gloria Anzaldúa. Reprinted by permission of Third Woman Press.

5. Louise Erdrich, "Two Languages in Mind, but Just One in the Heart," *New York Times*, May 22, 2000, E-1. Copyright © 2000 by Louise Erdrich. Reprinted with permission of the Wylie Agency.

6. Michele M. Serros, "Mi Problema," in *Chicana Falsa and Other Stories of Death, Identity, and Oxnard* (Valencia, CA: Lalo Press, 1993), 33–34. Copyright © 1993 by Michele M. Serros. Reprinted by permission of the author.

7. Gloria Anzaldúa, excerpt from "How to Tame a Wild Tongue." Reprinted from *Borderlands/La Frontera: The New Mestiza.* (San Francisco: Aunt Lute Books, 1987), 58–59. Copyright © 1987, 1999 by Gloria Anzaldúa, reproduced with permission from Aunt Lute Books.

8. Rosario Morales, "I Recognize You," in *Getting Home Alive* (Ithaca, NY: Firebrand Books, 1986), 145–46. © 1986 by Aurora Levins Morales and Rosario Morales. Reprinted by permission of the author, and Firebrand Books, Milford, Connecticut.

9. Eva Hoffman, "The New World," in *Lost in Translation: A Life in a New Language* (New York: E.P. Dutton, 1989), 271–80. Copyright © 1989 by Eva Hoffman. Used by permission of Dutton, a division of Penguin Putnam.

10. Benjamin Alire Sáenz, "I Want to Write an American Poem," in *Currents from the Dancing River: Contemporary Latino Fiction, Non-Fiction, and Poetry*, ed. Ray González (Orlando, FL: Harcourt Brace, 1994), 522–36. Copyright © 1992 by Benjamin Alire Sáenz. Used by permission of the author.

11. Abby Figueroa, "Speaking Spanglish," *Cultura ES*, número 13 (novembre–dicembre 1998): 11–12. Copyright © by *Cultura ES*. Reprinted by permission of the author.

12. Gina Valdés, "English con Salsa," *Revista Chicano-Riqueña/The Americas Review* 21, no. 1 (Spring 1993): 49–50. Reprinted with permission from the publisher of *Revista Chicano-Riqueña*, Arte Público Press—University of Houston.

Index

~

About the Authors

A Spokane/Coeur d'Alene novelist, poet, short-story writer, and screenwriter, **Sherman Alexie** has recently served as Creative Advisor to the Sundance Institute. His first book, a volume of short stories, *The Lone Ranger and Tonto Fistfight in Heaven*, received a PEN/Hemingway Award for Best First Book of Fiction. Alexie is an American Book Winner and Wordcraft Circle Writer of the Year. Alexie has published fourteen books to date, including *The Business of Fancydancing, The Toughest Indian in the World,* and *Indian Killer;* and he wrote the screenplay of the award-winning film *Smoke Signals,* about two Indian boys on a journey. He lives in Seattle with his wife and two sons.

Paula Gunn Allen, a Laguna Sioux Indian was born in New Mexico and grew up in the Pueblo culture. Her first book, *Blind Lion Poems*, was published in 1974. She has participated in the National Endowment for the Arts Creative Writing Fellowship. Allen recently retired from her position as Professor of English/Creative Writing/American Indian Studies at the University of California at Los Angeles.

Gloria Anzaldúa—lesbian writer, poet, and social theorist—has taught feminism, Chicana and Chicano Studies, and creative writing at numerous colleges. Anzaldúa received the National Endowment of the Arts Award and the Before Columbus Award for her book *This Bridge Called My Back: Writings of Women of Color.* Her 1987 book *Borderlands/La Frontera: The New Mestiza* combines Spanish and English poetry, memoir, and historical analysis. Her powerful ideas have generated new theorizing in Chicana/o Studies.

Currently the Director of the Center for the Study of Black Literature and Culture at University of Pennsylvania, **Michael Awkward** studies how race construction, gender, and community influence the representation of African Americans in literature, film, music, and other forms of cultural expression. He is the author of *Scenes of Instruction: A Memoir* and *Negotiating Differences: Race, Gender and Politics of Personality.*

Abandoned as a child and incarcerated as an adult, **Jimmy Santiago Baca** discovered language as a tool to transform oneself. His first major collection of poems is entitled *Immigrants in Our Own Land.* Baca was awarded the American Book Award in poetry from the Before Columbus Foundation in 1988 for his book *Martin and Meditations on the South Valley.* He published two books of poetry in 2002, *C-Train* and *13 Mexicans,* as well as a novel, *A Place to Stand: The Making of a Poet.*

Poet, essayist, artist, and activist **José Antonio Burciaga** was born in El Paso, Texas, but until his recent passing, lived most of his adult life in California. He was an accomplished figure in the Chicano literary and art world. Among many other roles, he was a founding member of the comedy troupe Culture Clash, a published poet, and a gifted humorist. He had an uncanny ability to go back and forth between English and Spanish, both in his work and in the way he spoke. His voice, his style of writing is quintessentially Chicano.

Antonia I. Castañeda was born in Crystal City, Tejas. She received her Ph.D. in U.S. History from Stanford University and is Associate Professor of History at St. Mary's University, where she held the O'Connor Chair in Colonial Texas and Spanish Borderlands history, 1999–2001. A feminist historian and activist, Castañeda works with several community-based institutions, including the Esperanza Peace and Justice Center, the Guadalupe Cultural Arts Center, and the Hispanas Unidas Institute.

Virginia P. Collier is Professor of Bilingual/Multicultural/ESL Education at George Mason University. She is best known for her award-winning research studies on school effectiveness for linguistically and culturally diverse students. She is coauthor, with Carlos Ovando and Mary Carol Combs, of the third edition of *Bilingual and ESL Classrooms: Teaching in Multicultural Contexts.* In addition, she has over forty other publications, including her popular monograph *Promoting Academic Success for ESL Students.*

Mary Carol Combs is Research Scientist in the Bureau of Applied Research in Anthropology at University of Arizona. Dr. Combs's scholarly interests include bilingual education policy and law, language planning, indigenous language revitalization and development, and bilingual and ESL teacher preparation. She is a former director of the English Plus Information Clearinghouse, a national clearinghouse on language rights and public policy. She is coauthor, along with Carlos Ovando and Virginia Collier, of the third edition of *Bilingual and ESL Classrooms: Teaching in Multicultural Contexts.*

Having grown up in a segregated community of Baton Rouge, **Lisa Delpit** has had firsthand experience as a minority student in public education. Delpit was one of the first students to integrate the Catholic schools of her town. Education reform has become Delpit's passion—specifically, teaching strategies for African American students. Her essays have been incorporated into a book, *Other People's Children: Cultural Conflict in the Classroom.*

Rubén Donato is Associate Professor of Education at the University of Colorado, Boulder. Professor Donato is an educational historian. His research ranges from the educational histories of Mexican Americans to current educational policy issues that affect United States Latinos.

With French-Ojibwe and German-American ancestry, **Louise Erdrich** weaves her rich history into her poems, stories, novels, and essays. Erdrich's works include *The Beet Queen, Tracks, Tales of a Burning Love, Love Medicine,* and many others. She has been awarded the 1975 Academy of Poets Prize as well as the Best Fiction Award from the American Academy and Institute of Arts and Letters. In 2000 she opened a bookstore, The Birchbark House, in Minnesota.

Rhina Espaillat has two poetry collections in print: *Lapsing to Grace* and *Where the Horizons Go.* Espaillat, who was born in the Dominican Republic, writes in both English and Spanish. She also runs a monthly workshop called "The Powwow River Poets" and was recently awarded the Richard Wilbur Award. Her third book is entitled *Rehearsing Absence.*

One Salvadoran mother + one Guatemalteco father + a multiethnic urban landscape = **Abby Figueroa**, writer. She has been publishing her work since 1994 in various local newspapers, literary magazines, and Internet media. As editor of *BOCA Magazine* from 1998 to 2000, she helped create its unflappable and wry voice. Abby lives, writes, and teaches in Los Angeles.

Phil George writes: My given name is 'Two Swans Ascending From Still Waters'. I am Nez Percé-Tsimshian, a member of Seven Drum Religion, Nespelem Longhouse; great-grandson of Chief Tawatoy. I love Wallowa, grandmas, wardancing, and frybread.

Maria Mazziotti Gillan is Director of the Creative Writing Program at Binghamton University and Director of the Poetry Center at Passaic Community College. Gillan has been awarded the Firman Houghton Poetry Award from the Poetry Club of New England, the National Poetry Book Award from Salmon Run Press, and the American Library Association Editors' Choice booklist for *Growing Up in Ethnic America*.

Norma González is Associate Professor in the Department of Education, Culture, and Society at the University of Utah. Her work ranges from Latino language socialization, language ideologies, to school–community partnerships. Her writings have appeared in *Anthropology and Education Quarterly, Education and Urban Society,* and *Journal of Applied Behavioral Sciences*. Her books include *I Am My Language: Discourses of Women and Children in the Borderlands* and a coedited volume, *Classroom Diversity: Connecting Curriculum to Students' Lives*.

Janet Campbell Hale grew up on the Yakima reservation in central Washington and the Coeur d'Alene reservation in northern Idaho. She moved often, usually with only her mother, who tried to escape her violent alcoholic husband. At age twenty-three, she published *The Owl's Song*. Hale has taught at several universities. In 1985, she was a Pulitzer Prize nominee for her book *The Jailing of Cecelia Capture*. Her most recent book is *Women on the Run*.

Rosemary Henze is Associate Professor at the Linguistics and Language Development Department of San José State University. Dr. Henze worked as a researcher and consultant in K–12 public schools. Her work focuses on issues such as educational equity, bilingual education, literacy development, ethnic relations, school leadership, and indigenous language renewal.

Born in Poland in 1945, **Eva Hoffman** served as an editor and writer of the *New York Times* from 1979 to 1990. Hoffman has written many books including one of her most well-known works, *Lost in Translation*. Her most recent book is *Shtetl: The Life and Death of a Small Town and the World of Polish Jews*. Hoffman also taught at various institutions, such as Columbia University, University of Minnesota, and Tufts College.

Distinguished Professor of English at City College in New York, **bell hooks** is mainly known as a feminist thinker. hooks was influenced by Paulo Freire's views on education as the practice of freedom. At age nineteen, she published her first book, *Ain't I a Woman? Black Women and Feminism*.

Daughter of Chinese immigrants, **Maxine Hong Kingston** calls her early years in school as the "silent years." Despite this rough beginning, she earned a scholarship to the University of California, Berkeley. Hong Kingston became involved in the antiwar movement but decided to leave the country when it became too violent. Though she never felt at home in Hawaii, her seventeen-year stay gave her time to work on her first two books, including *The Woman Warrior*. She currently teaches at University of California, Berkeley.

Herbert Kohl is a nationally renowned school reformer who has written over thirty books on education. He recently published *Should We Burn Babar? Essays on Children's Literature and the Power of Stories*. Kohl has taught at all levels, serving as a teacher in Harlem for many years and later moving to institutions of higher education, such as Carleton College and University of California, Berkeley. Currently, he is the Director of the Center for Teaching Excellence and Social Justice at the University of San Francisco School of Education.

A contemporary intellectual, **Julia Kristeva** was recently Visiting Professor at Columbia University. Kristeva combines the disciplines of philosophy, linguistics, semiotics, literary theory, and psychoanalysis into her work. Kristeva was awarded the 1997 Chevalière de la Légion d'Honneur for her thirty years of work, which has been translated into ten languages.

William Labov is one of the nation's most distinguished linguists. He is Professor of Linguistics at University of Pennsylvania. Labov directs the Phonological Atlas of North America and coedits the journal *Language Variation and Change*. His four best-known books are *The Social Stratification of English in New York City, Language in the Inner City,* and *Principles of Linguistic Change, volumes I* and *II*.

Tamara Lucas is Associate Professor in the Department of Educational Foundations at Montclair State University. She received her Ph.D. from Stanford's School of Education. Beyond university teaching, she has worked extensively in public schools to improve the education of culturally and linguistically diverse students, and she explored the experiences of diverse students in secondary schools. Most recently she published *Into, through, and beyond Secondary School: Critical Transitions for Immigrant Youths* and *Educating Culturally Responsive Teachers: A Coherent Approach*, with Ana María Villegas.

Luis C. Moll is Professor at the University of Arizona School of Education. His research centers on bilingual literacy learning, community analysis, and child development. He is best known for the inquiry-oriented "Funds of

Knowledge" approach, for the professional development of teachers. This approach seeks to improve classroom participation and student interest by drawing upon their own home and community resources. His writing appears in journals such as *Theory into Practice, Urban Education, Educational Researcher, Anthropology and Education Quarterly,* and *Language Arts.*

The first Latina to be accepted to Harvard Law School, **Margaret Montoya** is Professor of Law at University of New Mexico. Her research is on race, ethnicity, gender, and language. Montoya's publications have been included in several popular anthologies, including *The Latino/a Condition: Law, History and Narratives; Critical Race Feminism;* and *Speaking Chicana.*

An author of poetry, nonfiction, and children's books, **Pat Mora** believes in connecting communities through literature and literacy. Mora has been an English teacher at all levels and was recognized in 1999 as Distinguished Visiting Professor at University of New Mexico. She has been both a judge and a recipient of the National Endowment for the Arts Poetry Fellowship.

Rosario Morales (in her own words): I am a New York Puerto Rican living in Cambridge, Massachusetts, a feminist, independentista, and communist since 1949. I married, I've farmed in Puerto Rico, I've studied science and anthropology, and I've raised three children. In my fifties I broke a lifetime of "silence" to write.

Joe Nieto, a Santo Domingo Indian schooled both in public and Indian schools, has fought all his life. After serving in the Navy, he fought alcohol to a draw. He has been clean since 1980. He once fought to see his children; he now has full custody of them. He fought fires all over the Southwest for over a decade, at times as a member of a Hot Shot fire fighting crew. Now he breaks horses, and works in the Santa Fe Indian Hospital.

Simon J. Ortiz was born in Albuquerque and raised in the Acoma Pueblo culture. He served as the Lieutenant Governor of the Pueblo of Acoma, as well as the consulting editor of the Pueblo of Acoma Press. Ortiz has taught at numerous institutions, including San Diego State University, Institute of American Indian Arts, Navajo Community College, University of New Mexico, and currently at the University of Toronto.

Carlos J. Ovando is Associate Dean for Teacher Preparation and Professor of Curriculum and Instruction in the College of Education at Arizona State University. Throughout his career Ovando has been interested in examining factors that contribute to the academic achievement of language minority students and ethnically diverse groups, writing extensively in educational journals. His books include *Bilingual and ESL Classroom: Teaching in Multicultural Contexts*, with Virginia Collier and Mary Carol Combs; *The Politics of Multiculturalism and Bilingual Education: Teachers and Students Caught in the Cross-Fire*, with Peter McLaren; and *Institutionalizing Inequity in Multicultural School Communities*, with Colleen Larson.

Kit Yuen Quan is an FOB* who after twenty years is finally putting both feet on shore. Now she manages her own Learning to Learn Adventures. One of her remedies for symptoms of internalized oppression is the Chinese BLT (bakery, library, tai chi). At last word, she was the office manager and bookkeeper at Spinsters/Aunt Lute Book Company.

Currently teaching at Yale University, **Delphine Red Shirt** just published her latest work, *Turtle Lung Woman's Granddaughter*. Red Shirt is from the Ogala Sioux tribe, and she grew up on a reservation in Nebraska. At the United Nations, she was the chair of the NGO Committee on the International Decade of the World's Indigenous Peoples.

John R. Rickford is Professor of Linguistics at Stanford University. He became the Director of the African and African-American Studies Department in 1998. In the same year, he was honored as the Martin Luther King Jr. Centennial Professor. Rickford has an interest in sociolinguistics. His most recent book is *Spoken Soul: The Story of Black English*.

Alberto Alvaro Ríos is Regents Professor of English at Arizona State University. He is the author of eight books and chapbooks of poetry, three collections of short stories, and a memoir. His books of poems include, most recently, *The Smallest Muscle in the Human Body,* for which he was named finalist for the 2002 National Book Award, as well as *Teodoro Luna's Two Kisses, The Warrington Poems, Five Indiscretions*, and *Whispering to Fool the Wind*. His collections of short stories include *The Curtain of Trees* and *The Iguana Killer*. Ríos's work has been reprinted in over 175 literary anthologies.

Founder of Tia Chucha Press, **Luis Rodríguez** is also the founder of Youth Struggling for Survival, an organization established to help at-risk youth through arts, community activities, leadership, and more. Rodríguez was

---

*"Fresh Off the Boat." American high schoolers coined this term to malign Asian refugees when they began arriving in large numbers. Immigrants have now taken over the term to affirm their distinctive identity.

awarded the Carl Sandburg Literary Award, the Chicago Sun-Times Book Award, and the New York Times Notable Book for his book/memoir *Always Running: La Vida Loca, Gang Days in L.A.* He is also the author of *Poems across the Pavement* and *The Concrete River*.

Richard Rodriguez is an editor of the Pacific News Service, a nonprofit media organization, as well as a contributing editor for *Harper's Magazine, U.S. News and World Report*, and the Sunday opinion section of the *Los Angeles Times.* Rodriguez has been featured in the *New York Times,* the *Wall Street Journal,* among others. He is also the author of *An Argument with My Mexican Father* and two documentaries. He was awarded the Frankel Medal from the National Endowment for the Humanities.

Armand Garnet Ruffo is an Obijwe poet and English professor at Carleton University. He is the Associate Director for the Centre for Aboriginal Education, Research and Culture. Ruffo has also written several essays, short stories, and plays. He is the author of *Ghost Woman: A Windigo Tale* and *Grey Owl: The Mystery of Archie Belaney.*

Benjamin Alire Sáenz was born in southern New Mexico, not fifty miles away from the U.S.–Mexico border. He has tried unsuccessfully to leave the border behind his entire life—but he has always returned. He is a novelist, poet, artist, essayist, and an author of two bilingual children's books. He was the Wallace E. Stegner fellow in poetry at Stanford University, was awarded a Lannan Foundation literary fellowship, and an American Book Award. He teaches in the bilingual M.F.A. program at the University of Texas, El Paso. His most recent book is *Elegies in Blue.*

Juanita M. Sánchez is a native New Mexican of Chicana/Indian ancestry. Currently she is a machinist and shop steward. She has a B.A. in psychology and an M.A. in Human Resources Development. She holds the rank of captain in the Army Reserves. Her work has been published in several anthologies and numerous local publications. She sponsors the Festival of Women's Poetry, which promotes poets who are either Third World women or women of color. Presently she lives with her two dogs and cats, in an adobe house in the northwest valley of Albuquerque.

Otto Santa Ana is Associate Professor of Chicana and Chicano Studies at UCLA. He is a sociolinguist and discourse analyst. He has written a dozen articles about the languages of Chicanos and the education of language minority children. His first book, *Brown Tide Rising: Metaphors of Latinos in Contemporary*

American Public Discourse, was awarded Best Book of 2002 on Ethnic and Racial Political Ideology from the Race and Ethnicity Section of the American Political Science Association.

National Public Radio humorist and commentator **David Sedaris** currently lives in Paris, France. He was named Humorist of the Year 2001 by *Time* magazine, and he is the third recipient of the Thurber Prize for American Humor. Sedaris taught writing at the Art Institute of Chicago. He has also written plays with his sister, Amy Sedaris.

Spoken-word artist, writer, and poet **Michele M. Serros**, began her writing career while she was still a community college student. Since her first book, *Chicana Falsa and Other Stories of Death, Identity, and Oxnard*, Serros has released a spoken-word compact disc, has toured with Lollapalooza as a "road poet," and has been named by *Newsweek* as "one of the top young women to watch for in the new century." She is currently working on a young-adult novel tentatively titled *Notes for a Medium Brown Girl*.

Catherine E. Snow is Shattuck Professor of Education at Harvard Graduate School of Education, specializing in children's language and literature development. Her studies focus on how oral language skills are acquired and how they relate to literacy development. Snow has chaired two national panels: the National Academy of Sciences committee and the Rand Reading Study Group. She has also explored such topics as bilingual education and policy in the United States and developing nations, as well as testing policy.

Daniel G. Solórzano is a Professor of Social Science and Comparative Education at UCLA. His research interests include studies of underrepresented student access to, and graduation from, higher education. His current work applies Critical Race Theory to examine the college admissions process for minority high school students. The titles of his writing include "Critical Race Theory, Marginality, and the Experience of Minority Students in Higher Education"; "Critical Race Theory, Racial and Gender Microaggressions, and the Experiences of Chicana and Chicano Scholars"; and "Images and Words that Wound: Critical Race Theory, Racial Stereotyping and Teacher Education."

Ronald Solórzano is Associate Professor of Education at Occidental College, and he received his Ph.D. from UCLA. He taught in Los Angeles Unified School District for thirteen years and at East Los Angeles Community College for seven years. Professor Solórzano has published in the areas of school effects, teacher assessment, bilingual education, and state teaching standards.

A published author since the age of eight, **Amy Tan** was awarded the National Book Award and the *Los Angeles Times* Book Award for *The Joy Luck Club*. Tan is the author of *The Bonesetter's Daughter, The Kitchen God's Wife,* and *The 1000 Secret Senses.*

Gina Valdés was raised on both sides of the U.S./Mexico border. She has taught Chicano literature and culture as well as bilingual creative writing at universities throughout the United States. Her poetry and fiction have been published in anthologies in the United States, Mexico, and Europe. Her works include *Comiendo Lumbre (Eating Fire)* and *Puentes y Fronteras (Bridges and Borders).*

Guadalupe Valdés is Professor of Education, Spanish, and Portuguese at Stanford University. Her research explores issues of bilingualism relevant to teachers in training (instruction methods, typologies, measurement, and the role of education in national policies on immigration). Specifically, she studies the processes of language acquisition by learners in different circumstances—those learning a second language in a classroom setting and those who must learn two languages to adapt to immediate family-based or work-based communicative needs within an immigrant community. Her research in these areas has made her one of the most eminent experts on Spanish–English bilingualism in the United States.

Richard Valencia is Professor of Educational Psychology at University of Texas, Austin. His research interests are the intellectual and academic development of racial/ethnic minority children, psychometric evaluation of intelligence and achievement tests, social and psychological foundations of minority schooling, minority school failure and success, and teacher testing and prospective minority teachers. He is well known for his books, including *Chicano School Failure and Success: Research and Policy Agendas for the 1990s*, which has recently appeared in a second edition. His new book, *Intelligence Testing and Minority Students: Foundations, Performance Factors, and Assessment Issues*, is co-written by Lisa A. Suzuki.

Nana Veary (1908–1993) has been described as the "embodiment of the spirit of Aloha." She was reared by her Hawaiian elders in an environment where language, fishing, healing, building, and all aspects of life were firmly rooted in nature. It was a Hawai'i in which children planted by the moon and strangers were greeted with reverence.

Graduate of UCLA where she received an Ahmanson Undergraduate Research Scholarship, **Erika Villegas** now pursues a master's degree in education while working on behalf of language minority students. Growing up as a second-language learner herself, she identifies with their struggles and focuses her energies on their constructions of success. With a background in educational psychology, constructivist pedagogy, balanced literacy education, and English-language development, she is a dedicated classroom teacher and advocate of bilingual education.

Carole Yazzie-Shaw (in her own words): I am Navajo. I was born in a small Catholic mission at Tsénitsaa deez'áhí, Rock Point, Arizona. I went to school in Gallup and later received my bachelor's degree in sociology at the University of New Mexico. This was where I met my best friend, Curt Shaw, whom I married, and we now live in Albuquerque, New Mexico.

Ofelia Zepeda is a remarkable scholar and an accomplished poet. She was raised in Arizona, a member of the Tohono 'O'odham Nation. Professor Zepeda is on the faculties of Linguistics and American Indian Studies at the University of Arizona, Tucson. She wrote *A Papago Grammar,* the first pedagogical grammar of the 'O'odham language. She is a cofounder and codirector of the American Indian Language Development Institute. Her poetry books include *Ocean Power: Poems from the Desert* and *Jewed 'I-hoi / Earth Movements.* She was recognized with a MacArthur Fellowship for her "extraordinary originality and dedication in her creative pursuits" on American Indian language issues.